T0265595

LIBERAL BULLIES

LIBERAL BULLIES

What Psychology Teaches Us
about the Left's Authoritarian Problem
—*and How to Fix It*

LUKE CONWAY

PITCHSTONE PUBLISHING
DURHAM, NORTH CAROLINA

PITCHSTONE PUBLISHING
DURHAM, NORTH CAROLINA
WWW.PITCHSTONEBOOKS.COM

This edition published by arrangement with Swift Press Ltd.

Printed in the United States of America

Library of Congress Cataloging-in-Publication Data

Names: Conway, Luke, author.
Title: Liberal bullies : what psychology teaches us about the left's authoritarian
   problem-and how to fix it / Luke Conway.
Description: Durham, North Carolina : Pitchstone Publishing, [2024] |
   Includes bibliographical references and index. | Summary: "Liberal
   Bullies argues that the political left has an urgent and rising problem
   with authoritarianism. An alarmingly high percentage of self-identified
   progressives are punitive, bullying, and intolerant of disagreement-and
   the problem is getting worse. Using his own cutting-edge research to
   analyze contemporary politics, noted psychologist Luke Conway shows that
   it's not just right-wingers and fascists who long for an authority
   figure to crush their enemies, silence opponents, and restore order. A
   persistent proportion of left-wingers demonstrate authoritarian
   tendencies, and they're becoming more emboldened. On issues ranging from
   schooling and vaccine mandates to critical race theory and gender
   ideology, they are increasingly advocating censorship over free debate,
   disregarding the rule of law, and dehumanizing their opponents. These
   tendencies are part of an accelerating "threat circle" of mutual hatred
   and fear between left and right that could tear apart our basic
   democratic norms. Concluding with an eloquent call for firm but rational
   resistance to this rising tide of authoritarianism, Liberal Bullies is
   for everyone who is concerned about cancel culture and the hyperpartisan
   war zone that our political arena has become"— Provided by publisher.
Identifiers: LCCN 2023044652 (print) | LCCN 2023044653 (ebook) | ISBN
   9781634312547 (hardcover) | ISBN 9781634312554 (ebook)
Subjects: LCSH: Liberalism—United States. | Authoritarianism—United
   States. | Right and left (Political science)—United States. | Political
   culture—United States. | United States—Politics and government—21st
   century.
Classification: LCC JC574.2.U6 C657 2024 (print) | LCC JC574.2.U6 (ebook)
   | DDC 320.530973—dc23/eng/20231115
LC record available at https://lccn.loc.gov/2023044652
LC ebook record available at https://lccn.loc.gov/2023044653

CONTENTS

INTRODUCTION

I remember the moment I became truly worried about liberal bullies.

I had just presented evidence to my university's Faculty Senate on a resolution concerning vaccine and mask mandates. I was a long-time liberal,[1] but I had never just unthinkingly walked the party line; and this was one of those instances where I had gone against the mainstream academic position. In stating my opposition to these mandates, I had cited research from Brown University[2] and Yale University (co-authored with a Stanford University scholar),[3] and quoted a top researcher at the University of Minnesota.[4] And then I sat down expecting the predictable, yawning, biased responses.

Rarely have I ever been more wrong.

What came instead was a cannonade of vitriol unlike anything I have ever experienced in academia. Suddenly, I wasn't a scientist who had presented evidence from Ivy League universities and made arguments; I was a *heretic* who had dared oppose the current left-wing orthodoxy. Among other things, a colleague called the research I had presented 'conspiracy theories that anyone could get off of the internet,' to uproarious support from the rest of the Faculty Senate.

That was my moment. I knew that if research from Yale, Stanford, Brown, and the University of Minnesota could be called 'conspiracy theories anyone could get off of the internet,' something new and afoul was afoot. This wasn't just the usual and predictable bias; this was something truly different. It was time to start getting genuinely worried.

The Warning Signs Were All There

Truthfully, I should have seen this coming sooner.

In the summer of 2018, Pedro Pascal – star of the hit Disney show *The Mandalorian* – tweeted two pictures that compared the US to Nazi Germany.[5] Roughly three years later, Gina Carano, his co-star on the show, posted a tweet that similarly compared the US to Nazi Germany. Pascal's tweet went largely unnoticed and was active (as far as I can tell) until he deleted his Twitter account in November 2022.[6] Gina Carano, on the other hand, was forced under immense social pressure to delete her tweet, and Disney *fired her anyway*. Disney did so with a very harsh dismissal essentially claiming she was a mean and racist person.[7] Why did Pascal keep his job and Carano lose hers? After all, polling showed that a whopping 72% of Americans, upon reading Carano's tweet, did not think she should be fired for it.[8] It is hard to get 72% of Americans to agree that 'Rocky Road ice cream tastes good' these days, much less to agree on something *political*. But Carano was fired nonetheless. Why was she fired, while Pascal kept his job?

Maybe it is pure coincidence that Pascal's post criticized *conservatives* and Carano's post criticized *liberals*.

But I don't think it *is* pure coincidence. In fact, Carano's firing is indicative of a growing syndrome of leftist authoritarians who want authority figures to crush their opponents with ruthless ambition. And a lot of people in my home country are beginning to wonder about all these bullying, strong-handed, punitive, angry liberals roaming the internet and getting people fired. Many average Americans woke up one day to a world where they suddenly had to speak *just so* and act *in a certain way* to simply keep their jobs and their social lives intact. They woke up in a world where it is commonplace for people in the media to actually *say* they want their left-wing president to rule 'with an iron fist'.[9] And the people waking up to this increasingly left-wing authoritarian world want answers. Where did all these liberal authoritarians come from? How many of them are there? What drives them? What are they like? Why are they canceling and firing people? And what can we do about it?

In this book, I answer these questions by providing a comprehensive psychological look at who left-wing authoritarians are, how the modern authoritarian movement grew, and how we can stop it. In the first section of the book (Chapter 1), I lay out the case that left-wing authoritarianism is a real and pervasive problem. In so doing, I discuss what authoritarianism is, how it differs from positive instances of mere obedience to authority, and why you should care about it. Even if it hasn't touched your life yet, there is a very real chance that it will, and this section highlights that fact.

In the second section of the book (Chapters 2–6), each chapter diagnoses one characteristic of the left-wing authoritarian movement. To understand the cure, you have to first understand the disease. Thus, in this middle section, I dig deeply into the psychology of what makes a left-wing authoritarian person tick by discussing cutting-edge research in my own field.

In the third section of the book (Chapters 7–9), I talk about where left-wing authoritarianism came from – and what we

3

can do about it. By showing direct parallels between what you might see in your everyday life and what we can prove by science, I hope to make the modern science of authoritarianism come alive for you.

I don't know how you personally feel about liberal bullies at this moment, but if you are concerned about them, you aren't alone. For example, in the spring of 2020, our research lab debated prominent New York University professor John Jost's lab on left-wing authoritarianism.[10] At that time, left-wing authoritarianism felt somewhat on the fringe of my field of social psychology. I was thus a bit surprised when our debate-style symposium was accepted (the acceptance rate for these prestigious symposia is 35%). I was even more surprised when I checked out the room the morning of the debate and realized that the organizers had put us in one of the large ballrooms – instead of placing us in a small side room as I had expected. I began to imagine the embarrassment of a small crowd in a large ballroom. After all, this was a fringe topic in the field: Who would show up?

So imagine my shock when the large ballroom was nearly full with inquisitive people for what turned out to be a hotly contested, vigorous, and entertaining session. And I realized then that this topic was not so fringe after all. People – even the overwhelmingly liberal group of people known as social psychologists – *really* seemed to care about left-wing authoritarianism.

Maybe you have experienced liberal bullies yourself. Maybe you think leftist authoritarians aren't really that big a problem and the whole thing will just blow over. Maybe you find yourself uncertain what to think or who to believe.

No matter where you land on these issues or what your political background is, I hope this book is for you. You'll see in these pages that I'm a former liberal with many liberal sympathies. You'll see that I think conservative authoritarians are a huge problem too, and that we have to solve both liberal and conservative authoritarian issues together. My goal here isn't to bash liberals – it is to provide an objective psychological account of what is really happening in both the US and other parts of the world.

Liberal bullies are a worldwide reality that, I strongly believe, will only become more powerful if we don't do something about it. Fortunately, psychology research tells us exactly what to do – and I'm going to tell you all about that too. This isn't something that's going to go away on its own, but it isn't a hopeless fight either. It is possible to curb authoritarianism on both sides, and I'm going to show you how.

CHAPTER 1

AUTHORITARIAN FOLLOWERS, RIGHT *AND* LEFT

In the movie *The Avengers*, Loki – playing the part of the consummate authoritarian leader – orders a group of average Germans to kneel before him.[1] It seems to work, as almost everyone complies. But one solitary man refuses, saying that he will 'not [kneel] to men like you'. Loki arrogantly asserts, 'There are no men like me.' Then the German man utters the great hidden truth of authoritarian psychology: 'There are *always* men like you.'

Probably the most common misconception about authoritarianism is that it is largely about the authority figures in charge, the Loki types of the world. In fact, that is often the direction the conversation turns when I present evidence of left-wing authoritarianism. On *The Rick Ungar Show*, for example, one of the guests criticized our lab's work because it didn't clearly identify left-wing authoritarian leaders. An alarmingly high percentage of news stories about authoritarianism in the last seven years also referenced one particular right-wing leader: Donald Trump.

It is easy to see why there is a focus on authoritarian leadership. 'Authoritarian' has 'authority' – that is, the person in charge – built into the *word*. When people think 'authoritarian'

7

they often think of the leaders. So it's only natural to think that the authoritarian problem is only a problem with leadership.

Nothing could be further from the truth.

The hidden truth of authoritarian psychology is that *there are always people like that.* There are always people who will fill the power vacuum, who want to rule and order and dictate. Every movement has authoritarian leaders. Every movement has people who want to gain power and use it harshly. Every movement has leaders who wish to control, manipulate, and crush. So to spend time talking about authoritarianism as if what changes is in the leadership is futile. Nothing changes in the leadership. What changes is in the people they presume to lead.

Indeed, leaders are irrelevant if no one will obey them. It requires a lust in the masses for authoritarians to punish their enemies, to create and enforce norms for which dissent is not allowed, to promote intolerance and hatred. Authoritarian leaders are pathetic stooges if the masses are uninterested in them. So 'Are there authoritarian leaders?' isn't the primary question – the primary question is 'Will the people submit?' It doesn't matter if Congresswoman Maxine Waters tells protestors to 'get more confrontational' if they don't like a trial verdict;[2] it only matters if everyone thinks that kind of authoritarian fear-mongering is OK. Will they submit? Do they want leaders to boss others about, to lead them to aggression?

This truth maps onto decades of authoritarianism research in my own field of social psychology. That research has largely been built around personality and attitude scales that measure authoritarianism.[3] These scales are not built to measure authoritarian leaders; rather, they are built to measure authoritarian *followers.* They include items like this: 'Our country desperately needs a mighty leader who will do what has to be done to destroy the radical new ways and sinfulness that are ruining us.' That item doesn't say 'I want to lead my people to destroy my enemies.' It isn't a measurement of the leader. It is a measurement of the follower.

Thus, most of what we know about authoritarianism – most of the actual data used in the primary questionnaires that have come to define what we think about authoritarianism – is about the people who follow, and not the people who lead.

Scientific work justifies the importance of studying followers. In one study, for example, our lab evaluated whether we could predict changes in authoritarian leadership from the psychological traits of the populace. Did changes in the average authoritarian tendencies of the populace predict future authoritarian governments, or did changes in authoritarian leadership predict changes in the followers? In other words, which come first – authoritarian followers or authoritarian leaders?

Our work over a 30-year span suggests that changes in the authoritarian status of governments were predicted by the predisposal of the populace to authoritarian followership traits like collectivism; but authoritarian governmental changes had comparatively little effect on followers' psychology.[4] This work suggests that certain psychological features predispose followers to accept authoritarian dictatorships. This empirical fact is quite remarkable. So many things influence the rise of dictators that have nothing to do with the internal culture – military power, foreign politics, the status of a nation's immediate neighbors – that it would seem like the cultural beliefs of the followers in the populace hardly matter. And yet not only do they matter, they matter primarily. They are central. An authoritarian dictator may take over a country, but if the people never wanted that to happen, it won't last. A democracy may be installed from the outside, but if the people want authoritarian leadership, it won't last.

Thus, when we come to the potential for left-wing authoritarianism, the primary question we should be asking is not 'Are there authoritarian leaders on the left who will grab power and enforce dictates?' The real question is 'Do lots of left-wing people want authoritarian leaders to crush their enemies?'

Obeying Authority Isn't the Problem

Perhaps we move too fast. Let's take a step back and ask a broader question: What are authoritarian followers like?

And the first thing to get straight is that, to a psychologist, 'authoritarian' doesn't just mean 'obeying authority' or 'ordering someone to do something'. Parents who punish their kids for being mean to their siblings aren't authoritarian leaders. People who obey the speed limits aren't authoritarian followers. Authoritarianism means something specifically nastier. Authoritarians don't merely enforce reasonable rules or obey those rules – they want a strong leader to crush and silence their opponents. They want that leader to hurt people for the benefit of their group.

The authoritarian is thus vastly different than the person who merely complies with authority. In fact, merely obeying authority is largely a positive thing as far as it goes. If students in my classes refused to do what I ask of them, no one would ever learn. If they interrupted my lectures to discuss Taylor Swift, or yelled at their fellow students about line dancing, or wrote 'Luke stinks' on top of the notes I was trying to write on the board, then there would be little point in my class. Their obedience accomplishes a positive goal. We teach children to respect their teachers because it is a positive thing to respect their teachers.

Similarly, we want people to obey the law. We want them to respect the authority that tells them 'do not murder'. We're glad when people obediently decide not to drink and drive, when they follow directives to evacuate burning buildings in an orderly manner, and when they refuse to vandalize our property. Obeying authority in this way isn't authoritarianism, because we don't want those things primarily to hurt or crush or silence anyone. We just want people to behave well.

Authoritarians also want people to obey – but they differ in several respects from those who *merely* obey. The classic definition of authoritarianism is that authoritarians want a strong authority figure to hurt others (called 'authoritarian aggression'), to enforce radical group norms (called 'authoritarian conventionalism'), and to require submission to those norms (called 'authoritarian submission').[5] Authoritarians want to obey strong authority figures, but they are largely motivated by a desire to have their group *dominate other groups.*

In the words of the most famous authoritarianism researcher of all time, Bob Altemeyer, authoritarians

> support unjust and illegal acts by governments. They support police who abuse their power ... After viewing a film about [psychologist Stanley] Milgram's famous 'obedience' experiments, they tended to blame the Teacher and the Learner for what happened more than most people do, but not the authority, the Experimenter. In turn, they themselves aggress in laboratory experiments involving electric shock, when authority sanctions it. They harbor many prejudices against many minorities,

accepting stereotypes uncritically. In fact, most highly prejudiced persons turn out to be either social dominators or right-wing authoritarians. High RWAs strongly believe in punishment, and admit that they derive personal pleasure from administering it to 'wrongdoers'.[6]

This isn't merely obedience – it is a particularly nasty and aggressive kind of obedience. Authoritarians aren't especially interested in obeying the law – they are actually less likely to obey the law if their own authority commands them not to.

The distinction between good and bad authority can be seen in remarkable work on parenting by Cal Berkeley professor Diana Baumrind. This work suggests there are two primary dimensions of parenting: Responsiveness/Warmth and Authority/Control. How parents score on these two dimensions defines their parenting style.[7] Parents who are low on both responsiveness and authority are Neglectful parents who basically don't attend to their children at all. Parents who score high on responsiveness but low on authority are Indulgent parents who spoil their kids.

It is the contrast of the two high-authority parent types that is most relevant here. Parents who score high on authority but low on responsiveness are Authoritarian parents who are strict, dogmatic, and uncaring. However, parents who score high on authority but also score high on responsiveness are Authoritative. They expect obedience but they listen to their children and show warmth to them.

In my experience, it occasionally surprises some Americans that lots of research suggests kids have the best outcomes under Authoritative parents. Indulgent and Neglectful parents tend to raise unhappy and unsuccessful kids. So parents with no authority

at all don't do very well. Parents who have nothing but authority – cold authoritarians – also don't do well. But parents with
a combination of authority and responsiveness raise successful
kids at very high rates.[8]

This work highlights an important point for our larger study of
authoritarianism. The proper substitute for authoritarianism isn't
chaos. The proper substitute is good authority that is responsive
to the populace. We need leaders. Authoritarianism is essentially
a desire to put strong-but-bad leaders in power. The proper substitute for authoritarianism isn't to put no leaders in power, but
to put responsive and warm leaders in power. We shouldn't want
less leadership; we should want *better* leadership.

Authoritarianism to *What?*

That leads us to another common misconception about authoritarian followers. I think we tend to imagine authoritarians as
the kind of folk who indiscriminately obey any authority figure
who happens to walk by. After all, aren't authoritarians obedient
sheep who just do what they're told? If an authoritarian is walking down the street and someone orders them to do something,
wouldn't they be more likely than non-authoritarians to do it?

But a moment's reflection shows how wrong that view is.
Imagine an authoritarian Trump supporter walking down the
street and subsequently being commanded by Joe Biden to support climate change research. Do you see? It matters very much
to an authoritarian *who* is giving the command and *what* the
command is about. Authoritarianism is highly domain-specific:
Authoritarians get very attached to particular leaders in particular
domains, but they aren't likely to obey just any old leader.

This means that people can be authoritarian about almost anything. If people really hate bats, they might form an authoritarian movement to kill bats. But if people think that bats are awesome, they might be just as likely to form an authoritarian movement to *save* bats. Authoritarians *are* more likely to seek out and obey authority figures, yes – but only authority figures who care about their preferred domain. And that domain can literally be anything. That means one of the questions we have to ask about authoritarians is: Authoritarianism to *what?*

Consider the religion-versus-science dichotomy. We commonly associate authoritarianism with religion. And rightly so – religion is often one of the most pernicious purveyors of authoritarian evils.[9] People less commonly associate science with authoritarianism; and yet an increasing amount of evidence shows that science isn't a cure-all for authoritarian ills and, in fact, can actually serve as a conduit for them. For example, in one of my favorite studies, participants were told to do something they believed would seriously harm a fish.[10] (Don't worry, fish-lovers, the fish was actually a very lifelike robot – but participants didn't know that.) Beforehand, the researchers put some of these people in a 'scientific mindset' by having them write about science, while other control participants were not. Did approaching the situation with a scientific approach make participants less likely to obey the authoritarian command to harm a presumably innocent fish? Not at all. In fact, the opposite occurred: Putting people in a scientific mindset made them *more* likely to obey scientific authority to inject toxic chemicals into a fish.

This example illustrates the complex and domain-specific nature of authoritarian behavior. Putting people in a science-loving mindset can make them more authoritarian if the authority figure in question is a scientist asking them to do immoral things. This is important because, psychologically speaking, there is no reason that liberals can't be just as authoritarian as conservatives, if the situational domain meets the right set of authority figures for the right kind of people.

So that brings us to the question: Is that convergence of situations, leaders, and people currently happening on the left? Do we currently have a left-wing authoritarian problem? The answer to this question is scientifically indisputable:

Without a doubt.

Left-Wing Authoritarian Leaders

What has happened in the Trump era, the media convinced itself, the corporate media, that the real threats to the United States were no longer the CIA, and the Pentagon, and the NSA, and Wall Street and Silicon Valley, all of whom are on their side in trying to undermine Trump. It's the Trump movement and people who are conservative. Those are criminals in their eyes. And they've moved their media lens from the people who used to be the target of it – people in power centers – to individual citizens whose only crime is that they have the wrong ideology. And they are using their vast resources, the *Washington Post* is owned by Jeff Bezos, not to challenge actual power centers, but to destroy and wreck the lives and reputations of people who they regard as having the wrong politics. That's all this is about.[11]

– Pulitzer Prize–winning journalist
Glenn Greenwald

We are going to spend a lot of time in this book diagnosing left-wing authoritarian followers. But of course, leaders do matter too. For one thing, in a democracy, the success of left-wing authoritarian leaders is in part a marker of how authoritarian the populace is. If people want a strong leader to crush their enemies, they are more likely to vote for strong leaders who say they will crush their enemies. If people want leaders to silence their foes, they will follow media personalities who argue for censorship of their foes.

So it is still important that we complement evidence based on scientific research of authoritarian followers with evidence that there are left-wing authoritarian leaders. We'll see in Chapter 6 that liberals in the US are especially reticent to admit their own leaders are authoritarian – even when they obviously are. As noted earlier, I've been asked a lot about instances of left-wing authoritarian leadership – generally with the idea that there really aren't a lot of examples. Left-wingers don't like to see their own authoritarian leaders as authoritarian.

To be honest, I find this kind of questioning quite startling. My problem in preparing material for this book was not 'Can I find enough material from left-wing authoritarian leaders that I can fill a book?' No; my problem was rather the opposite. I am bombarded by obvious examples of left-wing authoritarian leaders on a near daily basis, and it was hard to winnow these examples down to fit the comparatively small space I had. As it is for Glenn Greenwald, it is obvious to any casual observer that there are a lot of left-wing authoritarian leaders in politics and in the media who are using their 'vast resources' to 'wreck the lives of people who they regard as having the wrong politics'.

If you are interested in the larger picture, you can go to our website at leftwingauthoritarianism.org, where we have a 'left-wing authoritarianism tracker'. I will here list only a few examples. Consider Justin Trudeau, the prime minister of Canada. Trudeau seized the assets of Canadian truckers because he disagreed with them politically. He vilified them. He stopped their peaceful protests. Glenn Greenwald said of the treatment of these truckers: 'The tactics Trudeau is employing are a decade in the making, and are part of a much broader plan to criminalize and then crush dissent,' noting in another tweet that 'episodes like this demonstrate just how propaganda functions. We're so well-trained to instantly recognize these tyrannical attacks on dissent as autocratic and tyrannical when used by enemies of the West, but barred from seeing them the same way when used by our own governments.'[12]

Indeed, Trudeau has consistently used autocratic and authoritarian measures to stop his political enemies from protesting against him peacefully. He's stolen millions of dollars of their money and sent the police after them, all because they *disagreed with him*.

It's probably no coincidence that Trudeau has praised leftist authoritarian leaders in other countries, saying of China that 'there's a level of admiration I actually have for China. Because their basic dictatorship is allowing them to actually turn their economy around on a dime'[13] and of former Cuban dictator Fidel Castro that he is a 'remarkable leader'.[14]

Western Europe, too, abounds with liberal authoritarian leadership. For example, one study of European Union nations during the Covid pandemic not only revealed deeply authoritarian leadership, but also provided a sober warning about the post-pandemic Western world. The author summarizes the findings this way:

> The multifaceted analysis carried out in this study on linkages between private companies and state security agencies, pandemic legislation, and essential good classifications in the realm of shopping reveals that during the pandemic, liberal democracies implemented policies that are akin to authoritarian liberalism and that a post-pandemic social order is likelier to be defined by an overt sense of authoritarian liberalism rather than some of the incremental erosions of constitutional democracy that scholars have associated with democratic backsliding over the last decade.[15]

This study suggests that Europeans are in danger of ceding their world to overtly liberal bullies. But this isn't just a problem for Europeans. And that brings us to … Dr Tony Fauci, the *de facto* leader of the Covid response in the US. As one example, read what Fauci says about a US court – the legitimate entity in this particular case for deciding what is legally appropriate – making a decision he disagrees with:

> I'm surprised and disappointed because those types of things really are the purview of the CDC. This is a public health issue and for a court to come in, and you look at the rationale for that it's not particularly firm. We are concerned about that, about the courts getting involved in things that are unequivocally a public health decision. This is a CDC issue, should not have been a court issue … So for a court to come in and interfere in that is really unfortunate. It's unfortunate because

it's against public health principles, number one. And number two, is because that's no place for courts to do that. This is a CDC decision.[16]

This is absolutely chilling. One of the authoritarianism items on the well-respected World Values Survey says this: 'Having experts, not government, make decisions according to what they think is best for the country.' In other words, authoritarians want their own side's individual expert to be able to override governments and laws. Authoritarians want to exert power over others to restrict their freedoms. So authoritarian experts don't want to bother with democracy and consensus.

Fauci's statement could be taken word for word from the authoritarianism questionnaire. Forget the government; forget the laws; forget checks and balances; forget all that legal stuff, *let the experts decide unilaterally*. Never mind that this isn't just a public health decision, it is a decision with implications for freedom, for human psychology, for all kinds of things. There is a reason that we don't let one single-issue expert of any ilk unilaterally decide what impacts the freedoms of the entire country. But Tony Fauci thinks he should have the power to force people to wear masks. It's not surprising that Fauci also tried to dismiss people who criticized him as attacking science itself (after all, in his words, attacking him is 'really criticizing science, because I represent science'[17]) and that he told unvaccinated people to just 'get over it'.[18] That's what authoritarians do – they claim they know what's best for you and tell you that if you have questions, you should 'get over it' because they are 'science'.

Similarly, California governor Gavin Newsom signed a bill making it illegal for doctors to say certain things to their patients about Covid-19.[19] In short, doctors must state the liberal party orthodoxy or be quiet – an orthodoxy that, as we'll see in Chapter 3, is at least worth questioning. Newsom wants to take away doctors' rights, rights likely guaranteed by the First Amendment of the US Constitution, to talk honestly with their patients about their own opinions. (Indeed, the bill was in fact later overturned in court.[20]) The common denominator across Fauci and Newsom that defines them as authoritarian is that they want power to be centralized into their own hands to exert on their political enemies. I'm happy for Fauci to have an opinion, I just don't think he should be allowed to force it on the whole country. I'm fine for Gavin Newsom to have an opinion, but it is glaringly authoritarian for him to demand that it be shared by every doctor in his state.

The situation isn't any better in academic circles. For example, at the Society for Personality and Social Psychology's (SPSP) 2024 conference, a poster presentation was canceled by SPSP leadership *after it had been accepted through the normal scientific process.* The reason? The poster contained statements offensive to authoritarian progressive groups.[21] Such blatant bullying by academic liberals is commonplace these days. Klaus Fiedler, one of the most respected academics in my field, was forced to resign as editor of a top journal because he facilitated scientific critique of a paper promoting progressive values.[22] Tracy Høeg was fired from her position at UC Davis for daring to present data that questioned the progressive Covid orthodoxy.[23] More broadly, the whole country witnessed an outpouring of academic left-wing authoritarianism after the Hamas invasion of Israel on October 7, 2023; to name just one example, a Cornell professor expressed that he found the massacre of Jews 'exhilarating'.[24] In each of these cases, liberal leaders engaged in classic authoritarian behaviors: They used their positions of power to censor, fire, or dehumanize their enemies.

I could go on with these examples for ages. But I don't have to do that here, because you will see scores of such examples in the pages of this book. You will see authoritarian leftists censor, bully, silence, harass, and destroy their enemies. You will see leftists ignore the law. You will see them hate and hurt and steal – all in the name of their authoritarian cause. They won't call it that; but it is clearly authoritarian all the same. And in this book, we are going to both diagnose the psychology of left-wing authoritarianism *and* discuss the cure for it.

The Rather Large Right-Wing Elephant in the Room

The proverbial elephant in any room for liberal authoritarians is this: Why the heck aren't we talking about *conservative* authoritarians instead? After all, the skeptic says, haven't right-wing authoritarians caused a ton of grief, suppressed a lot of people, and killed a lot of people? Are we just going to ignore Hitler? Are we just going to ignore the KKK? Are we just going to ignore the God Hates Gays movement of Westboro Baptist Church in Kansas? Wasn't the infamous 'Moral Majority' a tool for right-wing authoritarians to bludgeon those different from them? Wasn't Trump really a right-wing authoritarian?

I get that kind of skepticism a lot. And what I've consistently said is this: Yes, right-wing authoritarians are a big problem. I don't like conservative authoritarians any more than I like liberal authoritarians. I think both kinds are dangerous and both kinds should be stopped.

But part of my reason for writing a book on left-wing authoritarianism in particular is this: The two types of authoritarianism have to be dealt with *together*. As we'll see in Chapter 7, we ultimately cannot treat conservative and liberal authoritarianism independently. They are a part of the same package. If we only deal with authoritarianism on one side of the political spectrum, we are doomed to failure.

So yes, right-wing authoritarians are a real problem too – they are currently causing havoc in my own country and around the world. But I'm not going to spend a lot of time diagnosing them, because people in my field have spent 50 years doing nothing but diagnosing conservative authoritarians. You can find any number of articles or books on the psychology of right-wing authoritarians. But to my knowledge, no psychologist has written a comprehensive book on the psychology of left-wing authoritarians. And, in fact, most psychologists – wrongly, as we'll illustrate throughout this book – have treated authoritarianism as if it is really mostly (and sometimes only) a right-wing problem.

But we'll never solve our problems this way. As long as we refuse to address right-wing *and* left-wing authoritarianism together, we may be doomed to an ever-increasing cycle of authoritarian scorching. So the first order of business is to better understand how many left-wing authoritarians there are, what these left-wing authoritarians are like, and how they are similar to – and different from – right-wing authoritarians.

The Appreciably Smaller Left-Wing Elephant in the Room: The 'Classical Liberal'

On the other side of the proverbial elephant herd lies a different objection to this book: That *true* liberalism would never support authoritarianism, and thus most cases of seemingly authoritarian liberals are not actually 'liberal' bullies.

I've heard that kind of comment a lot, too, and we will address this issue more completely in Chapter 6. Here, however, it is worth tackling the definitional question at the heart of this elephant: What do I mean by the word 'liberal' in *liberal bullies*? What exactly is the 'left-wing' in *left-wing authoritarianism*?

Political labels are not perfect, monolithic monikers. What counts as a 'liberal' in one place might not count as a 'liberal' in another. For example, our lab has pointed out that a 'liberal' in New York is pretty different than a 'liberal' in Montana, and both are pretty different than a 'liberal' in Russia.[25] Colleagues I've worked with from around the world have frequently commented that 'liberals' in (for example) New Zealand and Western Europe are not really like 'liberals' in the US in many ways. Of course, there are many similarities in the actual beliefs of those liberal persons across places too: Liberals across the globe are more likely to accept communist and socialist philosophies, tend to favor governmental social programs, and are more likely to support climate activism. But nonetheless, the differences between people calling themselves 'liberal' make it hard to definitively label anyone a *true* liberal.

From a scientific point of view, this measurement problem is hardly unique – it is essentially baked into most psychological or ideological categories. No two extraverts are alike, either. No two sociopaths are alike. And yet extraversion and sociopathy are still meaningful measurement categories. 'Liberal', in the same vein, cannot possibly capture a one-size-fits-all set of beliefs. That is one of the reasons why, in this book, I primarily rely on a tried-and-true way to measure such constructs: Asking people how they think of themselves. As such, I generally take 'left-wing' or 'liberal' to mean 'someone who self-identifies as a left-winger/liberal' or 'someone who identifies with a political party that is largely considered liberal'. While not without its problems, this approach cuts across both cultural differences and potential reframing biases and allows the terms to be defined at the local level by the people most competent to judge them.

Against that backdrop, let's return to the elephant in our room. Liberalism historically has some of its roots in free speech, equality, democracy, and the formation of consensus through dialogue.[26] These roots are fundamentally anti-authoritarian, and the branches of this anti-authoritarianism can be seen in self-identified liberals' own views of their group right down to the present in modern America – so much so that the terms 'illiberalism' and 'authoritarianism' are often used as synonyms.[27] Thus, how can we legitimately say there is such a thing as a 'liberal bully'?

On the one hand, I think liberals who claim that liberalism is inherently anti-authoritarian have a point. If you are one of those liberals, then we are likely kindred spirits, and I suspect you will find quite a bit to like in this book. I, too, would love to see liberalism return to its roots in free speech, equality, and open dialogue. That view has come to be called 'classical liberalism' and that's the kind of liberal I was, when I used the word 'liberal' to describe myself. (I have not substantively changed any of my views except my view on what the term 'liberal' means to most liberals. With some qualifications, I still largely hold the same beliefs I did when I called myself a 'liberal'.)

On the other hand, there are legitimate reasons to think that claiming most liberal bullies are not *really* liberal goes too far in its semantic sleight of hand.

Consider a parable. Suppose that some people create an organization devoted to the free exchange of ideas about ice cream called the National Ice Cream Exchange (NICE). Originally, there were many and varied opinions welcome in the group – but over time, NICE began to stand primarily for one thing: The removal of all ice cream types except plain vanilla. They pushed for legislation banning everything but vanilla. They tried to get anyone who said 'Rocky Road is great' canceled on Twitter. So, while at the beginning NICE really stood for the open exchange of ideas about ice cream, by the end the majority of its members either really supported the vanilla-only agenda or didn't openly oppose it, and those few who stood out in favor of a free ice cream culture were largely ridiculed by the people in charge of NICE.

Now imagine that, if I tried to point out that NICE stood for anti-Rocky Road authoritarian measures, you said to me, 'But you are defining NICE in the wrong way. Sure, there are a few bad actors there, but the *true* spirit of NICE is open discussion, the principle on which it was founded.' I would respond to you by saying, 'If the majority of the people of NICE succeed in passing legislation to stop me from eating Rocky Road, then that's what NICE stands for. The fact that a few people in NICE are actually ... nice ... can't change the fact that the organization now stands for authoritarianism.'

This analogy is exaggerated. All the same, I'm not sure it is very helpful to try and skirt around the facts on the ground. Are we going to *really* call the many, *many* authoritarian Democrats in the US 'conservatives'? That would be bordering on the empirically absurd, given that 'Democrat' overlaps so strongly with 'Liberal' in the US that the two items are considered a part of the same scale measuring political ideology.[28] And as we'll see throughout this book, an alarming number of people calling themselves liberals are in favor of authoritarian measures.

As a result, the most empirically justified and honest way of communicating about someone who calls themselves a liberal and is also a bully is to do the straightforward thing and call them a 'liberal bully'. *They* have called themselves liberals. *They* are implementing policies that most people agree are liberal policies (for example, the climate agenda) with authoritarian tactics. At some point, pointing to a few – seemingly shrinking – strands of liberalism that stand opposed to authoritarianism is not a very effective argument. That classical liberal elephant in our room has become increasingly small.

A second reason to be skeptical is this: If we are going to pick an issue on which to draw the 'true' line between liberals and conservatives, *classical liberalism* is an odd choice. That's in part because classical liberalism has made strong historical inroads in conservative circles, particularly amongst American Republicans.[29] Former US Republican Speaker of the House Paul Ryan said, 'I really call myself a classical liberal more than a conservative.'[30] Grove City College (where I work) is considered one of the most conservative academic institutions in the US, and yet it has strong ties to the Ludwig von Mises classical liberalism school.[31] As such, classical liberalism doesn't provide the clearest demarcation line between typical liberal and conservative persons. While liberals no doubt have historically believed in classical liberalism more than conservatives – and our own data capture the echoes of that difference even today – if we were picking specific ideological issues on which to separate liberals from conservatives, classical liberalism wouldn't be in the top ten.

Classical liberals have the goal right. They want to bring liberals around the world back to their roots: Back to open dialogue, to free speech, to civil rights, to equality. I do too. In fact, I really, *really* wish those liberals would succeed in my home country at bringing American Democrats back to a saner, less authoritarian approach to government. But they haven't succeeded so far and very little evidence suggests that they will do so on their own. If they do – if Democrats become the bastion for free speech and open dialogue that I used to hope they were – then I will rewrite this section in the future.

I'm not holding my breath. As we'll see shortly, rather than fixing their own authoritarianism problems, in recent history liberal elites have created a slanted playing field that essentially recasts all liberal authoritarians as conservatives.

The Shards-of-Glass Problem

Our data are directly contrary to theories that dismiss the possibility of left-wing authoritarianism.

– Peter Suedfeld (Emeritus Professor at the University of British Columbia) and colleagues, in 1994

Almost 30 years ago, award-winning research giant Peter Suedfeld warned that our field was too blasé about left-wing authoritarianism. Suedfeld is one of the most important scientists in the history of the field: He's the past president of the world's largest political psychology organization; he's changed the face of two completely separate major areas of research; and he's won multiple lifetime awards for his scientific work (including the Order of Canada, one of the highest civilian honors in that country[32]). You would think, with such a warning from such an academic legend, that researchers would have paid more attention.

But they didn't. In fact, what has happened since then can be summed up in one sad sentence: Academics have really, *really* botched authoritarianism research. It's important for you, as the intelligent citizen I take you for, to understand this. Part of the problem here is that academics created a tilted playing field that made it hard for us to truly solve the authoritarian problem – because they made it hard to identify left-wing authoritarians at all.

You may wonder: Given that there were plenty of warning signs, noted by famous people such as Peter Suedfeld, why *haven't* we spent more time on left-wing authoritarians as a field? Understanding that question is a clue to understanding the authoritarian problem itself, so we're going to dig in a bit on the history of left-wing authoritarian research in social psychology.

One of the most cited reasons for academics' subsequent dismissal of liberal authoritarianism as a meaningful construct is that the most influential authoritarian researcher of all time, Bob Altemeyer, attempted to measure left-wing authoritarianism in the mid-to-late 1990s – and largely failed to find any evidence of it. In his words: 'The "authoritarian on the left" has been as scarce as hens' teeth in my samples.'

Altemeyer is one of the best academics in the history of our field, and I have no end of respect for him. But this oft-cited statement has done more than almost any other sentence in academic history to muddy the authoritarianism waters. And we can learn a lot by looking at the left-wing authoritarianism questionnaire he developed on which this evidence is based.

Reading the items on Altemeyer's left-wing authoritarian (LWA) questionnaire was one of the single most stunning moments of my academic career. I had heard the lack of evidence for LWA for a long time before I saw those items. And the moment I started reading, I could immediately tell something was completely wrong. I began to suspect that, great academic though he was, Bob Altemeyer hadn't tried very hard to seek out liberal authoritarians.

Because his LWA scale and his right-wing authoritarian (RWA) scale weren't remotely comparable.

To understand his error, first consider another parable. Imagine I wanted to decide whether there were more broccoli lovers or donut lovers in the world. So I designed a single item for each food type and gave it to thousands of people. As seen in the 'Glass Shards' figure, my broccoli item said 'I like to eat broccoli', whereas my donut item said 'I like to eat donuts filled with glass shards.'

Image how happy broccoli lovers were when the results came back: There were thousands of broccoli lovers out there, but donut lovers were 'as rare as hens' teeth'! However, could we trust those data? No. The flaw in this design is evident. I didn't give a parallel test because I put glass shards on only one side of the food aisle. My test likely didn't tell me anything about broccoli or donuts; rather, it told me that, regardless of what food it is in, people do not like to eat glass shards. As the bottom left of the figure shows, if you reversed the scenario and put the glass shards in broccoli instead, you'd almost certainly get the opposite result. This was never about donuts or broccoli, but about shards.

Glass Shards: A Comparative Parable		Authoritarianism: Literal Comparison	
BROCCOLI	DONUTS	RWA	LWA
'I like to eat broccoli.'	'I like to eat donuts filled with glass shards.'	'Let's submit to authorities who crush evil ways.'	'Let's submit to authorities who crush evil ways by joining a violent liberal revolution that attempts to overthrow the government.'
Results: Moderate-to-high scores.	Results: Very low scores.	Results: Moderate-to-high scores.	Results: Very low scores.
Conclusion: 'Lots of broccoli lovers'.	Conclusion: Donut-lovers 'as rare as hen's teeth'.	Conclusion: 'Lots of people high in RWA.'	Conclusion: 'As rare as hen's teeth … the Loch Ness Monster.'

The Hypothetical Reversal		The Hypothetical Reversal	
BROCCOLI	DONUTS	RWA	LWA
'I like to eat broccoli filled with glass shards.'	'I like to eat donuts.'	'Let's submit to authorities who crush evil ways by joining a violent conservative revolution that attempts to overthrow the government.'	'Let's submit to authorities who crush evil ways.'
Results: Very low scores.	Results: Moderate-to-high scores.	Results: Very low scores	Results: Moderate scores.
Conclusion: 'Like looking for the Loch Ness Monster.'	Conclusion: 'Lots of donut lovers.'	Conclusion: 'The conservative authoritarian is a myth.'	Conclusion: 'Liberal authoritarians are quite abundant everywhere.'

Altemeyer put metaphorical glass shards exclusively on the left-wing side of the authoritarian measurement aisle. For example, Altemeyer's LWA scale requires participants who score high on the questionnaire to support a violent revolution to overthrow the established government. In fact, 20 of the 22 items on Altemeyer's LWA scale reference a revolutionary movement. You can see this yourself in the 'Altemeyer's LWA Scale' list below. A representative item says: 'The members of the Establishment deserve to be dealt with harshly, without mercy, when they are finally overthrown.' By contrast, *none* of the items on any of Altemeyer's RWA scales makes a single reference to violent upheavals overthrowing the establishment.

Few people, conservative or liberal, want to uproot their lives to join a revolution to topple the government. Even most *authoritarians* are not like that, on either side of the political aisle. So when you throw those revolutionary glass shards only on the liberal side, you don't get a lot of liberal authoritarians. But that doesn't mean liberals are less authoritarian than conservatives; rather, it means that, like conservatives, most liberals – even most liberal authoritarians – don't want to join a violent revolution. If Altemeyer instead had put the glass shards on the conservative side, we'd be talking today about how hard it was to find those darned elusive *right-wing* authoritarians.

Altemeyer's LWA Scale
(Revolutionary Elements in Bold)

1. Communism has its flaws, but the basic idea of **overthrowing the right-wing Establishment** and giving its wealth to the poor is still a very good one.

2. Socialism will never work, so people should **treat left-wing revolutionaries** as the dangerous troublemakers they are.

3. People should do whatever a **left-wing revolutionary movement** against the Establishment decides.

4. The last thing our country needs is a **revolutionary movement demanding total submission** to its leaders, conformity among its members, and attack upon the Establishment.

5. The conservative, right-wing Establishment will never give up its power peacefully, so a **revolutionary movement is justified in using violence to crush it.**

6. There is a dangerous tendency for left-wing, anti-Establishment, **revolutionary movements to demand too much conformity** and blind obedience from their members.

7. Anyone who truly wants to help our country should support **left-wing revolutionary leaders stomp out the Establishment,** and then devote themselves to the new way of life ahead.

8. **Socialist revolutions require great leadership.** When a strong, determined rebel leads the attack on the Establishment, that person deserves our complete faith and support.

9. When a leftist, anti-Establishment movement begins dictating to its members whom they can associate with, where they can shop, and what they can eat, it's time to leave it.

10. The conservative Establishment has so much power and is so unfair, we have to **submit to the leaders and rules of a revolutionary movement** in order to destroy them.

11. Our present society has its problems, but it would be a great mistake to think any **leftist leader who wants to overthrow the Establishment** has 'the answers'.

12. The members of the Establishment deserve to be dealt with harshly, without mercy, **when they are finally overthrown.**

13. It would be a dreadful mistake for people in our country to unite behind leftist leaders, submit to their authority, and **launch attacks upon the Establishment.**

14. Even a **revolutionary left-wing movement dedicated to overthrowing the present,** totally unjust right-wing system does NOT have the right to tell its members how to act, dress, think, etc.

15. A **leftist revolutionary movement** is quite justified in attacking the Establishment, and in demanding obedience and conformity from its members.

16. It would be wrong to try to solve our problems by **acts of violence** against the conservative Establishment.

17. We should devotedly follow determined leaders who will fight the Establishment.

18. If certain people refuse to accept the historic restructuring of society that will come **when the Establishment is overthrown,** they will have to be removed and smashed.

19. If people who want to **overthrow the Establishment let revolutionary leaders** become important authorities in their lives, they are just exchanging one set of masters for another.

20. Even though the Establishment groups who control our country are quite repressive and unfair, society should only be reformed through NON-violent means.

21. If the 'Have-Nots' in our **country are ever going to overthrow the 'Haves,'** and give them the harsh treatment they fully deserve, the 'Have-Nots' must follow the rules and leaders of the revolutionary movement.

22. One of the worst things people could do in America now would to be to support the **left-wing, revolutionary forces trying to overthrow the Establishment.**

33

In fact, whereas Altemeyer's RWA scale reads like a measure of general authoritarianism, Altemeyer's LWA scale reads like a screening instrument for joining a terrorist group. As a result, the fact that few people scored high on Altemeyer's LWA scale tells us little about left-wing authoritarianism. Rather, it simply tells us the obvious fact that, whether left-wing or right-wing, few people want to endorse, let alone join, a violent military movement designed to attack and overthrow something else. However, historically, much of academia's dismissal of LWA was based on this clearly flawed evidence from Altemeyer.

And thus academics largely ignored left-wing authoritarians for two decades.

Why We're Bad at Solving the Glass-Shards Problem

How might we go about solving the glass-shards problem?

One way is to write measurements that have absolutely no ideological content at all. I get this kind of suggestion a lot. Why not write an authoritarianism questionnaire that doesn't mention anything 'right-wing' or 'left-wing'? Why not just ask people 'Do you want an authority figure to crush your enemies' without mentioning who the authority figure is and who the enemies are?

This sounds nice, and if someone can figure out how to do it, I'd be all in. However, the history of our field shows that we are bad at this. Consider a case study. In one of the most famous papers in psychology history, John Jost and his colleagues argued that conservatives were uniquely prone to rigid thinking (called 'cognitive rigidity'), whereas liberals were uniquely open-minded.[33] Part of this evidence was based on measurements of rigidity referred to as 'dogmatism'. We'll cover the larger evidence on this construct in Chapter 2, but for the moment I want to focus on the measurement issue. The claim of Jost and colleagues was that, because these dogmatism measurements don't contain any conservative or liberal content – they are, in the parlance of my field, 'value-neutral' or 'ideologically neutral' – they can be used as a *pure* test of how dogmatic liberals and conservatives are. Using these tests, it turns out that conservatives consistently scored higher on typical dogmatism measurements. Therefore, of course, conservatives are uniquely dogmatic. Those pesky and rigid conservatives are the problem.

However, the 'dogmatism' questionnaires they used turn out not to be so ideologically neutral after all. In particular, those scales contained domains of content – such as dogmatism about religion – that would make liberals, and not conservatives, score low on them. Liberals thus may score lower on those questionnaires, not because they are less dogmatic, but because they are less religious. If I asked you 'Do you believe dogmatically in the Bible?' and you are a liberal atheist, you might reply 'no' because you aren't dogmatic. But you might also reply 'no' even if you are *extremely* dogmatic about your own beliefs because you don't believe in your opponents' religion.

It isn't just us that noticed this problem, and the results have been nothing short of farcical. As it happens, a few years after Jost and colleagues' paper came out, another group of well-known researchers did a separate large analysis of the relationship between conservatism and cognitive rigidity.[34] In Jost and colleagues' analysis, dogmatism was used as a measurement of rigidity. However, in this later analysis of conservatism and rigidity, Van Hiel and colleagues used the *exact same dogmatism* measurement as a measurement of – wait for it – conservatism.

If you want to understand why a lot of us independent thinkers are skeptical of evidence on this kind of thing, think about that for five minutes. Quite comically, in separate analyses of the conservatism–rigidity relationship, one set of researchers used dogmatism as a *conservatism* measurement and the other set used it as a *rigidity* measurement. Jost trumpets dogmatism as 'ideologically neutral' while Van Hiel actually uses it as an ideological measure. When it comes to dogmatism, we can't seem to tell the difference between the independent and dependent measures.

The Common Sense Thing Altemeyer Should Have Done

So writing valueless questionnaires doesn't seem especially fruitful because we simply aren't very good at it. And that leads us to the most common-sense way of removing the shards of glass. Rather than trying to create ideologically neutral measurements, a better way is to create appropriately parallel measurements that keep all of the key language for whatever thing you are trying to measure the same – so no shards of glass – but purposefully change *only* the ideological content.

It's easiest to see the value of this with an example. We did this in our own research by simply rewriting the dogmatism items in question to deal with liberal domains instead of conservative ones, while keeping the dogmatism language identical. For example, a scale targeted to conservatives had an item that read: 'A **religious** group which tolerates too much difference of opinion among its own members cannot exist for long.' The parallel dogmatism questionnaire targeted to liberals had an item that read: 'An **environmental** group which tolerates too much difference of opinion among its own members cannot exist for long.' We kept the same dogmatism-related words and only changed the target group. Thus, unlike in Altemeyer's scale, we don't have any additional shards of glass thrown into one side or the other. Instead, we purposefully ensure that one scale targets conservatives and one scale targets liberals, but that all the rest of the language is the same.

What happens when you do that? What happens when you provide a fair and balanced test of dogmatism that removes shards of glass and doesn't introduce bias in measurement? Liberals are just as dogmatic as conservatives are – in fact, if anything, fairly consistently in our work, there was more dogmatism on the liberal side.[35]

Stripping Away the Shards

> I will argue that we should never bend standards of evidence and
> proof, no matter how morally inspiring the cause. It is not enough,
> moreover, just to admonish everyone to be fair-minded; we need to
> institutionalize procedures that apply the same methodological and
> logical standards to politically popular and unpopular hypotheses
> alike (no small order in an ideologically skewed subfield where
> most researchers and reviewers hold left-of-center values).
>
> – University of Pennsylvania professor Phil Tetlock

And that brings us back to authoritarianism. Penn professor Phil Tetlock notes in this quote that we have to use the same standards of judgment on all sides of a political question. Translation to our present case: 'If doing thing X makes conservatives authoritarian, then doing thing X – to an exactly equivalent degree – ought also to make liberals authoritarian.'

Altemeyer's RWA scale – on which we based our own LWA

scale – has historically been, and still is, by far the most extensively used measurement of the right-wing authoritarianism construct. For example, we showed empirically that 79% of the scales from recent research that measured RWA used a version based on Altemeyer's scale.[36] So nearly everyone agrees that Altemeyer's scale is the gold standard for authoritarianism measurement. Given this, it is important that we apply the same standards of evidence to judging LWA that have been used to arrive at that conclusion for RWA.

In our lab's award-winning and influential work[37] on left-wing authoritarianism in the US, we did the simple, common-sense thing that I imagined Altemeyer would have originally done. Namely, we followed the 'parallel scales' shard-stripping strategy: We took his original RWA scale and created parallel items that focused on left-wing authoritarian content. These items keep as much of the same authoritarian language as possible from the original scale, but substitute liberal groups as targets of positive things, and conservative groups as targets of negative things. The figure below lists one illustrative example.

RWA/LWA Example

Altemeyer RWA item	Conway et al. LWA item
It's always better to trust the judgment of the proper authorities *in government and religion* than to listen to the noisy rabble-rousers in our society who are trying to create doubts in people's minds.	It's always better to trust the judgment of the proper authorities in science with respect to issues like *global warming and evolution* than to listen to the noisy rabble-rousers in our society who are trying to create doubts in people's minds.

Using this strategy, we find almost as much, and by some metrics more, evidence for left-wing authoritarianism in the US as we do for right-wing authoritarianism. And it is important to remember parallel standards of evidence here. We have to be fair. Consider that participants who score high on both the RWA and our new LWA scale agree that (italicized words are direct quotes from the LWA scale) *our country needs a mighty leader*, that the leader should *destroy* opponents; that people should *trust the judgment of the proper authorities*, avoid listening to *noisy rabble-rousers in our society who are trying to create doubts in people's minds, put some tough leaders in power who oppose those values and silence the troublemakers*, and *smash* the beliefs of opponents; that *what our country really needs is a strong, determined leader who will crush the evil*; that society should *strongly punish those* they disagree with. They also deny that an opponent has a right to *be wherever he or she wants to be*, and support the statement that the country would be better off if certain groups *would just shut up and accept their group's proper place in society*. These items hit all of the hallmarks of the consensus conceptualization of the *authoritarian* person.

For decades, it has been assumed that if people agree with those statements when the targets of authoritarianism are conservative and the outgroups are liberal, then they are indeed authoritarians. Therefore, if people agree with those statements when the targets of authoritarianism are liberal and the outgroups are conservative, we must – applying the same standard – also agree that they are authoritarians. If we grant that someone saying they want to 'put some tough leaders in power who oppose those values and silence the troublemakers' is authoritarian when referring to right-wing leaders, then we also have to grant that someone saying the exact same thing when referring to left-wing leaders is also an authoritarian.

We Have a Real Left-Wing Authoritarian Problem

Indeed, once we strip away the shards-of-glass problem from authoritarian measurement – once we truly apply a fair standard to both sides – it becomes clear that the scientific evidence tells a consistent story: An alarmingly high percentage of left-wing people around the world are currently authoritarian. That includes our lab's work on left-wing authoritarianism in the US – work revealing that liberals are just as likely as conservatives to endorse items indicating they want authority figures to crush their enemies, silence opponents, and restore order. In fact, as with dogmatism, in many of our studies the highest average score for authoritarianism has generally been for liberals on the LWA scale. So if anything, our data suggest that liberals are currently slightly *more* prone to authoritarian beliefs than US conservatives are.

But I don't want to make too much of the percentages. I think a wider arc reveals that there are probably still more conservative authoritarians in the US than liberal ones. Rather, what I want instead to point out is this: By any metric from our own data, there are a *lot* of liberal authoritarians in the world right now – in the US and beyond.

We will cover this and much other work throughout this book. As we will see, those same liberals show predictable dogmatism, attitude extremism, and other markers of rigidity. This is the exact same kind of evidence (often using the exact same wording) that has been used for decades to advocate for the dangers of right-wing authoritarianism; thus, by fair standards of scientific evidence, we should be equally concerned about the dangers of left-wing authoritarianism.

Is this a small problem constrained to just a handful of liberals? Unfortunately, the answer to that question is no. As one way of quantifying this, for this book I re-analyzed our own data using metrics for authoritarianism suggested by Van Hiel and colleagues.[38] First, they used a metric representing how many people scored above the midpoint of the scale. Using this metric, we found that 45% of our samples were left-wing authoritarians, while 32% were right-wing authoritarians. Because that probably overestimates the actual percentage, Van Hiel also used a marker of more *extreme* authoritarianism – if people scored in the upper 80% of the scale. That kind of extreme score is generally pretty rare for a scale with such negative language, and thus one wouldn't expect too many people to reach that standard. And yet we found 8% of our sample were extreme left-wing authoritarians, compared to 7% of extreme right-wing authoritarians. If one extrapolates from these data to the general population, that means there are literally *tens of millions* of left-wing authoritarians in the US alone, and many of them hold very extreme views.

A different way of arriving at the percentage of left-wing authoritarians in the US got us to a similar conclusion. Instead of asking people about themselves, we asked average Americans to tell us about other people in their world. Specifically, we asked them how many left- and right-wing authoritarians they knew in their lives. I discuss these data in more detail in Chapter 6, but here I want to point out the bigger picture that's relevant to our current question. These data alarmingly reveal that average

Americans (even most American liberals) identify a high number of left-wing authoritarians in their actual lives. Extrapolating from those data about other people would, like our method of identifying individual authoritarians from their data about themselves, suggest the existence of *tens of millions* of left-wing authoritarians in the US alone.[39]

Triangulating Evidence

It isn't just our lab that has woken up to this growing left-wing authoritarianism threat. As we will see throughout these pages, there is also an emerging revolution of academic data outside of our lab, revealing a large body of evidence that left-wing authoritarians in the US and elsewhere are extremely authoritarian. This includes work in the US published in major research outlets that says, among other things, liberals more broadly are often just as prone as conservatives to possess traits considered hallmarks of authoritarianism, including resistance to change,[40] cognitive rigidity in attitude formation,[41] opinion certainty,[42] sweeping biases,[43] and racism.[44]

Much of that work was developed with an entirely different goal than ours and without our direct involvement. This is important because of a logical principle known as 'triangulation'. Triangulation suggests that the more independent sources of information ultimately point to the same conclusion, the more confident we can be in the conclusion itself. And that is even more the case when the sources look at the issue from a completely different starting point. If I tell you that Rocky Road ice cream is great, you might think twice about trying it. After all, I might be biased. But if three different people from three different countries tell you it's great, it increases your trust in that information. And that is especially the case if you know that one of them focused on its health value (lots of dairy!), one focused on its taste (chocolate tastes great!), and another focused on its texture (just the right ratio of chunky stuff to soft stuff!). To the degree that sources of information give you *different* perspectives that lead to the same conclusion, this suggests that Rocky Road is truly great.

That's partially what happened in left-wing authoritarianism research. For example, rather than trying to develop a parallel scale to the most-used RWA scale, as our lab did, researchers at Emory University (including Tom Costello and the beloved – and tragically now deceased – Scott Lilienfeld) wrote their own LWA scale 'from the bottom up'.[45] They essentially started from scratch, ignoring prior RWA research. Remarkably, using a completely different method of scale development than ours and developing it completely independently from our research program, our LWA scale and theirs are very highly correlated and show similar effects. This highlights that no matter how you approach the issue, left-wing authoritarianism is alive and well.

Indeed, the Emory researchers have shown, among other things, that left-wing authoritarians have a strong tendency to punish their political adversaries in experimental research.[46] This dovetails with multiple exemplars of such liberal authoritarian aggression seen in everyday life. Consider that Winston Marshall (founding member of the hit band Mumford & Sons) was ostracized and harassed online because he stuck up for a journalist who reported bad things about the left-wing group Antifa. It caused such trauma to the band that Marshall felt forced to leave, commenting: 'I could remain in the band and continue to self-censor but it will erode my sense of integrity. Gnaw my conscience. I've already felt that beginning.'[47]

Left-Wing Authoritarianism is a Worldwide Problem

Left-wing authoritarianism isn't constrained to just the US; it is a worldwide problem. Indeed, a long history of (often ignored) research reveals that authoritarianism sometimes has left-wing roots in Europe and beyond.[48] Building on this work, we were interested in evaluating the scope of left-wing authoritarianism around the globe. To do so, we used the authoritarianism scale on the well-validated World Values Survey. What we did was simple: We calculated whether authoritarian persons in each country were more likely to be right-wing or left-wing.[49] You can see a summary of the results in the table below.

We discovered that, while there is a tendency worldwide towards right-wing authoritarianism (as indicated by the larger number of countries on the right-hand side of the table) as we had expected, the tendency is extremely small – indeed much smaller than we had guessed beforehand – and in fact in many places, there was a tendency towards left-wing authoritarianism among the populace (the countries on the left-hand side). But even in countries that leaned towards right-wing authoritarianism, data suggest there would be *millions* of left-wing authoritarians. Consider the US, which has a slight leaning in this analysis towards right-wing authoritarianism: An effect size of '.02' means that there is almost no effect of political ideology on the likelihood of authoritarianism – which in turn means that authoritarianism occurs with nearly equal probability on both sides of the political aisle.

Authoritarianism Around the World
(From Conway et al., 2022)

LEFT-WING AUTHORITARIAN LEANING		RIGHT-WING AUTHORITARIAN LEANING	
Egypt	-.22	Yemen	.29
Estonia	-.16	Netherlands	.21
Uzbekistan	-.19	Argentina	.20
Azerbaijan	-.10	Chile	.19
Thailand	-.09	Spain	.18
Hong Kong	-.08	Uruguay	.18
Trinidad and Tobago	-.08	Morocco	.16
Algeria	-.08	Armenia	.12
Tunisia	-.06	Colombia	.11
Russia	-.04	Iraq	.10
Poland	-.03	Cyprus	.09
Georgia	-.03	Nigeria	.09
Palestine	-.03	Sweden	.08
Ukraine	-.03	South Korea	.08
Ecuador	-.03	Malaysia	.08
Australia	-.02	Germany	.07
Haiti	-.01	Belarus	.07
Turkey	-.01	Pakistan	.07
		Rwanda	.06
		Zimbabwe	.05
		Slovenia	.07

LEFT-WING AUTHORITARIAN LEANING (CONT.)	RIGHT-WING AUTHORITARIAN LEANING (CONT.)	
	Mexico	.04
	Kazakhstan	.04
	Kyrgyzstan	.03
	Lebanon	.03
	Libya	.03
	South Africa	.02
	United States	.02
	India	.02
	Taiwan	.02
	Romania	.02
	Philippines	.02
	Brazil	.01
	Ghana	.01
	Japan	.01

Effect sizes less than zero = more LWA.

Effect sizes greater than zero = more RWA.

This large body of evidence points to a very clear conclusion: Left-wing authoritarianism is a very real and very pervasive problem, not only in my own country, but throughout the world.

This suggests it is time for the world to collectively wake up a bit. Left-wing authoritarianism is not going anywhere on its own. If we are going to curb it, we need to actively fight it. And to actively fight it, we first need to fully understand it.

In each of the next five chapters, I dig deep into one aspect of the psychology of the left-wing authoritarian person. Then, having diagnosed the disease, in the concluding three chapters I offer some thoughts on the cure.

CHAPTER 2

INTELLECTUAL APATHY: A VIRUS THAT KILLS RATIONAL ARGUMENT

A post-truth democracy would no longer be a democracy.

– Jürgen Habermas, *Between Naturalism and Religion: Philosophical Essays*

German philosopher Jürgen Habermas argued for the importance of a public sphere – a place where groups could come together and argue rationally without fear of reprisal. If ever we came to devalue the truth exploration that happened in this sphere, we would be in danger of losing the essence of constructive democratic civilization. It would be a nightmare.

Left-wing authoritarians are currently making this nightmare dangerously close to a reality. You have likely heard of 'cancel culture'. Conservatives have of course done their fair share of 'canceling' over the years, and it is still a primary tactic of American Republicans. But when it comes to canceling, conservatives have absolutely *nothing* on modern liberals. Polling suggests that 50% of 'strong liberals' support the firing of Trump donors.[1] Think about that for a second. Half of 'strong liberals' think it is OK to fire people, not for being incompetent, not for breaking the law, but for political disagreements that *literally have nothing to do with their job*. And this isn't just talk. Actresses,[2] baseball personalities,[3] and Google employees[4] have all been fired for expressing conservative views.

The country has noticed. Polling data reveals that 62% of Americans (including 77% of Republicans and 52% of Democrats) are afraid to say what they think these days. They don't want to get fired or canceled. In fact, the only group of people in the country who aren't afraid to say what they think are the hard-line Marxist/progressives.[5] Those progressives, despite making up a comparatively small percentage of the country, have been ceded enormous power.

This has horrible downstream consequences for society. Cancel culture doesn't just cancel *people*. It cancels rational debate. Yes, cancel culture causes people who disagree with the mob's views to be silenced. But it *also* emboldens people *in* the mob to ignore reasonable arguments. The mind of an authoritarian isn't a thoughtful mind. In fact, one of the hallmarks of the modern left-wing authoritarian movement is its *intellectual apathy*.

As we'll see in this chapter, authoritarians not only possess a unique intellectual laziness, they also tend to spread their intellectual apathy to those around them like a virus. The consequence of this *authoritarian apathy virus* is an inability to have serious debates. And if we can't have serious debates, then – as Habermas predicted – we're not going to make it.

Why People Believe the Moon Landing Wasn't Real

I'll start with a seemingly odd angle of approach: Why do people believe fake news? Let's do a little experiment. Decide if you think each of the following six headlines represents something completely fake or something that really happened:

1. Because of the Lack of Men, Iceland Gives $5,000 Per Month to Immigrants Who Marry Icelandic Women!
2. Depression Symptoms Are Common Among Active Airline Pilots, International Survey Reveals
3. Gnarly! 6-Story Wave Is Revealed As Biggest Ever Recorded
4. Yahoo Suffers World's Biggest Hack Affecting 1 Billion Users
5. Billionaire Founder of Corona Beer Brewery Makes EVERYONE in his village a MILLIONAIRE in His Will
6. The Controversial Files: Fake Cigarettes Are Being Sold and Killing People, Here's How to Spot Counterfeit Packs

If you are scoring yourself, headlines 1, 5, and 6 are fake – they were news stories made up by researchers. Headlines 2, 3, and 4, however, represent real news headlines of events that really happened.

Now see if you can spot the bogus news in a different set of headlines:

1. Vladmir Putin 'Personally Involved' in US Hack, Report Claims
2. Sarah Palin Calls to Boycott Mall of America Because 'Santa Was Always White in the Bible'
3. Donald Trump Strikes Conciliatory Tone in Meeting with Tech Executives
4. Election Night: Hillary Was Drunk, Got Physical with Mook

and Podesta

5. Democrats Scramble to Prevent Their Own from Defecting to Trump
6. NYT David Brooks: 'Trump Needs to Decide If He Prefers to Resign, Be Impeached or Get Assassinated'
7. Trump to Ban All TV Shows that Promote Gay Activity Starting with *Empire* as President
8. Trump Lashes Out at *Vanity Fair*, One Day after It Lambastes His Restaurant

Headlines 2, 4, 6, and 7 are fake. Headlines 1, 3, 5, and 8 are actual headlines from real stories.

The world is a complicated place, and thus nobody perfectly discerns fake from real news all the time. But what factors influence why you might believe (or disbelieve) these kinds of fake news stories? To answer that question, Cornell University researcher Gordon Pennycook and his colleagues gave people headlines like the ones above.[6] Some of the headlines were true, some false. Further, some of the headlines were politically neutral (like the first set above), while some of them were politically loaded (like the second set).

Pennycook's findings were startling. What makes people better or worse at distinguishing real news from fake news turns out to be nothing at all like what I would have guessed. Decades of research in my field revealed the gigantic biases people have in favor of their own political groups. Thus, without seeing the data, the average political psychologist such as myself would have predicted the following: You'd be better at accurately identifying the first (neutral) set of articles than the second (political) set. If things are neutral, the reasoning goes, you wouldn't feel any special compunction to view them in a particular way. Because of that, you'd be an objective observer and would be more accurate.

The second set of political headlines, however, would have brought in your own political biases, making you more likely to believe what you wanted to see. So if you were a Democrat in the US, political-bias models would have said you'd be especially likely to believe fake news items 2 and 7 (because those make your political *opponents* look bad) but especially unlikely to believe fake news items 4 and 6 (because those make your *own* political group look bad). You'd also be especially likely to disbelieve true stories – such as about Trump striking a conciliatory tone with tech executives – that made your opponents look good.

As we'll see in Chapter 4, those political biases are real, and they help us understand authoritarianism. Pennycook's research, however, has smashed my pet political-bias theory of fake news to bits. In its place, it has substituted something else. This research suggests rather that what causes people to fall for fake news isn't bias; it's *intellectual laziness*.

Pennycook's team found that it didn't matter very much whether or not participants wanted a headline to be true. It didn't matter whether the headline was politically neutral or whether it supported or opposed participants' own political views. Rather, what mattered was their propensity to think reflectively about things in general.

To understand this, Pennycook also gave participants a standard test, called the Cognitive Reflection Test, of their likelihood of engaging in intellectual apathy. One of the items on this test is illustrative: 'A bat and ball cost $1.10 in total. The bat costs $1.00 more than the ball. How much does the ball cost?' If you don't think about it very much, you'll say 10 cents. About 65% of respondents in fact give that answer. But the other 35% reflect briefly and realize that 10 cents must obviously be wrong, because if the ball cost 10 cents, the bat would have to cost $1.10 and together they would equal $1.20.

If you are the kind of person who gets the bat-and-ball problem right (the answer is 5 cents), you are especially unlikely to fall for fake news headlines. That is true of you whether you are a Democrat or a Republican, or whether you are evaluating news that is neutral, news that you want to be true, or news that you desperately wish was untrue. In the words of the authors of the study: 'Our findings therefore suggest that susceptibility to fake news is driven more by lazy thinking than it is by partisan bias per se.' This has huge implications for our understanding of authoritarianism. Because guess which kind of persons are especially likely to be intellectually lazy?

That's right – authoritarian persons.

Authoritarians Are Intellectually Apathetic People

As we'll see in Chapter 4, authoritarians *do* of course have group-based political biases. Independent of that, however, they also simply don't like to think very hard. This connection between authoritarianism and intellectual apathy is well established in scientific circles. For example, Becky Choma and her colleagues found that authoritarians do much worse on the Cognitive Reflection Test used by Pennycook.[7] Authoritarians are especially unlikely to give that extra second of thought to figure out answers to questions, even for a task completely unrelated to politics.

Our lab ran a quick study to investigate if authoritarians' unwillingness to think hard would make them especially vulnerable to believing fake news at higher rates. Using similar headlines to those in the Pennycook study above, we found that authoritarians were indeed especially likely to think fake news (relative to true news) was true – regardless of its political orientation.[8] This suggests authoritarians are just generally lazy thinkers.

The evidence that authoritarians are especially cognitively lazy goes well beyond the Cognitive Reflection Test and fake news studies. Psychologists have long studied a constellation of personality variables known collectively as 'cognitive rigidity'. People high in rigidity really hate thinking hard about things. They dislike thoughtful reflection. They exhibit intellectual apathy. They shun serious intellectual questions. Research shows that high-rigidity persons ignore evidence and rational argument; instead, they focus on lazy, quick-and-easy heuristics that are functionally irrelevant to the argument itself.[9] Unsurprisingly given their unwillingness to engage in deep thinking, high-rigidity persons produce especially unhelpful and boring ideas; one study evaluated consultants at a Dutch company and found that those high in rigidity produced duller solutions with less creativity than their low-rigidity counterparts.[10]

Just like the Cognitive Reflection Test demonstrates, scientific research has shown for years that people high in authoritarianism score much higher on measurements of cognitive rigidity.[11] Authoritarians just don't like to think as much as other people do.

While most of the evidence discussed so far – due to the leftist bias in the field – has historically been about right-wing authoritarians, more recent evidence shows the same thing is true of left-wing authoritarians too. For example, our lab found that left-wing authoritarians were especially likely to hold rigid attitudes and score higher on personality measurements of cognitive rigidity – and that they did so at roughly the same rates as right-wing authoritarians.[12] Tom Costello's lab at Emory University developed a program of research completely independently of ours – and found an identical pattern, showing that left-wing authoritarian persons are also more likely to be intellectually apathetic.[13]

It turns out that no matter which side of the aisle you're on, authoritarianism kills deep thinking. It creates intellectual apathy. This intellectual apathy is harmless when it is merely an individual difference that exists in the minds of some people. After all, there is nothing inherently wrong with simply not enjoying deep thought. It is rather elitist to assume that everyone should be Stephen Hawking.

However, it is a problem when it co-occurs with the authoritarian mind. The reason for that is simple: Authoritarians don't just sit in their basements and play video games. No; authoritarians spread their intellectual apathy like a virus to everyone else. They impose their intellectual apathy on the rest of society.

Coming to a Town Near You: The Authoritarian Apathy Virus

For decades, academics have posited that many psychological traits spread through cultures much like a virus.[14] We don't mean, of course, that (for instance) extraversion is literally carried by a small biological organism. Rather, we mean that psychological traits possess properties that make them travel from person to person in ways metaphorically similar to a virus. Traits can 'infect' different 'hosts' and thus 'spread' through a population of people. And we can analyze the factors that make particular traits especially 'contagious'.

This metaphor has proven useful for understanding various aspects of the human condition. For example, my graduate advisor Mark Schaller and I used this metaphor to predict changes in the cultural content of stereotypes over a 70-year period.[15] The virus metaphor also helps explain many odd facts about our psychological world, such as the fact that personality traits tend to be organized geographically: Without knowing you at all, I can predict you are more likely to be anxious if you live in the northeastern US and are less open to experience if you live in the southeastern US.[16] This is in part because psychological traits are transmitted from person to person, much like viruses are, to people in close proximity. Our metaphor further helps explain why traits get weirdly lumped together in geographical space, such as why southerners tend to be conservative, eat grits, say 'y'all', and like college football.[17] Those traits actually have no direct relationship to each other, and yet they all come packaged with the same metaphorical virus – much like headaches, sniffly noses, and sore throats can come from the same virus.

Now I don't want to get too carried away with this metaphor, but I think it is especially useful for understanding the impact of authoritarian apathy. There are many properties of authoritarians' propensity to intellectual laziness that make it especially likely to be contagious. It is unlikely to stay inside the authoritarian mind, but rather – given the right set of circumstances (something we return to in Chapter 7) – it is prone to rapid distribution throughout society.

We can roughly split the reasons for its high contagiousness potential into two types of processes. First are what psychologists call 'implicit' processes – that is, things that are either unconscious or unintentional (or both). Lots and lots of things are contagious in this way. For example, research suggests that our emotional or sensory states are contagious.[18] If the person next to you is angry, you tend to get angry. If the person next to you is bored, you tend to become bored. I even ran a study once showing that if the person you are interacting with experiences time dragging on endlessly, then so do you.[19] And if the person next to you seems apathetic or uninterested, then you too tend to become apathetic or uninterested. This happens whether the person is actually trying to make you uninterested or bored or what-have-you, and it happens whether or not you are aware that they are influencing you.

Research reveals that one of the markers of the apathetic mind – that it produces simple thoughts – may be implicitly contagious as well. For example, in one well-known research program, Penn professor Phil Tetlock showed that you could predict the simplicity of the rhetoric from US and Soviet politicians during the Cold War by knowing the simplicity of the other side in the time frame immediately prior to each speech.[20] In other words, simplicity begat simplicity: US politicians became more simple as their Soviet counterparts did and vice versa.

Thus, it is likely that merely being in the presence of an apathetic authoritarian will make you more apathetic. It is probably partly for this reason that research shows authoritarian parents tend to pass on a lazy authoritarian mindset to their children. In fact, an amazing study by Dhont and colleagues showed that cognitive laziness is the mechanism by which parents tend to create authoritarian children.[21] This probably occurs because parents repeatedly model authoritarian apathy for their kids – even if they aren't intending to make them cognitively apathetic specifically.

Of course, many of the reasons that authoritarianism tends to spread intellectual apathy are in fact quite intentional. Psychologists call these 'explicit' processes. Authoritarians actively seek to silence those different from them. They want authority figures to punish dissenters. They don't like open debate. History and psychology both teach the same lesson about how that influences the spread of intellectual apathy. Look at what happened in Nazi Germany. Look at what happened in the Soviet Union.

From a psychological perspective, it's easy to see how this happens. For example, psychologists have identified one of the psychological consequences of a fear of speaking out, a process called 'pluralistic ignorance'.[22] The classic case of pluralistic ignorance is when everyone in a classroom doesn't understand the statistical reason for the probability value (or whatever) that the professor is talking about, but everyone is afraid to ask the question because they don't want to look stupid. The net result is that everyone else believes – falsely – that they are alone in their confusion. And then people stop thinking about it altogether on the assumption that critical thinking isn't welcome.

Why does this matter? Consider the famous studies run by Solomon Asch.[23] Asch had participants do a 'line-matching' task: They had to say whether a line was closer in length to one of three sample lines. In each case, there was one obvious answer and, left to their own devices, everyone gets all the problems right. Except that in Asch's paradigm, they weren't left to their own devices.

Participants were required to give all their answers out loud, one at a time. And in each session, all participants but one were 'confederates' – that is, trained accomplices of the experimenter.

After a few 'normal' rounds where everyone chose the same answer, something unexpected happened. To the horror of the real participant, all of the other 'participants' decided to publicly pick an obviously *wrong* answer. Then the real participant was asked to also share their own answer publicly, after hearing everyone else state a clearly wrong answer to the question. What did participants do? They often went along with the crowd and gave a wrong answer – because they assumed they were alone in their private dissent.

Authoritarianism magnifies that intellectual problem. In fact, the Asch studies have been performed all over the world, and research shows that you get more compliance in collectivistic countries that are more conducive to authoritarianism.[24] Why? There are likely many reasons for this, but authoritarianism makes everyone feel isolated and alone in their concern – and eventually people just give up thinking or caring.

On the flip side, authoritarianism causes the people in the majority to feel emboldened to ignore debate. Why should you bother listening to your opponents' arguments when you can simply ignore them, knowing that they will be punished by an authority figure sooner or later? A long history of research in social psychology shows that critical thinking often decreases in the majority when the minority is silenced.[25] Left to run its course with no metaphorical cure, this silencing will inevitably be fatal to Western society. We discuss some of those metaphorical cures in Chapters 8 and 9, but here I want to spend some time diagnosing the nature of the disease.

This intellectual apathy disease affects both left-wing and right-wing authoritarians, and both groups are equally capable of spreading the virus to a non-authoritarian audience. However, in my lifetime nowhere has this problem been more clearly exhibited than in the left-wing authoritarian squelching of debates on issues like Covid-19, the educational system, and biological sex. We turn to this evidence next.

Syllogistic Reasoning:
Died, August 2021, You Had a Good Run

Consider the case of Dr Scott Atlas, a decorated Stanford medical professor who worked with the Trump administration on Covid policy. Atlas served on a Covid task force run by Vice President Pence that included heavy-hitters such as Dr Fauci, Dr Robert Redfield, and Dr Deborah Birx. And his reflections about that experience are instructive:

> I'm listening to these people talk and I was stunned. I was stunned at the lack of knowledge, at the complete lack of knowing the data, at the lack of critical thinking ... in fact, I was the only one who had scientific papers in the task force meeting. I walked around the White House my entire time, in every task force meeting I went to, with a dozen, two dozen papers, all the new data. And I would go through the scientific papers whenever I spoke. And whenever I spoke about an issue, whether it was the schools opening, the risk to children, the immunity, no one there, none of these medical people, offered any data to rebut it. None of them. Not one. They never had any scientific paper to rebut it. They would just say I'm an outlier.[26]

Atlas isn't alone. Indeed, as I discussed in the introduction, I presented five arguments at my university's Faculty Senate that suggested both mask and vaccine mandates were not necessary. And of those five, how many of those arguments were met with scientific evidence on the other side? How many scientific studies were provided to counter my scientific studies?

The answer is: Exactly zero. No one provided a single piece of evidence to counter mine. No one critiqued the methods of the studies I cited. Instead, like Atlas, I was branded an 'outlier' and vilified. Objectively, I was one of the most decorated researchers at my former university, and my substantive arguments, based on research done at Ivy League universities, were completely dismissed as conspiracy theories. Disagreement is of course healthy, and I welcome it – but this wasn't disagreement so much as it was an assumption of my lunacy.

In fact, although no one cited research, one (and only one) person attempted to directly address an argument I made – and his answer is quite instructive. In my third argument, I had noted that vaccine mandates were likely unnecessary because if the vaccines were as effective as advertised – and I expressed that I believed they were indeed effective – then a mandate was unnecessary because the vaccines would protect the vaccinated from the unvaccinated. If this was a pandemic of the unvaccinated as had been claimed, then basic logic suggests it was *not* a pandemic of the vaccinated. So what do vaccinated people have to worry about? If you are vaccinated, why push a mandate to protect you from something that logic reveals you are not in danger from?

And my colleague's response to my argument? He spent quite a while telling me, in condescending tones, *how effective vaccines are*. He apparently didn't even notice that my whole argument was based on the presumption that *vaccines are effective*! So he had in essence simply defended my position; and neither he nor anyone else seemed to notice, and the mandate resolution passed with overwhelming support.

The Canceling of Debate in Higher Education

The spreading of the intellectual apathy virus is equally evident in ongoing debates about our educational system. Take one example from my own field. I'm a fellow of the Society for Personality and Social Psychologists (SPSP), the largest organization of social psychologists in the world. And as such, I keenly follow the online discussion forums associated with SPSP. In May 2020, someone posted a question to the primary SPSP listserv.[27] Essentially, this professor noted that their graduate program was considering dropping the GRE (a standardized test used for graduate admissions, much like the SAT or ACT is used for undergraduate admissions) and was interested to learn what others thought about it.

What followed was a kind of parable for the authoritarian dangers we face as a society – the real potential for the canceling of rational argument. There were 38 posts in total on the thread. Through post 19, there had been some reasonable back-and-forth on the pros and cons of the GRE test, with people presenting data on both sides. I did a rough 'vote-counting' to identify whether the tenor of each post was more positive or negative, and through the 19th post, there was a roughly equal split of people who supported versus opposed the GRE. The debate had been vigorous but largely cordial.

And then post 20 happened.

In post 20, a researcher at an R1 institution took issue with the debate itself:

> As a Black social psychologist, reading this thread has been troubling to say the least. It highlights just how out of touch this field is with respect to increasing access to PhD programs, particularly for Black applicants and applicants from marginalized backgrounds. It's disheartening to see scholars who I respect and whose own work investigates inequality advocate for a metric that is prohibitively expensive and minimally predictive. It demonstrates some of why, at least in my estimation, the few Black social psychologists associated with SPSP find it difficult to trust this association. This thread highlights your unrelenting investment in the academic institution that strives to maintain exclusivity while patting itself on the back for promoting diversity and inclusion.

That attack was quite different. It wasn't making a specific argument against the GRE – it was making an argument against the very debate itself. It didn't so much attack the merits of the GRE as attack the scholars involved in the debate – and the fact that we were even having a debate. 'It's disheartening to see scholars …' is an attack not on ideas, but on people. It's not even an attack on a narrow group of people – it's an attack on everyone involved, the whole field, *including* scholars (some of whom had posted on the thread in favor of the GRE) who were either from a poor background, or minority scholars, or both. It was an attack on the *thread* (which 'highlights your unrelenting investment in the academic institution that strives to maintain exclusivity'), which is to say, the *debate*.

And everyone noticed. The authoritarian apathy virus had been planted and was about to spread.

The tenor of the debate changed after that. There was less discussion of evidence. There was less back-and-forth. What had been a fairly equal split in terms of posts became more lopsided in favor of ditching the GRE. There was far less pushback and, indeed, a shift away from the original question in favor of personal narratives related to diversity.

What happened is quite clear. I'm not sure if my colleague intended to invoke an authoritarian norm in post 20; but whether intended or not, the only reason such a post was effective is because people are afraid of liberal authoritarians. My colleague suggested that simply debating the merits of the GRE is racist. That dubious assumption went almost entirely unchallenged, because we all know that doing so might be a career-ending decision. And in fact, the one brave person who did dare challenge the assumption was completely eviscerated by famous academics in the remainder of the thread. It was clear to everybody: Liberal authoritarians lurk in the wings to humiliate and ostracize you. And so it was that a reasonable debate about the merits of the GRE was squelched because someone planted fear of honest intellectual critique. That is how the authoritarian virus spreads. Cancel culture doesn't just cancel ideas – it cancels debate itself. It turns data-based and reason-based discussions into one-sided narratives where debate itself is the enemy.

This chilling effect of authoritarianism on real debate about the GRE isn't just an event isolated to one discussion board. It can be seen across the country. Authoritarians on the left are creating a huge mass of intellectual apathy in their wake. In fact, universities throughout the nation are canceling the GRE, the

SAT, and the ACT. One of the main (and often the only) objective mechanisms for comparing students in different places – one of the only truly objective 'colorblind' pieces of evidence – is being torn down. Is that because of a rational debate?

Answer: No. I was a part of this process first-hand. At the University of Montana (the university I worked at for 18 years), on November 17, 2021, the Graduate Council passed a 'GRE Resolution' that effectively banned all university departments from using the GRE. Why? They argued that (1) the GRE was ineffective because it didn't predict who would succeed in graduate school, and (2) the GRE violated equity concerns because it unfairly discriminated against minority groups. In their words: 'Numerous studies across different fields have revealed that the GRE score is not an accurate predictor of success (see sample collection of research and discussion below), and the financial hardships of preparing for and completing the GRE put obstacles in the way of recruiting a diverse body of graduate students.'

I'm actually not a huge fan of the GRE personally and haven't ever really used it seriously in making judgments about graduate students. So in case you are wondering, no, I'm not on the GRE's payroll. But the argument put forward by the Graduate Council was so thoughtless and inaccurate that it bordered on the absurd. For one thing, they claimed that 'numerous studies' show the GRE doesn't predict success and pointed to three links to three separate studies. It turns out that there are no words strong enough in the English language to describe how much of a mischaracterization of evidence this is. Incredible? Comical? Horrifying? Even a quick Google Scholar search using 'GRE Predictive Validity' reveals, in three seconds, a highly cited meta-analysis in a major journal by Kuncel and colleagues.[28] The graduate school cited three studies at random and claimed that 'numerous studies' support their case. Do you know how many independent studies were evaluated in Kuncel and colleagues' highly circulated paper?

The answer is over 1,700 studies. And that's just the number of independent *samples*. They actually gleaned from those samples over 6,000 tests on over 80,000 participants. And what happens when you don't just cherry-pick three studies at random, but in fact look for every study you can find? What happens when you do an *actual* scientific analysis of the predictive validity of the GRE? Here are the words of the authors of the meta-analysis of over 1,700 studies: 'The results indicated that the GRE and UGPA are generalizably valid predictors of graduate grade point average, 1st-year graduate grade point average, comprehensive examination scores, publication citation counts, and faculty ratings.'

To put this in perspective, the graduate school's argument was basically like saying, 'We found three people in a town of 1,700 who hate ice cream and so we're going to declare no one in the world can eat ice cream because obviously people don't like it.' One might be forgiven for wondering why they didn't at least bother asking the other 1,697 residents first!

I'm not trying to convince you to take the GRE, but I want you to see something. There are reasons to be skeptical of the GRE. Some minority groups do perform more poorly on it (others perform better, which is why one of the groups pushing back against these equity policies are Asians, who consistently outperform whites). I don't think the test is perfect. But there are also plenty of reasons to keep it around – it is predictive of student success, it offers the only chance to compare students from different environments on a standardized test, many minority group members think it is the best chance they have to overcome biases, and we know from experience that such objective tests are generally less biased than other, more subjective factors like letters of recommendation.

And here is my point: The debate that *should* have happened never happened.

What should have happened is that all the thousands of studies that supported the GRE, all the tens of independent reasons for keeping it, should have been weighed against the real difficulties it poses. That would have been a vigorous and useful debate and likely would have solved a lot of problems.

But that's not what happened. What *did* happen is, without any real pushback, the University of Montana Graduate Council (like so many other universities around the country) merely dropped the GRE. They did so on completely faulty grounds while radically mischaracterizing the state of the evidence. They effectively canceled a needed debate due to a political goal – an equity goal. When I tried to push back against this decision in a faculty email thread, I got a response that ignored both of the substantive arguments I had made and spent most of the time discussing 'social justice' issues.

We didn't have a debate that day. I was worn down by the intellectual apathy and concerned for my job, and thus decided it wasn't worth my effort to continue the fight. The virus won.

This is an all-too-frequent pattern across the US right now in almost every area of educational life. One of my former students sent me an email expressing the problem in general terms: 'I've personally seen this in one of my classes and had to drop it due to getting graded harsher for having more conservative views and speaking up about them instead of pretending to be liberal in my discussion posts.' What could have been a vigorous and stimulating debate from across the political spectrum was cut short because a professor bullied a student into submission – and rather than submit, the student left the class. It is infuriating for the individual student that they had to go through that. But it is an intellectual tragedy for *everyone* that the debate itself was cut short. Rather than arguing for a particular perspective, a professor instead chose to bludgeon students – and we all lose.

Biological Sex Isn't Real?

This apathy for argument isn't just about sociological test data; it has affected discussions of even the most basic biology. Consider the case of Dr Kathleen Stock, a former professor at the University of Sussex in England. Dr Stock wrote a book questioning the idea that gender identity is more important than biological sex. She was then characterized by emboldened left-wing authoritarians as 'transphobic' and 'bigoted', among other labels. (She completely denies that those things are true about her, and I can find no evidence to suggest that they are.) However, after all the social pressure to fire her, she eventually resigned. And what she said about her experience is very telling:

> In almost every university … there are a small group of people who are absolutely opposed to the sorts of things I say and instead of getting involved in arguing with me using reason, evidence – the traditional university methods – they tell their students in lectures that I pose a harm to trans students. They go on Twitter to say that I'm a bigot so thus creating an atmosphere in which students become much more extreme and much more empowered to do what they did, I guess.[29]

Note again the same left-wing authoritarian intellectual apathy, the same aversion to actual argument. What Dr Stock wanted was argument, reason, and evidence. What she got was the thoughtless authoritarian mob.

Why is this happening? What accounts for such massive groupthink that makes supposedly smart people cease to engage in scientific debate?[30] To me as a social psychologist, the answer to that question is quite plain: My academic colleagues are emboldened by left-wing authoritarian cancel culture. They know that as a presumed outlier, anyone speaking against the orthodoxy has to be afraid of being canceled (and indeed, I have also been silent on key issues for that exact reason – and I'm writing a book called *Liberal Bullies!*); they know that other people will be afraid to support such a person for *their* fear of being canceled, even if that person is not quite so much an outlier as they suppose, and thus they have little motivation for responding to an argument *with an argument*. Authoritarianism is necessarily thoughtless. There is little as stifling to good thinking as the belief that most of the world wants your opponent to completely shut up.

Squashing Gender Debates Isn't Just an Academic Professor Thing

On July 12, 2021, the US Senate convened to talk about abortion. In the process of doing so, Republican senator Josh Hawley had a heated exchange with Cal Berkeley law professor Khiara Bridges about biological gender.[31] In response to the Hawley–Bridges debate, liberal strategist Jessica Tarlov responded that she didn't think it was that important because no one watches a Senate hearing anyway.[32] Maybe you think that too. Let the elitist senator and the elitist Cal professor have their day. Who cares?

Honestly, I used to feel that way about political squabbling. However, the authoritarian attitudes conveyed by university academics have filtered down to affect the lives of real people throughout the US, Britain, and indeed the whole Western world. The virus just keeps spreading. And if we don't do something about it, debates are going to be canceled in your neighborhood too – and one day you are going to wish they weren't.

Consider the case of Marin Country Day School, an elite private school in the San Francisco Bay Area that charges $40,000 a year for each student.[33] Controversy emerged when the school changed its curriculum to focus on 'deconstructing the gender binary' – that is, that we should replace the notion of boys and girls with a relative spectrum of gender identity.

Personally, I can see both sides of this debate. Some people don't seem to subjectively fit their own biological sex, and I take their subjective view seriously. I've never wanted to exclude people who don't think they fit the binary distinction. I want them to be loved. I want them to be treated as equals. On the flip side, biological sex is nonetheless important. I don't think ignoring a categorical distinction that 99% of the human race would be able to correctly identify with minimal cues makes a lot of sense. This distinction would pass any scientific test we threw at it. In my area, we often accept an 80% level of agreement as evidence of a scientifically valid categorical distinction, and 90% is almost always considered high enough. That's for *trained coders*.

But biological sex can be identified at nearly perfect percentages with almost no training whatsoever. If we were applying a fair standard, we'd have to admit that it was *at the least* a useful categorical distinction. And this means that when we want inclusion beyond the binary – and I do – that doesn't mean we have to *throw out* the binary. That would wipe out the feminist movement. It would wipe out decades of research that tried to better understand differences and similarities between men and women.

So it seems clear that this area has some built-in tension. Solutions will require a full debate.

But Marin Country Day School wasn't interested in even a partial debate. Instead, it canceled debate and replaced it with authoritarian bullying. A lot of parents were upset about the new gender-based curriculum. But almost none of them spoke out. The reason? Good old-fashioned authoritarian fear.

As journalist Leighton Woodhouse noted:

> There were three classes in the second grade, with each class comprising about 20 students. Out of that, there was a core group of more than a dozen parents who were the angriest. But no one would speak up. It didn't matter that most of the parents were affluent. They feared school administrators. They fretted that MCDS would say bad things about their kids or deny admission to their kids' younger siblings or not write recommendations for their kids if they tried to transfer to another school.

In fact, Woodhouse reached out to many of these parents for comment: 'Several parents I reached out to indicated that they wanted to talk but were scared. One father said he'd call me from a pay phone, if only there were pay phones.'

That doesn't sound to me like a healthy and well-functioning school where debate on a key issue is welcomed. It doesn't sound to me like critical thinking is encouraged. It rather sounds like the Watergate scandal. An American dad would only talk from a pay phone? Are you kidding me? What is, this, *All the President's Men*? Is the man Deep Throat, for crying out loud? I thought we were talking about classes for seven-year-old second-graders. And are we serious about parents being *that* afraid to speak out?

Actually, evidence suggests their fear was justified. The vice president of the school's Diversity, Equity and Inclusion (DEI) Committee challenged the school's policy. He emailed the head of the school: 'The curriculum at MCDS seems to be based on trendy political theory instead of pedagogy that has strong empirical support ... The majority of the families have and are witnessing their children experiencing high levels of stress, pain, sadness and asking questions that many parents are not ready or equipped to answer and all because of the Gender self identity activity.'

Among the responses to this email, two stand out. First, the head of the school said that parents anonymously protesting the curriculum had left many LGBTQ+ faculty 'with feelings of unsafety'. So basically having a different opinion had made people feel unsafe. Second, the DEI vice president who had dared lodge a reasonable argument expressing the concerns of parents was removed from the DEI committee a month later.

It wasn't just the DEI VP who suffered. Two parents who spoke out – Paul and Beka Sinclair – were treated brutally. Their story is complicated and involves them making a mistake they admitted to in reaching out to a conservative organization that sent emails they did not approve of. But the upshot is this: A lot of parents weren't happy. They were afraid to speak out. One set of parents did speak out. They weren't treated very well and subsequently decided to move their children (five and eight years old) to another private school. The kids were both accepted to start in the fall at the new school.

But even given that they were going to be leaving their old school anyway, their kids were kicked out of Marin Country Day School before the end of the spring term. And, because of the hubbub the Sinclair parents had created at their former school, their children were subsequently kicked out of the *other* private school, which had already accepted them, before they even got to start. In describing why he was rescinding the admission the children had already earned, the school administrator noted: 'We are now understandably concerned about your questioning of the "science around human identity development" and your assertion that there is a "political motive to deconstruct the gender binary".' He went on to say that 'reasonable people' could be 'offended by your presence on campus'. (They didn't get their almost $12,000 admission fee back.)

'Reasonable people' could be offended by their 'presence'? So just the presence of people who had publicly expressed that they didn't want their children being taught sexual gender identity in the second grade, who thought biological sex was real and not a manufactured construct – indeed, the mere presence of those people's *kids* could offend the 'reasonable'?

Well, what sort of horrible monsters are these folks who would offend reasonable people? Are the Sinclairs radical right-wing QAnon supporters? Hardly. In describing Paul Sinclair, the article notes:

He didn't think of himself as a political person, but he wanted

other parents to know what was happening at MCDS. 'I'm
from Canada,' he told me. 'I view myself as a centrist. I am by
no means – well, let's just say I'm not a Republican.' But he was
upset. He didn't want his kids hearing about all this stuff at such
an early age, and no one had bothered to ask him or any other
parents how they felt. The head of the school didn't seem to care
at all about parents' concerns.

So a centrist Canadian who isn't Republican doesn't like part of
the school curriculum, and his kids were denied admission to
another school because 'reasonable people' would be 'offended'?
When I read stuff like this, I think I went to sleep in the US and
woke up in China. What happened to the spirit of free speech?
What happened to rational debate?

This story makes it clear that this canceling of critical thinking
isn't unique to one school in the area. Indeed, a parent at another
school in the county said this: 'We all experience this very progressive, liberal lifestyle that I love. But that open-mindedness is
turning into homogeneity. We want our kids to be critical thinkers. We want diversity of thought. But if we're teaching them
there's only one way, and that you're at risk if you disagree – I
think that's the last thing we want to teach our kids.'

I want to tell that parent: Don't say that kind of thing *too*
loudly. Apparently, reasonable people might be offended and
your five-year-old child may not be allowed to go to school. If
you don't believe me, listen to Beka Sinclair:

You can't say obvious, uncontroversial things anymore. We're
asked to lie over and over, and because we all do it so much we
seem to have forgotten that that's what we're doing, that we're

taking part in a charade. Really, what I want is not to feel like I'm on an ideological island, like I'm crazy for having an opinion that other people don't have, and for being punished for that. This is not how people outside elite culture were raised. But elite culture doesn't care about open or liberal society. It cares about power, and it will throw everything else away before it gives that up. It will gaslight everyone else into submission.

Again, social psychology shows why this is happening. It happens because authoritarian apathy is contagious. It happens because when people are afraid, they will shut up. And when minority voices don't speak up, the majority voices don't have to engage in reasonable debate.

The End of Civilization: Data? Please, I Don't Need Data

So far, we've seen that the left-wing authoritarian apathy virus is currently contagious. It is spreading like wildfire. It is wearing people down. It is making it increasingly difficult for people to have debates about important issues that matter to them.

The ultimate result of this left-wing authoritarian intellectual apathy is that facts become irrelevant. The more we allow leftists to bludgeon us, the more they can make decisions that are disconnected from reality.

Although we've seen some examples of facts being ignored, in none of them did the authoritarians actually *claim* that facts didn't matter. But at the very far end of the authoritarian spectrum – once we get to the edge of the apathy cliff – authoritarians actually publicly declare that facts are irrelevant.

Consider one example in debates over gun control. In the summer of 2022, after the Supreme Court had overturned the legitimacy of New York's over-restrictive gun laws, the state signed into law ... an even more severe set of gun restrictions.[34] Those restrictions border on scarily authoritarian. Not only do they essentially ignore the Supreme Court – and thus the established rule of law – they are frankly creepy. To carry a gun, applicants have to demonstrate that they have 'the essential character, temperament and judgment necessary to be entrusted with a weapon and to use it only in a manner that does not endanger oneself or others'. And how will that be determined? Among other things, an applicant is required to show 'no less than four character references who can attest to the applicant's good moral character' and must submit 'a list of former and current social media accounts' from the previous three years.

So in an extremely liberal state run by extremely liberal persons, to get a carry permit for a gun, all those liberals need to approve your social media accounts? Yeah, I really trust *that*. Come on, conservatives, what could possibly go wrong?

I realize that, to those outside of the US, this may seem an odd debate. But here, the right to carry a gun is literally given the same legal status as the right to religion or free speech. It is in the Second Amendment to the Constitution. I'm not raising the issue here because I disapprove of New York's law – although I do disapprove. New York can frankly do whatever it wants as far as I'm concerned. Rather, I'm raising the issue here because I want you to see what happened next.

Anne McCloy is a news anchor at CBS Albany, and she was at a press conference for New York governor Kathy Hochul. McCloy asked: 'Do you have the numbers to show that it's the concealed-carry permit holders that are committing crimes? ... the lawful gun owner will say that you're attacking the wrong person.' McCloy further noted that 'it's really the people that are getting these guns illegally that are causing the violence, not the people going and getting the permit legally'.

Now, hit the pause button for a second. Whatever else you think about gun ownership, if you are going to pass a gun law because you think it protects people, you ought to care about evidence related to the causal relationship between your restriction and said protection. It may not be the whole argument, but it ought to matter. And, in point of fact, I used to be in favor of strong gun restrictions, but I changed my mind because of evidence and argument. As McCloy notes, there is quite a bit of common sense involved in saying that punishing legal gun owners likely will not stop people from committing crimes, because presumably the criminals will not be especially likely to obey gun laws. I don't own a gun and I'm married to an anti-gun pacifist, but nonetheless, I think people should have the right to carry them legally.

But here's what I want you to see. We could have a great debate about that. We could present evidence on all sides. But what did Kathy Hochul, governor of one of the most important political entities in the world (the great state of New York – I love you, Rochester!), say in response to this set of reasonable questions about empirical evidence? Here's what she said:

> I don't need to have numbers. I don't have to have a data point to point to say this is going to [matter]. All I know is that I have a responsibility to the people of this state to have sensible gun safety laws ... I don't need a data point to make the case that I have a responsibility to protect the people of this state.

That's the new left going to the edge of the cliff. That's evidence of the authoritarian apathy virus. That's what happens when you aren't used to being seriously challenged because you know you can simply do what you want and silence your enemies. You stop thinking it is important to come up with persuasive arguments. You don't 'need to have numbers' because ... you are the authoritarian in charge, and your virus has rendered your opposition tired and mute.

If it hasn't already, this virus is coming to your town too – unless we work together to find a cure. And if we don't do something about it, if we don't collectively find a cure, this authoritarian intellectual apathy virus will become a full-blown pandemic.

CHAPTER 3

MISINFORMATION OBSESSION: THE PSYCHOLOGY OF THE ELEPHANT'S TUSK

All truth passes through three stages. First, it is ridiculed. Second, it is violently opposed. Third, it is accepted as being self-evident.

– Philosopher Arthur Schopenhauer (attributed)

Modern authoritarians love the word 'misinformation'. It represents a reincarnation of the oldest page in the historical authoritarian playbook. One of the defining elements of authoritarian regimes, both past and present, both right-wing and left-wing, is that they try to control informational dissent. Only one narrative is permitted, while others are dismissed as non-factual, censored, and often completely removed from public discourse entirely.[1]

Sound familiar? If you live in the US, it likely does. Because that trait has defined an increasingly large part of political discourse for the last four years of life here on my side of the pond. Rather than responding to arguments and information in the way

a free democracy would – with better arguments and better information – American leftists have instead worked to censor, bully,
intimidate, and fire people who have said things that they didn't
like. And one of their preferred methods is the subject of this
chapter: They have simply borrowed from that old authoritarian
playbook and labeled everything they disagree with as 'misinformation' or 'disinformation'.[2] They have a *misinformation obsession*.

In my opinion, this has been the single most destructive thing
that's happened over the last few years. In fact, if I could personally
advocate for one change in modern Western culture, it would be
to take the words 'misinformation' and 'disinformation' (and their
meaner linguistic cousin 'conspiracy theory') out of the public
lexicon. Those kinds of words are the driving forces behind an
alarmingly high percentage of modern authoritarian bludgeoning.

That doesn't mean there is no such thing as misinformation,
of course. Some of what is out there that is labeled 'misinformation' is, in fact, wrong. But that's not the point. The point is that
in a free society one has a *right* to misinformation. In America,
my right to spread misinformation is literally guaranteed in the
First Amendment.[3] The reason is simple: Only a lunatic – or
an authoritarian – believes that they have a perfect barometer
for *all* informational truth. We get at the truth of information
only by degrees; and one person's misinformation is another
person's truth. As Schopenhauer said, what turns out to be true
is frequently ridiculed and opposed. Thus, we figure out the truth
collectively, together, by putting all the facts from every perspective into play and then working it out in the public sphere. That's
why democratic systems are almost always purposefully set up to
be adversarial – let both sides claw it out. It may get ugly, sure,
but everyone still gets to speak.

Seeing the Whole Elephant

You don't have to look very far to see how dangerous it is to constantly label things as 'misinformation'. That's because today's misinformation is often tomorrow's truth. That's the nature of learning. We've seen this play out again and again (and again) in the last three years. Things that were repeatedly censored as 'misinformation' have subsequently proven not quite so misinformed after all. The *New York Post* was banned from Twitter for suggesting scandalous misinformation about Hunter Biden's laptop, and yet basically everyone now agrees that the story that got them banned was true.[4] Facebook banned *any* discussion of the Wuhan lab leak theory of Covid's origins as misinformation, and then was forced to reverse course after essentially everyone on all sides admitted that the idea was at least plausible.[5]

My point isn't, of course, that every bad theory out there will be proven true. My point is rather the opposite: To figure out what's true or not, we shouldn't predetermine the conclusion by simply censoring opinions we don't like as 'misinformation' – even if they contain facts we think are false. That is especially so when, as has been the case for the last three years, almost all the stuff labeled 'misinformation' has been on one side of the political aisle. Left-wing authoritarians are especially obsessed with weeding out conservative 'misinformation'.

So when the left-wing US government tried to create a 'Disinformation Governance Board' to censor its own citizens, I was suitably alarmed. I wasn't alone – the board was disbanded after a lot of protests from people on all sides. But more telling was what the head of the board while it lasted, Nina Jankowicz, said in bemoaning its untimely death: 'It's hard to imagine how we get back from this, when this is how our elected representatives are behaving – when we can't agree on, you know, what is the truth.'[6]

That's right, Nina. We can't agree on the truth, because the truth is complicated and only an arrogant narcissist with a God complex thinks they have *all* truth in their finite mind. So of course, we can't agree on the truth all the time ... and that's OK. But Nina Jankowicz, like many modern authoritarians, thinks we need to bludgeon consensus from the top down because it's a tragedy of some kind when we can't all agree on *what is the truth*.

That bludgeoning is dangerous. I used to assign an article in my Political Psychology class that argued that our major granting institutions (NIH, NSF) should force agreement among reviewers by requiring them to make judgments on a very narrow set of specific categories.[7] In doing so, the article argues, we'll get rid of all this horrible disagreement among reviewers because they'll be forced to focus on the important things. The author of the article draws on the age-old elephant analogy: If we just leave reviewers to their own devices, they will be like blind people all grabbing different parts of the elephant and we'll never know what's what.

Ironically, these kinds of top-down authoritarian arguments show exactly why authoritarianism fails at getting us closer to the truth. Yes, it is true that you can force agreement between reviewers by making them all grab the tusk of the elephant. But that's probably the very worst way to actually get to the truth of the *whole elephant*. Instead, your reviewers will falsely believe that an elephant is entirely made of ivory. They will imagine that an elephant is really just a sharp pointy thing. Sure, they will agree, but will this get them closer to understanding *an elephant*? Of course not.

In fact, if you want to understand the whole elephant, then precisely what you need is reviewer *disagreement*. You need different people with different perspectives to talk to each other without authoritarian guidance or fear of reprisal. You actually need people reaching for the tusk, and the leg, and the ears, and then working together to sort out what the heck is going on with that elephant. The one thing we know for sure is that if you force agreement, it will work at producing agreement – but it certainly doesn't get us a whole lot closer to the truth. Calling the rogue reviewers 'misinformed' for daring to describe the elephant's back only slows down the process of getting to the truth.

Unpackaging the Psychology of the Elephant

Our elephant analogy teaches us a great lesson in psychology. If you strip away the veneer of the misinformation obsession, underneath it you will find a psychological difficulty with admitting one doesn't know everything. When people reach out for the tusk and claim it is the elephant, it's often because they have a hard time admitting that maybe they don't really know what the animal looks like yet – and that bothers them. And when people become obsessed with other people's 'misinformation' it is often because they don't want their own view of the elephant as only a tusk to be challenged. It really bothers people to believe they could be wrong about elephants – and politics.

None of us should be too smug about this. In fact, research suggests that everyone can fall into this trap. In a classic and highly influential psychology study, Arie Kruglanski and colleagues revealed how little it takes to get people to seize on any old piece of elephant.[8] In the study, each participant engaged with another person they believed was a participant (but who was actually an accomplice of the experimenter) in a jury simulation. Before the jury 'deliberation' the participant got official-looking 'legal briefings' that suggested one or the other party in the case – which was about a lumber company suing an airline – had a stronger argument. Then the accomplice always tried to persuade the participant away from their initial position to take the other side.

The study had two catches. First, some participants were given a very weak case for their initial side – nothing very firm to hold on to – while the other participants were given a very strong case. Second, some participants were assigned to a 'noisy printer' condition where a super-obnoxious printer was operating in the background. (It was a dot matrix printer – can you guess what decade this study was conducted in? I told you it was a 'classic'.) Some participants did not have to endure this auditory bludgeoning.

What they found was that the noisy printer made people especially desirous to finish the case quickly – to grab on to whatever piece of the elephant seemed most solid to them. This meant that if they already had a solid case, the noisy printer made them (in the words of the researchers) 'freeze' on that case and reject everything the accomplice said. However, if they had a weak case, instead participants were especially likely to 'seize' on the persuasion attempt and go with whatever the accomplice argued. In either instance, any ambiguity was shoved by the wayside in favor of grabbing on to a single piece of the elephant and calling that the whole thing.

Happily, none of us has to endure that horrible assault on the ears known as the dot matrix printer anymore. And yet the principle remains. When things irritate or distract us – and our world bombards us with printer-like distractions – we tend to eschew ambiguities and want to believe we've got the thing figured out. Importantly, however, even though most people fall prey to seizing and freezing at least some of the time, there are also individual differences in people's propensity to tolerate ambiguity. In a separate study in that same paper, Kruglanski and colleagues showed that individuals who are more chronically motivated to avoid uncertainties are also more likely to seize upon whatever part of their (in this case, legal) elephant is most convenient and call it the whole shebang.

Based on what we've discussed so far in other chapters, I probably don't have to tell you that intolerance for uncertainty is part of the authoritarian mindset. And so it is: A lot of research evidence establishes that authoritarians really, *really* dislike uncertainty.[9] They don't like ambiguous ideas; they don't like ambiguous poems; heck, they don't even like ambiguous *pictures*.

For years, this kind of authoritarian intolerance for ambiguity was assumed to be mostly a conservative thing. And maybe that used to be the case. But it is undoubtedly not the case anymore. Mirroring modern work on left-wing authoritarianism, both liberals and conservatives these days seem equally subject to the ills of uncertainty intolerance. One remarkable study in 2021 tied this directly to activity in the brain.[10] In the study, liberals and conservatives watched political debates while hooked up to an fMRI machine, which allows researchers to track brain activity. The researchers were especially interested in polarized differences in brain functions between liberals and conservatives.

And what they found was quite incredible – they could predict the amount of polarization in the brain by a particular personality trait: Intolerance of uncertainty. This occurred equally for both liberals and conservatives. In their words: 'Participants less tolerant to uncertainty in daily life had more ideologically polarized brain responses than those who tolerate uncertainty. This was observed on both sides of the ideological aisle. This suggests that aversion to uncertainty governs how the brain processes political information to form black-and-white interpretations of inflammatory political content.'

Other recent work suggests that liberals might, in some circumstances, be *more* averse to uncertainty. In this work, researchers at Syracuse University evaluated the likelihood that conservatives and liberals would feel ambivalent about issues by looking at the degree to which they would report having 'mixed feelings'.[11] It is worth noting that, according to the researchers' account, they were expecting to find that liberals showed more ambivalence because, historically, liberals have shown more tolerance for uncertainty. But they found the exact opposite. Their own words are instructive: 'The results of five studies (total N = 1,049 participants) reveal instead that political *liberalism* is *negatively* associated with ambivalence. This finding held for both subjective and potential (i.e., formula-based) measures of ambivalence and for both politicized and nonpoliticized attitude objects.' In short, they found very robust evidence that, in fact, conservatives are actually more OK with having mixed feelings on topics than liberals are.

This should not be taken to mean – and the authors of the Syracuse study did not take it to mean – that conservatives are suddenly uniformly high in their ability to accept uncertainty across the board. Some studies still suggest that, depending on how it is measured, conservatives can be quite averse to uncertainty. But I raise this evidence here to make a different point: If you imagine that this uncertainty intolerance is, in the modern world, really just a right-wing problem, you've missed the metaphorical boat entirely.

Now, having stripped back the veneer, we can see more clearly how authoritarians become obsessed with misinformation. People who can't accept uncertainty are more likely to simultaneously believe misinformation and call out other people for believing 'misinformation' (quite remarkably, while believing things that are untrue themselves!). For example, one study early in the Covid pandemic showed that people high in intolerance for uncertainty were especially prone to latch on to hard-to-believe explanations of the pandemic, such as 'The US or UK (or another Western government) created or weaponized the coronavirus, intentionally introducing it to the population in an attempt to attack the Chinese economy' or 'Bill Gates (via the Bill and Melinda Gates Foundation) teamed with a UK-based company (Pirbright Institute) that produces Covid-19 vaccines to create the virus in order to profit from selling the vaccines'.[12] While of course anything is possible, these seem like especially unlikely explanations. People who have a hard time tolerating uncertainty want to latch on to the first thing they can find.

More importantly for our present point, however, is the fact that authoritarians are obsessed with misinformation *in other people*. And this is especially pronounced right now on the left. In a telling study, Joseph Manson compared the Covid-related attitudes of left-wing authoritarians and right-wing authoritarians.[13] There were many similarities between the two types of authoritarians: Both liberal and conservative authoritarians wanted more punishment for Covid rule-breakers, fewer legal protections for pandemic rule violators, mandatory tracking apps, immunity certificate requirements, and even protest restrictions. However, there was one striking difference: While conservative authoritarians did not support prohibiting misinformation about Covid, liberal authoritarians strongly wanted a focus on stopping it.

That's one of the defining traits of the liberal authoritarian movement. It is positively obsessed with 'prohibiting misinformation'. And the net result of this: If we don't do something about it, we're going to really lose sight of what an elephant looks like.

One does not have to look very hard to see this uncertainty-avoidance-inspired misinformation obsession – and its consequences – in modern American life. It's everywhere, happening all the time, almost every day. To illustrate, I'll cover a few examples.

The Gradual Downfall of Wikipedia

That brings us to one of the most dangerously authoritarian things I've seen in my lifetime: The other-worldly shifting of Wikipedia to a misinformation political machine. I used to trust Wikipedia. Indeed, I once wrote a blog piece in a series on four principles of epistemology with the heading 'Principle #4: Trust Wikipedia'.[14] My argument was that Wikipedia was the ultimate in democratic knowledge production, because it was ... everybody. It allowed us to get to the whole elephant by degrees because we could all write about whatever part we happened to see in our own way.

But I've lost faith in Wikipedia. Consider the case of Dr Scott Atlas, who we discussed in Chapter 2. Atlas has argued that, among other things, scientific evidence suggests face masks are not effective at slowing the spread of Covid.

Now you may or may not agree with Dr Atlas, but either way, it is worth considering the argument. I myself am a decorated researcher with a PhD from one of the top research institutions in the world and over $500,000 in grants from NIH to study health-related phenomena. As such, I have looked at much the same data and, while I think masks likely do have some positive benefit (so I'm not sure I would go as far as he would), Atlas clearly has a point worth thinking through. And it isn't just me, as the World Health Organization and a top University of Minnesota epidemiologist who worked as a Covid advisor for Biden (among many others) have also expressed doubts about the effectiveness of masks – at least the kind that people actually wear – in various ways.[15] But, whether you agree with Atlas or not, you should go read the data and make an argument.

But that's not how misinformation-obsessed authoritarians do things. Rather, they do what Wikipedia did to Atlas (italics added for emphasis): 'Atlas was selected by President Donald Trump in August 2020 to serve as an advisor on the White House Coronavirus Task Force. In that role, Atlas *spread misinformation* about Covid-19, including theories that face masks and social distancing were not effective in slowing the spread of the coronavirus.'[16]

I could go on. The whole Wikipedia article brands Atlas – who, I remind you, is a decorated Stanford professor repeating things also said by the World Health Organization – as a kind of conspiracy theorist nutball who completely opposes the scientific community. Note that it doesn't even say '*was accused of* spreading misinformation'. No, it literally just wipes him off the credibility map by saying he 'spread misinformation'. (And, predictably, Twitter also banned an Atlas tweet that said masks don't work, and he and a respected group of academics from other prestigious universities had seminars removed from YouTube.)

Whatever you believe about masks, I'm not sure it's a good thing to call a decorated researcher who cites a bunch of Ivy League studies a 'misinformation spreader'. But Wikipedia does, and so does the modern authoritarian left, because one of their defining traits is an obsession with other people's presumed misinformation. And if we allow that trait to flourish – well, that's how authoritarians win. And that's how we all lose. Because if we really want to get at big issues like effective pandemic policies, we really need everyone to report their own view of their part of the elephant.

Misinformation Obsession in Renewable Energy

Wikipedia isn't the only arena that illustrates this left-wing misinformation obsession. On June 9, 2022, Biden's top domestic climate adviser, Gina McCarthy, addressed the topic of disinformation on clean energy in an Axios interview. Her solution? Censorship of disinformation. 'The tech companies have to stop allowing specific individuals over and over again to spread disinformation,' McCarthy said. 'We need the tech companies to really jump in.'[17] The idea that liberals in the US government would pressure huge tech companies to censor American citizens might have been unthinkable ten years ago – it was certainly unthinkable to me when I was a liberal – but as this quote clearly demonstrates, it is a present-day reality in American life.

Indeed, getting big tech to censor or tag things deemed

'misinformation' is one of the pillars of the left-wing clean energy movement. In an article from March 2022 by Julia Simon of NPR, she decries how 'misinformation is derailing renewable energy projects across the United States'.[18] And what does she want to do about it? That's pretty clear: She wants to follow the old authoritarian playbook. She wants to be sure conservative opinions on the matter don't see much sunlight. In fact, despite the fact that Facebook was already trying to actively reduce the spread of anti-clean-energy posts, NPR actually pushed Facebook to do more to stop the spread of misinformation. To quote from the article:

> NPR reviewed dozens of posts from anti-wind and anti-solar groups. While some posts about climate change denial, lithium mining, and a quote misattributed to Winston Churchill were marked as inaccurate, there were dozens of posts with misleading information about renewable energy that were not tagged. NPR sent Facebook a sampling of the posts from anti-renewable community pages. Facebook spokesman Kevin McAlister said in an emailed statement, 'We take action against content that our fact-checking partners rate false as part of our comprehensive strategy to keep viral, provably false claims from spreading on our apps. The examples shared with us don't appear to meet that threshold as they have only ever been shared a handful of times over a period of several years.' ... Leah Stokes, an associate professor of political science at the University of California, Santa Barbara, says as resistance to wind and solar projects spreads on social media, the dangers of misinformation from these anti-renewable Facebook groups is growing.

What Simon wants is for Facebook to stop the spread of misinformation. Despite Facebook's 'comprehensive strategy' to keep information from 'spreading', NPR wants them to do more.

We've already shown what lies behind the psychology of this misinformation obsession – people like to believe in the certainty of their preferred position. They like to believe that green energy is a simple solution that will save the planet. They get satisfaction and meaning from that belief. But, you may wonder, is this *really* going to make us all miss the bigger picture? After all, in some sense, aren't we really just prohibiting people who are delusional and not actually looking at the elephant *at all* from speaking, by censoring obvious misinformation?

If you think that, this case is particularly instructive for you. So let's evaluate the potential loss of real knowledge in this case via censorship. We'll start with this question: Is the information that Simon wants to censor genuinely false in a meaningful way? Out of curiosity, I did my own fact checking of the lithium post cited in the quote above – one of the posts that was tagged by Facebook as 'partly false'. It wasn't at all what I expected. I had imagined that I'd find some clear evidence of major misinformation presented in a somewhat biased way by the censors. I figured I'd mostly find stuff that didn't contribute much to our metaphorical elephant. What I found startled even me, the person writing a book about how liberal bullies are taking over the country.

To be clear, I'm of course not claiming that this one case covers all possible cases. There are no doubt examples of censorship that are more accurately performed. Yet sometimes it is worth digging deeper into a small sample – as opposed to an aerial view of a large sample – to test the assumptions at the roots of an enterprise. Large data swaths can mask deeper logical problems. NPR has made a claim, and here I evaluate that claim with reasoned argument.

With those caveats, here is the Facebook post on Lithium batteries in total:

DID YOU KNOW? There are four main kinds of batteries used in electric cars: lithium-ion, nickel-metal hydride, lead-acid, and ultracapacitors. Below is a picture of a lithium mine where they dig it out with diesel powered equipment and haul it with diesel trucks and process it with coal fired power plants so you can drive a electric car and hug trees.[19]

Then there was a picture of a fairly ugly mine that reminded me of the Berkeley Pit mine in Butte, Montana.

The post was tagged by Facebook as having 'partly false information'. There was a link to an article in *USA Today* which explained the false information tag. The link summary said 'Fact Check: Post incorrectly IDs nickel mine, lacks context on electric cars'. I read the *USA Today* critique in the link and, yep, that's an accurate summary of what it said. They tagged it as misinformation because of a misidentified picture and a lack of context.

Does the fact that the post got the wrong mine type and 'lacks context' make it misinformation? Absolutely not. It is not misinformation in any meaningful sense, not in any way that changes the basic arguments of the post. I once co-authored an article called 'Integrative complexity of 41 US presidents'.[20] My co-author (who is now a tenured professor at Cornell University) and I were embarrassed to later discover that we had actually miscounted the number of presidents in our study – it turned out to be 40 and not 41. (Naturally, we blame Grover Cleveland for daring to have two non-consecutive terms.) Did the science fall to pieces because the title of our article had the wrong number? No. That fact does not in any way invalidate the primary conclusions of our study; it is literally irrelevant to them. None of our statistics would be any different. None of our methods would be any different. The miscounting is a mere superficial detail that occurred late in the process, after the study was complete, and had no bearing on anything whatsoever.

So should the whole study be retracted as 'misinformation' or tagged as 'partly false'? Should the conclusions that liberal presidents were more complex than conservative presidents, or that presidential complexity tends to drop over the course of their first four terms, be labeled as misinformation because we miscounted something completely unrelated to those conclusions? Of course not. Those findings have actually been replicated and have withstood scientific scrutiny for 16 years.[21] We didn't base any of our conclusions on the number of presidents. The error is entirely superficial and thus not relevant.

That strikes me as much the case here. Note that the post itself lists nickel as one of the main kinds of battery, something that even the *USA Today* critique admitted was true. It then shows a picture of a nickel mine but calls it a lithium mine. So they got the naming of the picture wrong, but does that change anything about their point? Not that I can see. Imagine that I said to you: 'You shouldn't eat donuts. Research shows that donuts from all chains, but especially Shipley's and Jack N Jill's, are bad for you. Look at this picture of a glazed donut from Shipley's, you can see the fat dripping off of it.' It would hardly make a difference if you pointed out, 'Ha! Those aren't glazed donuts from Shipley's, they are clearly from *Jack N Jill's*.'

My point is still the same – donuts are bad for you. That is still a picture of a donut. In fact, it is a picture of a donut from one of the food chains I specifically named. It hardly matters what the picture is, it still makes the same point. While of course we'd prefer total accuracy, labeling something as 'partly false' because of an irrelevant detail hardly seems worth Facebook's time. And it is patently misleading, as it implies the conclusions stated in the post are false – when in fact, as far as I can tell, there is little false information there and the conclusions seem largely true upon further evaluation.

And the 'lack of context' argument? That may be the single most dangerous criteria for judging something as false that I've ever seen. *Everything on earth* lacks context. Several years ago, I was invited to give the keynote graduation speech for the University of Montana's Department of Psychology ceremony. (This isn't as great an honor as it sounds. While the speech was given to a large audience that nearly filled a room that holds over a thousand people, the stated reason for asking me specifically was that 'literally we can't find anyone else to give the speech this year'.) For one of my five points, I told the audience that I had searched human history to find a piece of advice that was entirely context-free.

And, lo and behold, I found one: *Never eat poison ivy*. I assured my audience that this piece of advice would always hold true and would never need to be qualified by the surrounding context. There was never a circumstance where they should eat poison ivy. Afterwards, a graduate came up to me and said, 'What if someone was holding my children hostage and told me that they would kill them unless I ate a piece of poison ivy? Would your advice hold in *that* context?' I had to admit that no, they had found a situation that made my principle – like basically everything else – qualified by context.

If 'lacks context' is your criteria for labeling something as 'partly false' then you better get out a very, *very* long metaphorical censorship pen. In fact, 'lacks context' would literally be a reason for calling almost anything 'partly false'. Einstein's theory of relativity? Better not post it, Facebook will label it 'partly false' because it 'lacks context'. (It clearly did and clearly does – see quantum physics). *Avatar* is the highest-grossing film of all time? Partly false, lacks context. Ask what happens when you adjust for inflation. Move over, *Avatar*, hello, *Gone with the Wind* (which wasn't even in the top 200 for unadjusted gross), *Star Wars*, *The Sound of Music*, and *E.T.* Heck, *Avatar* isn't even in the top ten when accounting for inflation.[22] Everything could have more context.

The larger point is simple. Everything has flaws. If you pick anything apart long enough, you'll find its weaknesses. That's why athletes are often better entering professional sports drafts as young prospects with a lot of unknowns than after a lot of information is compiled on them. Eventually, flaws will be found. Everyone like me who has submitted hundreds of papers to professional journals knows that reviewers will pick apart every idea, every paragraph, until there is some flaw exposed. Nothing is perfect. Given this, it is reasonable to ask: Are the Facebook employees spending this much time evaluating liberal posts that they politically agree with as much as the conservative ones they don't like? Social psychology and common sense – and experience – tell us the answer. No, they are not. Thus, what gets labeled as 'partly false' due to context or a mislabeled (but irrelevant) mine picture or any one of hundreds of other vague reasons, are almost invariably conservative posts. Doubtless many of them do contain misinformation; but what about liberal misinformation?

One is rather left with the feeling that censorship isn't about misinformation at all, but about political bullying. Out of curiosity, I googled 'eating poison ivy' and was alarmed to see the number of serious articles that addressed the question. While quite a few, including University of Pennsylvania Medicine, argued that you should not eat it, some sources – including an article called 'Can you eat poison ivy?' – actually argued that not only was it possible, it was good for you.[23] Sorry, University of Pennsylvania researchers – and common sense! – apparently this is not the settled debate I would have assumed. Regardless, Facebook would be compelled by its standards to declare both sides 'partly false' if it were to apply its weird misinformation approach to the issue. But to my knowledge, they haven't done that.

Why? That misinformation approach seems reserved for anti-left-wing rhetoric. If the far left ever decides poison ivy is good for you, watch out! One day we will wake up to find University of Pennsylvania researchers who tell you not to eat poison ivy tagged as spreading 'partly false information' because they accidentally attached a picture of a poison sumac leaf, or didn't provide all the facts about mosquito bites for context. Sound far-fetched? It's actually not that much more far-fetched than calling an otherwise accurate post that mostly presented common-sense information about mining 'partly false' because the picture was of the wrong mine and the post 'lacked context'.

The larger point is this: We absolutely, positively *are* missing out on important information about our metaphorical green energy elephant by censoring conservative posts on the issue. And there is a great danger in authoritarians' inability to handle uncertainty causing them to dismiss a huge percentage of the possible data in the world. If we start dismissing most people's views of their part of the elephant, then how are we ever going to learn what an elephant really looks like?

CHAPTER 4

INCONSISTENCY: GROUPS IN, PRINCIPLE OUT

As human beings, we have a hard time applying standards consistently. A few years ago, my family vacationed in Sandpoint, Idaho. We got there late at night, and we were hungry. Unfortunately, the only thing open was a local grocery store. I went to the counter where they served hot food and rather brazenly ordered a breakfast burrito. Was this a smart thing to do? No. I'm pretty sure under 'bad food decision' in the dictionary it says 'ordering a breakfast burrito at a small-town grocery store at night'.

The dictionary wisdom played out in this instance. The first thing that happened was the lady behind the counter chewed me out for ordering something that they currently weren't serving because it wasn't breakfast time. After I pointed to the sign behind the counter that literally said 'Breakfast Served Anytime', she changed course and started cussing out the manager for putting the sign there in the first place. Then, with small-town ethics as her guide, she basically insisted that she was sending me home with a breakfast burrito whether I wanted one or not. Only it turned out that the more I saw of it, the less I wanted it. They didn't have any normal ingredients at that time of night to put in it – only stuff that had been sitting around covered in flies all day that you probably shouldn't put in a burrito of any kind, breakfast or otherwise. This included ranch dressing (burrito heresy!) and something she called 'ham' but which I'm pretty sure was actually chunks of an old hot dog.

For those of you that don't know, a hot dog is made of ... gross stuff. I wrote down some of the ingredients listed on the package of a hot dog once. Here they are:

Mechanically separated pork meat, pork fat, cereal fillers, unknown animal intestine, water, salt, pepper[1]

How can they not know what *species of animal intestines* is in the hot dog I'm eating? Did they pick up random roadkill? My point is that unknown animal intestine in my night-time Sandpoint burrito didn't get any better for being eaten by flies all day long. And the tortilla felt like cardboard.

But I ate the thing anyway, intestines at all.

Now the question is: Why did I eat this horrid thing? And here's the point of the story. If you asked other people around me why I did that, they'd say, 'Luke is prone to making bad food decisions.' They would recall many times in the past that I have made similarly bad decisions, like the time I made and subsequently drank a mixture of milk, Diet Coke, pickles, chocolate, mayonnaise (!), whipped cream, and yogurt; or the time I ate a bagel that had been run through 50 college students' armpits, chewed up, spit on the ground, and then rolled in mud. 'These are not things normal people do,' they'd say with cruel heartless logic, 'and Luke does them all the time. Thus, this cross-situational consistency that is unique to Luke suggests the reason he ate that Sandpoint burrito is something about him.' In other words, they'd give a thoroughly rational answer to the question based on a logical principle.

If you asked me, however, I would have said this: 'I ate that gross burrito because I was hungry late at night and anyone would have done much the same in that specific situation.'

Do you see? When it comes to ourselves, we have a hard time using the same standard of judgment that we'd use on other people. We view ourselves through a biased lens that avoids rational thought. I preferred not to think about my poor eating tendencies, so I deflected that discussion – which might ultimately have led me to take responsibility for my own actions in an unpleasant way – onto something conveniently situational. It is practically proverbial wisdom that the person who passes me on the road is an insane maniac hell-bent on vehicular destruction, while the person I have to pass because they are driving more slowly than me is clearly an outdated grandmother who shouldn't have a license. Humans aren't very good at seeing our own actions through a consistently applied principle. We aren't good at thinking, 'Maybe *I'm* the one who is the maniac for driving too fast around the person I called a grandmother,' or, 'Maybe *I'm* the grandmother for forcing a reasonably paced driver to pass me on the highway.'

In other words, we are really bad at looking at ourselves through a rational lens that applies the same principle to ourselves that we would apply to others.

A *lot* of research suggests that it isn't just me. One of my favorite studies of all time happened in the mid-1970s.[2] West and colleagues were trying to better understand how things like Watergate could happen. So they went to a college campus and asked people if they'd be willing to sign up for a study that, as it turns out, would force them to commit a burglary. An alarmingly high percentage of students agreed to sign the consent form exonerating the experimenters of liability and thus agreed to participate in the heist. But the real story is how they described their own behavior.

When researchers told other people about the behavior of the burglars, those other people said 'Well, there must be something about those people that made them do that – they must have bad impulse control or a love of science or something.' However, when they asked the burglars *themselves* why they agreed to commit a crime, they said basically anything on earth *except* something that would implicate themselves: The experimenter pressured me, I didn't read the form, I was having a bad day, and so on. You see, we're not very good at looking at ourselves through a consistently applied principle. We don't view ourselves using the same standards that we apply to other people.

Why? Because we have a horse in the race. And anytime we have a horse in the race, anytime we can be emotionally affected by judgments we make in ourselves or other people, we tend to be less rational.

The Tribal Mentality

This bit of psychology is incredibly important for understanding left-wing authoritarianism. It turns out that one of the things that influences us the most to make irrationally inconsistent judgments are the groups we and others belong to. We have a tendency to want to protect *our tribe*. We don't view the other group through the same lens as our group.

A classic social psychology paradigm illustrates how deep this tribal lens goes. In this research, people are randomly assigned to be members of one of two groups with people they've never met. Imagine going to a research study where you draw a name out of a hat that assigns you to either 'Group A' or 'Group B'. You then participate in an activity with a group of people you've never met, against a group of people you've never met, where group assignment was determined randomly. You'd think that, in that instance, you wouldn't really care much about the groups.

You'd be wrong. It turns out in this research, called the 'minimal groups paradigm', people behave in surprisingly unprincipled ways. They judge their own group members as more competent and as having more positive personality traits than that *other* group. They give their own group members more resources than the other group.[3] They even feel better about themselves if they show discriminatory behavior against the other group![4] After all, they seem to say, 'I'm a "Group A" guy now. Those are my people. I don't like that *other* group.'

As a reminder: That's the other group comprised of people that I've never met, who were assigned to that group during the study by drawing a name out of a hat.

But although all people do this to some degree, some are especially prone to it. And as we'll see, no one is more willing to throw consistent principle out the window in favor of their own group than an authoritarian. A tribal us-versus-them mentality forms the backbone of the authoritarian person's psyche. Authoritarians do not want the same standard applied to their own groups that they apply to other groups.

Authoritarians Care a Lot More
than Normal about Groups

Everyone cares about their own groups. It is natural to care more about your family than about your neighbor's family. Few people go to a football game and cheer on both teams equally. And mostly, this kind of group-based mentality is OK. To want to belong is to be human. There is nothing wrong with feeling more at home with your family than with strangers. There is nothing wrong with failing to celebrate vigorously when the Cleveland Browns score a touchdown against your beloved Pittsburgh Steelers.

But authoritarians are absolutely *obsessed* with a tribal mentality. Recall that, as we saw in Chapter 1, authoritarians don't just follow any old authority figure in their vicinity who commands them to do something. Imagine an authoritarian walking down the street. And on that street, here comes a crazy person issuing a positively insane command: 'The end of the world is near, you must obey me, get down on your knees right now and ask for forgiveness.' Will the authoritarian person submit to the crazy command?

The answer depends on how that command fits into the group-based world of the authoritarian person. More than most people, the authoritarian will say yes if the crazy command comes from someone who is a member of the group the authoritarian cares about.

Now imagine an authoritarian on the street hearing a different command, one that is not crazy at all, something like 'Do not hit this aging grandmother with a stick'. Authoritarians would actually be *less* likely to obey that command than most people *if* the command comes from someone who is a member of an *enemy* group. That aging grandmother had better watch out. The authoritarian is looking for a stick, because someone who isn't in their group ordered them to go stickless.

Thus, if Donald Trump gives a crazy command, conservative authoritarians will follow it. But if Donald Trump gives a *reasonable* command, will liberal authoritarians follow it? Not for anything in the world. They'd be less likely than regular liberals, or independents, or politically uninterested people to follow a reasonable command from their political group's enemy leader.

The point is, authoritarians are especially prone to dogmatically follow their own group's leaders while dismissing other group's leaders – and followers – as inferior. Authoritarianism is thus inherently divisive. That's why in our own work we find that authoritarians on both sides really like it when their group leaders stick it to the other group's leaders.[5] Authoritarians really dig divisiveness. It's totally their thing to divide the world into us versus them. To a lot of liberal Americans, Democrat Nancy Pelosi ripping up Republican Donald Trump's State of the Union Speech on national television was horrible. It was a very petty and divisive thing to do. But our research shows that liberal authoritarians thought it was awesome. Why? They *like* their leaders to divide their world in two.

Authoritarians Really Do Not Like Consistently Applied Principles

A second problem can arise if you have not examined your ideas for consistency. You may use double standards in your thinking, and right-wing authoritarians do, over and over. They would sentence gay protestors who incite an attack on opponents to much longer prison terms than antigay protestors who commit the same crime. They would punish a 'hippie' more than they would punish an accountant for the same crime. They would punish a prisoner for beating another prisoner in jail more than they would a chief of detectives who did the same thing. They believe in 'majority rights' when they are in the majority, and 'minority rights' when they are in the minority.[6]

> – Bob Altemeyer and Bruce Hunsberger,
> researchers into right-wing authoritarianism

If you or I say that on YouTube, they'll take it down or flag it with a misinformation flag, but Bill Gates is allowed to say it.[7]

> – Phil Kerpen, conservative pundit

One of the clear practical implications of this divisive, us/them mentality is that authoritarians believe that *groups* matter more than *principles*. Authoritarians are especially likely to engage in all the group-based biases we've discussed so far. They are particularly likely to throw out rational principle and substitute it with group bias. They have a harder time than most people applying principles consistently across different groups.

Bob Altemeyer, unarguably the most influential authoritarianism researcher of all time, illustrates (along with colleague Bruce Hunsberger) this very well in the above quote. Conservative authoritarians don't apply the same standards to people in groups they like as they do to people in groups they don't like. If conservatives commit a crime, it's OK. But liberals committing the same crime – let's take them down.

Now Altemeyer and Hunsberger, like most researchers up until recently, focused almost exclusively on right-wing authoritarians.

However, more than Altemeyer supposed, it turns out that the exact same inability to consistently apply principles defines a very large number of authoritarians on the left. Phil Kerpen is right. With left-wing authoritarians, it doesn't matter whether the thing is true. It doesn't matter what rational principle or evidence would say. It only matters that Bill Gates is *liberal*. He's a member of a group left-wing authoritarians approve of. If he wasn't – if the same thing was said by a conservative – it is wrong.

Consider the following items from well-validated scientific questionnaires related to authoritarianism. The first is from a left-wing authoritarianism scale and the second from a related social dominance orientation scale:

This country would work a lot better if certain groups of Christian troublemakers would just shut up and accept their group's proper place in society.

Some people are just more deserving than others.[8]

As shown by these and other scale items, one of the fundamental defining traits of people who score high on authoritarianism and social dominance is this: They don't believe the same standards apply to all people. They don't want *their* group to shut up and accept their proper place in society; they only want the *other* group to do so. They believe that some groups of people are simply more *deserving* than others.

Thus, there is nothing more psychologically antithetical to authoritarianism than a *principle* applied equally across both my group and yours. Authoritarians by nature actually *want* an inconsistent standard.

To what degree is this happening in the real world outside the laboratory? When we cast our eye to modern culture, do we see evidence that this psychological inconsistency occurs on the left side of the political spectrum? Below, we evaluate these questions. As we'll see, the resounding answer is that yes, there is an overwhelming array of evidence that the psychological data accumulated in laboratories around the world is in fact being played out in a town near you. Left-wing authoritarians are substituting liberal groups for (often liberal) principles.

As you evaluate the evidence below, keep those two sample items above in your head. Think about how well-established research fits almost seamlessly into our modern world. Leftist movements increasingly embrace an authoritarian worldview that wants to silence their enemies and believes that their groups are simply more deserving than their conservative counterparts.

We're Fine Beheading Trump, but Cheering on Brandon Is Just Too Far

Indeed, this *authoritarian inconsistency* is currently dominating modern public discourse. For example, consider the 'Let's Go Brandon' chant that turned into a hit song, clothing line, and multiple extremely popular memes. The chant started because fans at a racing event in the US were chanting (obvious for everyone to hear very plainly) 'F*** Joe Biden', but the announcer – who at that time was interviewing a racer named Brandon Brown – said to the camera, 'You can hear the chants from the crowd ... "Let's go Brandon".' The video went viral and 'Let's Go Brandon' became a right-wing chant representing both disdain for Biden and the growing sense that he was completely out of touch with the American people.[9]

In fact, on a cross-country trip in the spring of 2022, my family and I were trying in vain to find Sioux Falls on the map at an official government rest stop. Since Sioux Falls is by far the largest city in South Dakota, we found this very odd. How could we possibly miss the biggest city in the state on a giant computer map at an official state rest stop? We thought maybe we were going crazy, but after looking at some older maps, eventually we put together the story. It wasn't us. In reality, on the map at this official South Dakota rest stop, the rather large city of Sioux Falls had been replaced by the rather small suburb of – you guessed it – Brandon. It was other-worldly. Brandon had unofficially become the new symbol of opposition to the president.

And what was the liberal response to the whole Brandon escapade? During the height of the movement, a Southwest Airlines pilot was accused of saying 'Let's Go Brandon' over the intercom during a flight. The outrage among the left was overwhelming. But this outrage over a comparatively minor offense struck many as quite a double standard after four years of attacking Donald Trump at every turn. As Kat Rosenfield said of the incident:

> But let's leave aside the question of whether this even happened: it's become irrelevant. Let's also leave aside the question of what an appropriate response would be, if it had. Let's forget about everything except this, the heart of the complaint: that a man with a PA system and a captive audience of a hundred or so air travellers used this platform, however briefly, to slightly disrespect the president. And in response, the people in charge of our national conversation have called him a terrorist and demanded the man be fired … whoever he is. What? We've just come off four years of barely veiled innuendo about the size of Trump's

hands; of cheering on the Congresswoman who publicly referred
to him as a 'motherf*****'; of cartoons and T-shirts and statues
and giant inflatable blimps depicting the president as a big fat
babyman with a tiny little wiener. We defended the comedienne
who posed with a latex mock-up of the President's severed head.
But suddenly, in 2021, 'Let's go Brandon' is a step too far?[10]

Rosenfield illustrates *authoritarian inconsistency* perfectly. Calls on
authority figures to punish members of another group for a comparatively minor offense feel especially egregious when such calls
were absent as members of our own group did far worse things.
But note the psychology underlying the event: Authoritarians
do not care about the principle – what constitutes an offense for
either group – they care about using authorities to crush people
they don't like. Period. We don't care about whether it's reasonable, given the amount of vitriol we allowed versus Trump, to call
for the firing of someone who said 'Let's Go Brandon'. We just
want this pilot to (in the words of the validated authoritarianism
scale) 'shut up and accept his proper place in society'.

Of course, such biases are commonplace across the human
political landscape on all sides, but right now the left has become
noticeably untroubled by principle, and as a result is increasingly
replacing *standards* with *authoritarian mob-ism*. You can turn on
news outlets around the world and see examples of this every
day. Bill Gates states that 'we got vaccines that help you with
your health, but they only slightly reduce the transmissions'.[11]
It's of course fine for leftist Bill Gates to say maybe vaccines
don't work that well at reducing transmission, but, as noted in
the quote from Phil Kerpen we saw earlier, if a conservative says
the same thing, well, here comes the authoritarian mob. That mob

doesn't care about the actual question of whether vaccines stop Covid spread – they care instead about the fact that you aren't in their group.

In England, it's OK to fly a 'Black Lives Matter' banner, but if you are a Burnley football fan who flies a 'White Lives Matter' banner, you lose your job at an aerospace manufacturing company because they (in the company's words) 'do not condone or tolerate racism in any form'.[12] They do not seem to care that by that standard, a 'Black Lives Matter' banner would be equally racist – because they are not applying a consistent standard, only mob authoritarianism. Dr Tony Fauci railed on conservative outdoor events as dangerous super-spreaders (when the CDC's own standards said outdoor masking was unnecessary), but never commented on large liberal outdoor events, or even on Obama's large *indoor* birthday party where people danced maskless cheek-to-cheek (something that at the time was forbidden by the CDC's own standards).[13] The left-wing American Civil Liberties Union (ACLU), which has long stood against mandates of any kind on principle, suddenly said: 'Far from compromising them, vaccine mandates actually further civil liberties.'[14] San Francisco mayor London Breed was caught maskless indoors against her own strict mandates, and when criticized for the hypocrisy, said she didn't 'need the fun police to come in and micromanage and tell us what we should or shouldn't be doing' and that she 'got up and started dancing because I was feeling the spirit and I wasn't thinking about a mask'.[15] Apparently she was unaware that other people also wanted to 'feel the spirit' and didn't want the 'fun police' she herself instituted. But authoritarians don't care about principle; they only care which group you are in. Congresswoman Cori Bush was asked how she thought it was

OK to support defunding the police when she herself had an expensive and publicly funded armed guard, and she said, 'I have private security because my body is worth being on this planet.'[16] Apparently the average citizens dying from lack of armed police protection are *less* 'worth being on the planet'. Her answer was basically a line from the social dominance questionnaire: 'Some people are more deserving than others.' Get with my program or else you aren't my people. Incredibly, left-wing authoritarians are OK with that answer. Consistent principles aren't their thing.

Laws Are for 'Them'

Substituting *authoritarianism* for a consistent *principle* has even more insidious consequences than regrettable hypocrisy. Our lab has studied how societal-level authoritarianism gets instantiated in the laws of countries and states.[17] And one of the defining traits of authoritarians is that they like to impose rules on others, but don't like a democratically imposed fair standard that applies to them as well. Consider that on the well-validated and highly used World Values Survey, the measurement of authoritarianism largely centers around people's desire for the rule of law and government to be superseded by personalities and experts. Authoritarians on the World Values Survey want 'a strong leader who does not have to bother with parliament and elections' and they want 'experts, not government, to make decisions according to what they think is best for the country'.[18] In other words, authoritarians want leaders to make decisions independent of the rule of law, decisions that *they* agree with. They do not want decisions based on a common legal standard that applies equally to all sides.

Against that backdrop, it is worth considering that Joe Biden's administration has quite dangerously and publicly ignored US law and even Supreme Court rulings. For example, after repeatedly affirming he did not have the Constitutional power to restore his administration's eviction moratorium in light of the Supreme Court's ruling that he couldn't, he then brazenly said he was going to do it anyway. In the words of *USA Today*, 'The President of the United States stood before the nation and announced that he intended to break the law.'[19] The fact that Biden's shocking statement did not dominate CNN and other liberal outlets for weeks shows how authoritarianism has seeped into the left's thinking. When principle isn't your guide, you want your authority figures to break commonly accepted legal guidelines.

There is a trickle-down effect of this authoritarian attitude. Grace Trick, an American schoolteacher who immigrated from Argentina, was fired from her job in Oklahoma for refusing to wear a mask in school. Now you may agree or disagree with her decision. But there is no disagreement about the fact that she was fired *even though Oklahoma law explicitly prohibited mask mandates.* In other words, this firing was actually directly opposed to her own state's codified law. And this is what she said about that:

> Well, to be honest, it was deeply shocking to me when he made the announcement. All the sudden all these images from when I was young came to me. I remember watching in Argentina this news of this politician did this or this politician did that or millions of dollars were seized from this politician's house. So politicians believing that they were above the law. I truly never thought that this would happen here in the United States of

America. Not here. So I was just deeply saddened to see someone in power to believe they were above the law. You know, when I became a United States citizen, I took an oath to follow the law. We as educators should be a moral example to follow.[20]

Grace Trick knows full well what authoritarianism looks like, because she's seen the complete disregard for the principles of law from politicians in Argentina. But increasingly, as her case illustrates, this authoritarian double standard is coming to define the politics of the left in Western democracies as well.

Blind Résumé: Judging on Principle and Not Group Bias

I'm an avid college basketball fan. The game is fun; the atmosphere inside a college arena is mesmerizing; buzzer beaters are entertaining. But I also love the debates concerning who should or should not get into the holy grail of American college sports: The NCAA basketball tournament, or March Madness as it is affectionately known by aficionados. These debates are fascinating because they are at their root a study in stereotyping. People expect that traditional powers from traditional power conferences, like Duke or Syracuse, are better than smaller teams from smaller conferences, like George Mason or Virginia Commonwealth. And the discussion on major networks could be fodder for any Social Psychology class on the nature of prejudice. Essentially every commentator looks for every possible reason to show that Duke is more deserving than George Mason. That's the outcome they expect, and so almost every discussion is tilted in favor of Duke. As a result, it is hardly surprising that official computer metrics (metrics which are not directly subject to human bias), such as the Ratings Percentage Index (RPI), historically revealed that – statistically – the most highly rated teams that were excluded from the tournament were from small schools. Power schools have an empirically demonstrable unfair advantage over smaller schools in NCAA tournament selection. If we compared apples to apples, if we applied a fair standard consistently, more small schools would get in based on evidence.[21] But we don't. No matter what statistics say, no matter what evidence says, we tend to just assume that Duke is better than George Mason because ... well, they're Duke.

My favorite segments on sports television force commentators to cut through their biases and deal with actual evidence. One of those is called *Blind Résumé*. ESPN used this trick to present the statistical cases for two teams side by side without the accompanying team names, so commenters had to declare, on the spot for posterity, which résumé they believed was better, without knowing which team was which. And despite the fact that commenters – *college basketball* commenters, mind you, people paid to know everything about every team – were experts in the field, they often picked the smaller school in the blind comparison. I admit that I enjoyed watching them squirm, trying after the fact to reconcile their previously stated opinion that Duke should get in the tournament ahead of George Mason with the fact that, when the names were removed, they just picked George Mason's résumé over Duke's!

There is a reason Lady Justice is blind. We need more blind résumés. Blind résumés force us to apply evidence equally to both sides, devoid of our pre-existing biases. So let's play *Blind Résumé* with an example here to illustrate the LWA problem. Below, I'm going to present a real-life event, altering some of the details to hide the political implications until after you've seen the pertinent facts.

How we judge the case depends, of course, on the principle we bring to bear. For the sake of consistency, we'll use a very common-sense guide that most people would agree on. This guide revolves around how *mean* each party was being. We're going to ask questions like this: Which side was being more of a jerk? Which side was being too harsh, or too dogmatic, or too bullying?

Our *Blind Résumé* starts with two groups dining at a restaurant. In what is a very familiar American tale, one group thought another group was too loud and asked them to quiet down. The louder group thought they were just having a good time and didn't appreciate some fuddy-duddies invading their personal space – and said so.

As it happens, in this case both groups returned to their meals, and that would have ended things except that the groups confronted each other outside the restaurant. It isn't clear exactly how the confrontation started. But it is clear that it mostly involved two people. We'll call one of them 'Johnny' and the other 'Steve'. Here is where *Blind Résumé* comes in. Now imagine that, in the midst of the confrontation outside the restaurant, Johnny got right in Steve's face and called him a 'f****** b****'. In response, after a brief pause, Steve responded by calling Johnny an 'idiot' and then walked away from the scene.

Now, as an objective observer, what should our evaluation be? If we don't know anything about either side, if we are just trying to apply a principle of meanness, how should we judge this encounter? Which side used the most inappropriate or inflammatory language that would escalate a conflict?

And that seems clear: Both sides used inappropriate language, but Johnny used much, much harsher words. Johnny's language was considerably more inflammatory than Steve's, and in fact preceded Steve's insult. Johnny got up in Steve's face and basically yelled horrible things about him. Steve didn't exactly de-escalate the situation, but he certainly didn't match Johnny's horrible words, *and* he walked away. So Johnny seems far more to blame.

Now let's take our *Blind Résumé* a step further and evaluate what happened after the incident. Steve was upset about it and pursued retribution. And the end result of that retribution is that Johnny was *fired from his job* for this incident. Was Steve justified in getting Johnny fired for calling a random person at a restaurant a 'f***** b****'?

And if we honestly view that question from a neutral lens – a lens that doesn't know which person is the liberal and which person is the conservative – the answer to that second question also seems clear. No, Johnny should not have been fired. Trying to get him fired was mean. That's not what happens in a civilized and healthy society. In a healthy democracy, things that aren't relevant to your job and that aren't illegal do not get you fired. In a healthy democracy, people don't get fired for saying dumb stuff to a stranger in a restaurant in a weak moment. In a healthy democracy, either the two sides apologize to each other and make up, or they go home, spend time with their friends and families, and tell stories about the incident to their grandchildren years later. My point is, you don't have to like someone or make up with someone to go your separate ways after a public argument and not let a brief confrontation at a restaurant turn into a full-blown apocalypse.

It is an honest question to ask: Is that really the kind of society you want to live in? Where you might be fired for saying something unfortunate tonight – not to your boss or client, but to a random stranger who annoyed you at a restaurant? You should be asking that question right now, because if you live in the US, that is *exactly* the society you in fact *do* live in.

This case is one of many that illustrates the point. Only in this instance, it wasn't *Johnny* who was fired. It was *Steve*. Put down this book and think about that for three minutes. It wasn't the person who used the more inflammatory language who got the work ax. No; the person who was fired didn't scream 'f***** b****'. That screaming, cussing person was rewarded as a hero; it was the person who *responded to being screamed at* who was fired.

Now, to facilitate the résumé being truly blind, I purpose-fully altered some aspects of the story. What Steve actually said, represented in total, was 'You look like an idiot.' We'll see that this insult could indeed have been quite meaningful and deeply wounding to the recipient, perhaps more than merely calling that person an idiot would have been. But before we get to what happened next, I want you to see something. It is hard to come up with a reasonable justification for someone screaming 'f***** b****' at someone else outside a restaurant. Watching the video, it seems to me like Johnny is goading Steve, trying to get a response. Steve should have walked away sooner, no doubt – and he shouldn't have responded. But at a minimum, both parties are equally culpable, and most likely Johnny bears more of the blame.

But we don't live in a society that applies a principle fairly or equally. We live in a society that increasingly substitutes authoritarian tribalism for principle. Screaming an obscenity at a stranger outside a restaurant would normally be viewed as bad behavior. Responding to someone screaming at you by insulting them would in a fair society not be viewed as a fire-able offense.

And yet that is what happens in America – if the someone screaming is a liberal and the someone responding is a conservative. In this case, the incident revolved around a teenage boy celebrating prom wearing a dress. The teenager screamed the obscenity at a conservative company executive. The executive responded 'You look like an idiot' and walked away, thinking the incident regrettable but over.

But the teenager posted the video on TikTok, and celebrities took up the cause. In particular, comedian Kathy Griffin – who had once posted a video of herself with a lifelike severed head of Donald Trump – called his bosses. His bosses originally backed the executive. The left-wing authoritarian cancel culture crowd then went after the company's clients. Ultimately, they got the executive fired. As a result of a two-second moment in response to a teenager who was shouting obscenities at him, he lost his job and his income.[22]

Now, in an interview on Dan Bongino's *Canceled in the USA* TV show, the fired executive did not come off to me as especially likeable.[23] He did not seem particularly apologetic for his behavior, when I thought he should have been. Indeed, given the teenager's identity, claiming that he 'looked like an idiot' was quite an insult, and even though provoked, I don't think this was the right way to handle the situation.

So I'm not defending the executive's behavior here. What I'm defending is a fair standard of judgment. If we are going to eviscerate the conservative executive, then we need to apply the same standard to the rude teenager whose behavior was clearly worse. I don't think either of them should face repercussions; but if they do, they should face them (at a minimum) equally. In fact, it is worth noting that two teenagers – the teenage boy and his friend who was also there on the fateful night – not only got him fired and led to him getting death threats, they also sent him a taunting message on Twitter, saying 'Hope you like all the fame'. Imagine if the roles were reversed and a conservative had done that to a liberal executive! And how did the teenagers respond to all this? When interviewed, one of them said: 'Yes, I do think he deserved to lose his job. I'm not mad that he got fired, no.' The other one said: 'As I stand right now, I do think he got what he deserved.'[24]

Do these teenagers also think *they* should have suffered consequences for their terrible behavior? Do these teenagers think *they* should receive death threats for *their* awful actions? No. Did Kathy Griffin think these teenagers should apologize for their behavior, or be fired for engaging in mean-spirited bullying? Of course not. Left-wing authoritarians don't evaluate principle – they don't have to have the same standard applied to them, because *they are from the right group*. It isn't about principle at all to the authoritarian; it's about what group you belong to.

One of the teenagers summed up the attitude perfectly by saying this: 'Times are changing, people are changing – either get with it or just shut up.' *That's* the clincher. It doesn't matter that I said something worse about you. It doesn't matter who started the argument. It doesn't matter that the argument is completely irrelevant to your job. It doesn't matter that you received death threats and were called nasty names and publicly humiliated. It doesn't matter that you lost your income and your livelihood. It doesn't matter that if I had a job as an executive and said those things to you, I think I'd be a hero and certainly would not be fired. None of those principled arguments matter. No; *you* just need to get with the times; *you* just need to adopt my positions on things. And if you don't believe like I do, then you just need to *shut up*. Because my group is the one with the power and yours isn't. Get with the times, man.

When Nice People Defend Authoritarianism, It's Time To Speak Out

I've consistently been an apolitical person, both privately and within my own field. I've tried hard publicly not to take political sides. Now I of course have always had political opinions, some liberal, some conservative, some embarrassingly moderate. Overall, until recently I would have considered more of my opinions liberal than conservative.

Even when I called myself liberal, it always bothered me, though, that being 'apolitical' in my field meant that I was free to state *only* my liberal opinions. I knew I had to keep my conservative opinions to myself. In my field, liberal opinions make me a normal person; conservative opinions make me an ideologue. As a result, I have purposefully reined in any conservative opinions and I've generally been quite liberal in many of my public statements. In fact, even when I've protested liberal bullies, I've often done so privately.

Generally speaking, I was content with that state of things because my goal wasn't to make political statements, but to simply be allowed to do my own scientific thing free from influence. But one incident in particular convinced me it was time to speak out, and it was the double standard, the lack of principle, that was the primary motivator. I'm going to tell you what that incident was.

The Society of Experimental Social Psychology (SESP) is one of the most important organizations in my field. It is essentially an exclusive club for elite researchers. Fellows are elected each year and the membership can only grow by 5% in any year. It runs two of the most important journals in the field. It is often considered a highlight of one's career to be elected as a fellow. I certainly considered it a highlight of mine and I was proud to be elected a fellow.

After SESP's annual conference in 2021, SESP's Executive Committee sent out an alarming email. In it, they described a horrible racist talk that happened at the conference. In their words, 'even a single unfortunate event can reawaken and amplify concerns about the exclusivity of SESP', and they further noted that they had heard 'from multiple attendees of SESP 2021 who were upset about a specific talk given at this past convention. We thank those individuals for highlighting this issue.'

The email then proceeded to describe that the horror of this single talk had caused SESP to make large changes to its organization. Among them included developing a clear 'Diversity, Equity, and Inclusion' statement and a mandate to 'share this statement with every future speaker at SESP and ask them to keep the statement in mind as they prepare their talks'. The very worst part to me was that the person who gave the talk issued a groveling apology, sent with the Executive Committee's email, in which she flogged herself endlessly for engaging in such horrible behavior.

Given that this one single talk caused a major organization to completely alter its policies, you might imagine it was incredibly horrible. What vile monster reared its ugly head? What was in this racist talk that was so bad that SESP changed its policy? Was it support of the KKK? Was it use of the 'n' word to describe black people?

No. One of the speakers had used Kanye West (who is black) to illustrate 'narcissistic' pride and had used Bernie Sanders (who is white) to illustrate 'positive' pride.

Did the speaker specifically draw out a racist point, stating that black men are more narcissistic than white men? No. Did the speaker make any reference to race at all? No. Did the speaker have any history of racist behavior or language? No. In other words, was there any hint of actual racism involved? No. Rather, the speaker had used a narcissistic example of a black person to illustrate … narcissism.

As far as I can tell, there is no evidence of a systemic pattern of racism. There is no evidence, as far as I can tell, that my colleague in the field intended or even tried to use this in even a vaguely racist way. Instead, as far as I can tell, she simply chose an example that seemed appropriate involving an African American person being depicted in a less than flattering light. I can see how that would hit people the wrong way, don't get me wrong. It would almost certainly hit me the wrong way, too, if it involved one of my own groups. In fact, for this exact reason, in my own career I always try to use parallel examples with respect to groups – if I show a white person in a good light, I try to show a white person in a bad light. If I show a liberal in a bad light, I try to show a conservative in a bad light. So I get why this would rankle people.

But did this merit large-scale authoritarian nuclear warfare from the top down? Not at all. Rather, it seems more appropriate to the level of a private conversation with the speaker. In other words, how about just discussing amongst yourselves and moving forward? I have little doubt this response from SESP was well meaning, but we're going to change the entire face of the organization, we're going to make a colleague submit a groveling public apology, because … she used a reasonable example of her construct who happened to be black? Is the implication that we simply can never use an unflattering example of anyone unless they are a straight white man?

As that suggests, the real problem here is the lack of a principled standard. This double standard is the primary thing that has changed my public approach to this issue. Think about this for a second. Kanye West isn't just racially different than Bernie Sanders. He's also (a) more conservative and (b) more religious. So why aren't we demanding a groveling apology from our colleague for offending *conservatives*? Why aren't we demanding a groveling apology from my colleague for offending *religious people*? The answer is obvious – this isn't about a fair standard or even about diversity, but about a group-based political agenda. We don't like those conservatives very much, so it's fine to make fun of *them*. In fact, never mind using Donald Trump as an example of narcissism, which would obviously be appropriate. (Full disclosure – I used Donald Trump as a negative example of simple-mindedness in a recent conference talk myself. Perhaps in the spirit of SESP, I should issue a groveling apology to all people who were born in Queens, New York, since that's where Trump was born.) Having been to hundreds of talks given by social psychologists over the years, I can say with confidence it is obvious that it is open season on conservatives and religious people. Most of these attempts go well beyond simply using a conservative white guy as an example of narcissism or simplicity; most of them generalize to how bad conservatives or religious people are. And yet one example of a narcissistic black man used to illustrate narcissism causes one of the organizations to which I belong to change its entire policy, when conservatives and religious people in the field have had to suffer from overt attacks on their whole group for years?

Any standard must be fairly applied or else it will devolve into authoritarianism. And we also must have room to use reasonable examples without looking over our shoulder every third second for cancel culture. SESP's email made me feel like I'd joined a cult rather than a group of independent freethinkers.

After the incident, I reached out to one of the people in the field I most trusted, a liberal freethinker who is one of the nicest and best people I know. I had seen this person consistently say and do things that went against social and political norms. I trusted him as an honest straight-shooter. 'This man,' thought I, 'at least won't be subject to the left's authoritarian norms.' And he was in fact very nice and eloquent in his response – but it was a response that (much to my shock) actually defended SESP's authoritarianism. *That* was the last straw in my silence. I had hoped that one of the elder statesmen of the field, a liberal freethinker who never just accepted the status quo on either side, would tell me that things were being done to provide a correction to that horrible email. Instead of that, he just defended authoritarianism.

And this is a message to all liberal freethinkers out there: *This is the consequence of your silent defense of authoritarian inconsistency.* For ultimately, we cannot have a free society if we don't apply the same standard to all sides. And if the many millions of nice and good liberals don't wake up from this soon, it may be too late.

The liberal authoritarian virus is spreading.

CHAPTER 5

SIMPLICITY: AUTHORITARIAN BLACK-AND-WHITE THINKING, LITERALLY

What thoughts come to mind when you think about broccoli?

Maybe you think the same thing as former president of the US George H. W. Bush: 'I do not like broccoli. And I haven't liked it since I was a little kid, and my mother made me eat it. And I'm President of the United States, and I'm not going to eat any more broccoli.' (Hopefully you don't think you are the president. That would be a different kind of issue. We're talking just about broccoli here.) If so, you basically associate broccoli with one thing. It is *bad* and that's that. In fact, that's about as simple a thought as you can get. You've associated a single object (broccoli) with a single dimension (bad).[1]

If you think instead that broccoli has a really bad flavor, but a really great texture, you've thought something that is measurably more complex. You've identified two different parts of broccoli and admitted that these two things might actually point to different conclusions, one good and one bad.

We have a fancy, hyphenated word for this phenomenon in my field: *Multi-dimensionality*. Multi-dimensionality means associating more than one thing with a particular object. Although complexity has been defined in many ways by many scholars, a common thread across all those definitions is this: *Complexity equals multi-dimensionality*. In fact, I was once a part of a journal symposium on measuring the complexity of language with some of the top scholars in the field, and although we could barely agree on anything, the fact that *complexity = multi-dimensionality* seemed to be scandalously bordering on near-universal agreement.[2]

That means that if you think broccoli has both good and bad elements – if you can 'see both sides' of broccoli – you are thinking more complexly than if you can only see one side.

This distinction – simplicity versus complexity – turns out to be very important in our understanding of the left-wing authoritarian movement. As we'll see, left-wing authoritarians are especially prone to simplistic, black-and-white thinking on an issue that is increasingly defining modern America: Race.

We'll start by discussing how the language authoritarians use is a window into their (often) simple, black-and-white psychology.

The Linguistic Footprint of an Authoritarian

Authoritarians may or may not be more simple-minded about broccoli; but simple-mindedness about racial and political issues is a hallmark of the authoritarian mind.[3] This can be seen by approaching the problem at the other end. Specifically, can we identify authoritarians from the language they use? Do authoritarians leave a specific 'linguistic footprint' that allows us to recognize them from how they talk? It has been curiously quite difficult for linguistic analysts to pinpoint a specific linguistic profile for the authoritarian person. To my knowledge, the few scholarly attempts at creating an 'authoritarian' linguistic foot-print have all failed. In an age where, using only Facebook likes, linguistic analytic algorithms can predict someone's personal-ity traits better than that same person's friends (!), it is quite remarkable that authoritarians are that hard to linguistically pin down.[4] You can apparently talk in a lot of different ways and still be authoritarian. But one of the most consistent predictors of the authoritarian speaker is that they use simpler language than non-authoritarians.

Psychologists have constructed scientific methods for evaluat-ing the complexity or simplicity of people's thoughts. The most prominent among those is a measurement called 'integrative complexity', which was created and honed by Peter Suedfeld.[5] Using this system, scientists have been able to quantify how simple or complex people are on any given topic at any moment. And in one of the more influential political psychology papers of all time, Jost and colleagues performed a large meta-analysis on multiple *integrative complexity* studies and showed that people high in authoritarianism consistently use simpler political lan-guage.[6] They were focused only on authoritarians on the right, but research on left-wing authoritarians similarly reveals that simplicity – both linguistic simplicity and other forms of sim-plicity – is associated with authoritarians across the political spectrum.[7] We did a linguistic analysis of over 6,000 people ourselves using many different linguistic variables, and for both left- and right-wingers, simple language was one of the most consistent predictors of authoritarianism. The effect sizes weren't large – in keeping with typical linguistic effects – but they were pretty consistent.[8]

This provides a window into the mind of the typical authoritarian person. And from a psychological point of view, it makes a lot of sense: Authoritarians possess a lot of traits that are associated with simplicity. We've already evaluated some of those traits in Chapters 2 and 4. Authoritarians are intellectually lazy, and an unwillingness to think hard about things is associated with simple attitudes – in fact, it was one of the most consistent predictors of simple thinking in our own work.[9] Authoritarians are focused on groups and not principles, and dividing the world into us and them is not a formula for complex thinking. One research study showed that group biases occurred in part because people could not complexly parse causal information related to specific group traits – for example, racist people tend to focus on a simple story (blacks possess trait X) while non-racist people tend to understand that while blacks may on average possess trait X, it could emerge due to complex situational factors that mean it isn't a permanent feature of that group.[10] Further, authoritarians are extremists, and research shows extremists tend to be less complex – indeed, it is one of the most consistent predictors of complexity.[11]

Authoritarians are also aggressive, and a long history of research similarly ties simplicity to aggression.[12] To name just one example, terrorist groups sometimes do not fit the linguistic profile one would expect – they show greater social and affiliation language than the stereotype would suggest – but they are invariably less complex across the board than control groups. We once ran a study that was funded by the Department of Homeland Security. We found terrorist groups were consistently lower in complexity than control groups, even when the control groups themselves were comparable ideologues that shared many similar ideas *except* the endorsement of violence.[13]

In another study, we found that as terrorist groups became more creepily violent, they used simpler rhetoric. One of the ways you know that you have really gone to the dark side is when al-Qaeda – the people who flew planes into the Twin Towers – disavows you because you have become too violent. But when you do become *that creepy* and as a result turn into ISIS, you tend to become much simpler as a result.[14]

The point isn't that all authoritarians want to behead their enemies like ISIS. Rather, the point is that authoritarians of all ilks tend to be simple-minded. They focus on one dimension to the exclusion of others. One of the inevitable outcomes of this authoritarian simplicity is that everything tends to become a single-issue problem. The issues change from group to group, but the psychology remains the same. For many terrorist groups, the evil resides in the West. Rather than imagine the complicated world that the capitalistic US system actually produces, rather than analyze the many and varied causes of problems in their own countries (both internal and external), rather than that complex analysis, they tend to say, more simply, that 'Western ideas' produce all the bad things.

For many left-wing authoritarians in the US, their single issue is race. Rather than imagine the complicated world of inter-racial interactions to be the complex morass of psychological and moral factors that it in fact is, rather than imagine that humans are a mixed bag of good and bad motives, instead the modern leftist authoritarians think that almost every problem can be boiled down to one source: Conservative whites engaging in racism.

The Reduction of Complex Societal Issues
to One Variable: Meet Ibram X. Kendi

> Ibram X Kendi is as dumb as Obama is smart; as crude as
> Obama is nuanced; as authoritarian as Obama is liberal. On
> race, Democrats are going to have to choose between these two.
> Because they sure as hell can't pick both.[15]

>   – Andrew Sullivan, British-American author

An increasing number of people have wondered out loud, like
Andrew Sullivan, whether many modern 'antiracist' movements
(such as those led by Ibram X. Kendi) are actually dogmatic
authoritarianism in disguise. In my experience, an even larger
number have wondered *privately* if the constant playing of the
'you're racist' card has made legitimate discussions about race
less productive – but they've been afraid to say so out loud for
fear of being canceled.

But *are* these modern antiracism movements genuinely
authoritarian? Let's apply a psychological scientific lens to
examine the claim that Kendi's *antiracism* movement is, in fact,
destructively authoritarian. The answer is, without doubt, yes.
Kendi's movement embodies *authoritarian simplicity*, and it is
one of the most damaging traits of the left-wing authoritarian
movement.

Kendi's book *How to Be an Antiracist* was an international
bestseller and launched him into superstardom. In the book,
Kendi makes a startling claim: He argues that every single thing
you do or think falls into one of two categories – either you
are being a racist or you are actively opposing racism. In fine
authoritarian simplicity fashion, Kendi makes it absolutely clear

that there is no middle ground for considering something race-neutral or colorblind. If you believe something is 'neutral', then you are at that moment being a racist. If you don't think explicitly antiracist thoughts, then you are at that moment being a racist. If you believe you can debate the health care system, the price of peas, or the likelihood of Manchester City winning the Premier League title[16] without considering race, you're being racist.

Consider this statement from Kendi at a TED Talk question-and-answer session:

> And so what I'm trying to do with my work is to really get Americans to eliminate the concept of not racist from their vocabulary, and realize we're either being racist or antiracist. We're either expressing ideas that suggest certain racial groups are better or worse than others, superior or inferior than others. We're either being racist, or we're being antiracist. We're expressing notions that the racial groups are equals, despite any cultural or even ethnic differences. We're either supporting policies that are leading to racial inequities and injustice, like we saw in Louisville, where Breonna Taylor was murdered, or we're supporting policies and pushing policies that are leading to justice and equity for all.[17]

On the surface, few people I know would have a problem with trying to own racist tendencies in society, and thus much of what Kendi says actually resonates with me and other like-minded liberal Americans. But note at the end of that progression the strong emphasis on *policy*. This policy emphasis isn't an anomaly: it is in fact central to the antiracism movement. Elsewhere in the talk Kendi says:

One, for several decades now, every workplace has publicly pledged a commitment to diversity. Typically, they have diversity statements. I would basically rip up those diversity statements and write a new statement, and that's a statement committed to antiracism. And in that statement you would clearly define what a racist idea is, what an antiracist idea is, what a racist policy is and what an antiracist policy is. And you would state as a workplace that you're committed to having a culture of antiracist ideas and having an institution made up of antiracist policies. And so then everybody can measure everyone's ideas and the policies of that workplace based on that document.[18]

Note again the emphasis on transforming people's beliefs about policy from the top down. Note again the lack of nuance, the absolutist black/white, with-us-or-against-us mentality. *Rip up everything else. Measure everyone's ideas and policies by this one document that Kendi approves of.* I have spent a good portion of my career studying the complexity of thinking, and this is basically the textbook definition of low complexity.[19]

Now, you may wonder, what exactly are the policies I need to support that make me a good person? Practically speaking, how can I actually be an antiracist? Kendi was pressed on that and he offered two things: You must believe in universal health care and you must believe in financial reparations (income redistribution) for past wrongs. In his own words:

I mean, if someone was to force me to answer, I would probably say two, and that is, high-quality free health care for all … and then secondarily, I would say reparations. And many Americans claim that they believe in racial equality, they want to bring about racial equality. Many Americans recognize just how critical economic livelihood is for every person in this country, in this economic system. But then many Americans reject or are not supportive of reparations.[20]

To be clear: When pushed on what it means to be a good person, Kendi doesn't say that you should love your actual minority neighbor, or try to treat everyone fairly whatever their skin color, or engage in honest and sometimes painful discussions with people who aren't like you. No; Kendi repeatedly states that to be a good person you must endorse certain *policy positions* in a dogmatic black/white fashion. And when pushed on what policy positions people must endorse, he says universal health care and redistribution of income. In fact, as it turns out, every policy position Kendi advocates for is a political position of the far left. So, in summary, if you don't support these specific policy positions, you are going to be branded a racist and in danger of being canceled in the workplace and beyond. Submit to this reprogramming or else.

The consequences of this overly simple black/white dogma for public discourse are huge. In Kendi's left-wing authoritarian world, there is no room for debate about the policy positions themselves. So if I believe in equality (which I do) and I want everyone to have exactly equal health care (I do), but I don't think that universal health care is the best way to accomplish that goal (I have some doubts) – or if I raise points about the problems with universal health care actually possibly making life worse long-term for everyone (which lots and lots of sensible people of all stripes have raised), including blacks – I'm considered a racist.

Black-and-white authoritarianism such as this is society-killing. There has to be room for debate without canceling everyone you don't like by branding them a 'racist'. In fact, unlike what Kendi claims, many whites who don't like his movement have for a long time been willing to admit that they've benefited from white privilege. For a long time, many have been willing to admit they were born on metaphorical third base. Many whites are aware that they didn't hit the triple that got them there. For a long time, many whites have been willing to acknowledge that there is systemic racism. But incredibly, in Kendi's world, these persons are not allowed a space to debate what the best policies for creating the most equal and awesome society are, because if they challenge anything he believes about what leads to the best and most equal outcomes, they are considered racists. And *that* is an intellectual tragedy.

Everyone has prejudices. But among the large group of people who want to overcome their prejudices, there is little evidence that it helps to forgo honest discussion about whether or not many police violence incidents are justifiable, about why blacks want police in their neighborhoods more than whites, about whether or not we can afford universal health care, about whether universal health care will simply make health care worse for everyone, and on and on. Society needs more than this kind of left-wing authoritarian simplicity offers.

Racial discussions have to involve more than one-way traffic, and they can't reduce everything down to 'conservative white people are racist'. Almost no problem is a single-issue variable with a single-issue solution.

Ibram X. Kendi's mindset has permeated American culture. And nowhere has this authoritarian simplicity become more entrenched than in the American university.

Authoritarian Simplicity in Higher Education

This authoritarian simplicity about race is running the American university system right now. My former university, the University of Montana, is representative of this bracingly simplistic view of race. To illustrate, in February 2024, I went to the University of Montana's own pages dedicated to race and equity.

It is hard to overstate the shocking level of simplicity I found there.

One of the key resources was on UM's library page.[21] On that page, they recommend long lists of readings, links to external groups, and the like. And while it is unsurprising that every single resource was from a far-left authoritarian angle, it is nonetheless – for an old-school ex-liberal like me – bracing. You will find books from Kendi, of course, but scads and scads of other books dedicated to how horrible white people are, with titles including the words 'kill', 'rage', and (in a separate book, in case you didn't get the point yet) 'killing rage'.[22] Other book titles included 'fatal', 'stamped', 'reaped', 'oppression', 'systemic racism', 'rape', and 'white supremacy'.[23] In these books, it seems that white people are *doing* the bad stuff and minority ethnicities are *receiving* the bad stuff. Whites have the rage, minorities are killed and reaped and raped. There were several books on racist policing, a lot of books on Critical Race Theory, and a book promoting Marxism. There were links to far-left organizations like Black Lives Matter.

To be clear, it isn't like I want those books banned. I think we can learn from them. Some of these books contain important truths, and we should not run from those truths. In no way am I claiming that whites have never done the bad things the books say they have. Obviously, whites have a long history of racism.

Further, I'm not saying that the individual books themselves always ignore nuance. After all, this book is titled *Liberal Bullies* and yet, if you read its pages, you will find that I do not think all liberals are bullies – in fact, most of them aren't. You will also find that I am quite concerned about conservative bullies as well. But evaluating each individual book on this list is not the point. Rather, the point is about the message UM's webpage conveys to its own students and faculty. Each of those books focuses primarily on the ills associated with white people. And none of those books focuses primarily on other arguments that would provide a counterbalance to those points. No matter how nuanced and fair the individual books are, if your local library contained only books analyzing 'left-wing authoritarian ills', you would get a biased picture of the relationship between authoritarianism and ideology. That's because those books would be focusing primarily on the bad stuff on the left, and not focusing on the bad stuff on the right.

The same is true here. I simply could not shake the feeling that this list of books on race was an incredibly narrow, single-minded, dogmatic, authoritarian approach to the issue. Where were the books on black-on-black violence? Where were the books looking at white people who had tried to overturn slavery? Where were the books showing the positive benefits of capitalism or the glories of the First Amendment's ability to protect minorities? No; just like a library that only stocks information about left-wing authoritarians, this collection of books presented a completely skewed view of American institutions from a simplistic, far-left position.

And, as is often the case with overly simplistic analysis, it lacked intellectual credibility. Some of the things found there seemed designed more for a *Saturday Night Live* sketch than a university website. For example, you will find Reni Eddo-Lodge's *Why I'm No Longer Talking to White People about Race* literally right next to Robin DiAngelo's *White Fragility: Why It's So Hard for White People to Talk about Racism*. I can only wonder, tragically but comically, if maybe the reason it is so hard for white people to talk about race is because … no one will actually talk to them about race? One imagines a comedy skit where a supposedly fragile white person is desperately wandering the streets of San Francisco, looking for someone to talk to about their racism problem. They scream and scream 'Help me, I'm racist' in all the nooks and corners of the city, until they finally find a black person who, nobly holding out their hand, says: 'I'm sorry, white man, but I no longer talk to your kind of person about race.' The white person hangs his head and says, 'Ah, you got me, I'm soooooo fragile!'

While it is easy to laugh off such coincidences, the complete unwillingness to present alternative points of view – one of the hallmarks of authoritarian simplicity – was alarming. For example, one of the first things you see on UM's library website is a bit on *White Rage* by Emory University professor Carol Anderson. It is a shockingly one-sided leftist position. And it is disconnected from my world – I'm a white person and I feel little rage, and I know a lot of white people and few of them seem like they have suppressed rage. So rage is clearly not the right term to describe at least a fair number of white people, and if you don't believe me, try asking a lot of them.

Dr. Anderson proceeds from rage to criticize former New York mayor Rudy Giuliani for responding to a question by pointing out that his 'broken windows' policy is reducing crime. I'm not sure if she means this is an example of white rage or not, but her point was that this reduction in crime isn't working for blacks. She may be right, but that isn't my point – my point is that the other side is *never* presented. Where are the statistics on this page that show that blacks overwhelmingly *want* police in their neighborhoods?[24] Where are the statistics that show black lives are disproportionately *saved* by *increasing* the size of the police force?[25] This is a complicated issue and needs more complicated views than, or at least alternative views to, this one.

Micro-Aggressions, or How Everything White People Say Is Hostile but Everything Everyone Else Says Is a Legitimate Expression

Everywhere you go across almost every American university right now, this is what you find. Academic authoritarians have simplified race down to one basic idea: White conservatives are bad.

One of the resources referenced by the University of Montana – on their 'Inclusive Workspaces' page – was to a University of California, Davis, overview of 'micro-aggressions'. I'm guessing you've heard of micro-aggressions, but in case you haven't, micro-aggressions are basically subtle things you say to others that aren't overtly hostile but might carry messages of aggression beneath the surface.

It may surprise you to know that, in my field, the very existence of micro-aggressions as a meaningful construct has been challenged quite a bit. In one particularly influential paper, incredibly well-respected Emory University professor Scott Lilienfeld argued that micro-aggressions had basically been scientifically debunked as an idea.[26]

But I don't want to focus primarily on that debate. Rather, I want you to see how single-minded the micro-aggression proponents are in their practical recommendations.

Which takes us back to UC Davis's micro-aggressions tutorial. The tutorial links to a list of exemplar micro-aggressions produced by the University of Minnesota.[27]

I think everyone in the Western world should go read this list. I'm going to give you a few examples of things that it is aggressive to say to people of another race, according to (at a minimum) the University of Montana, the University of California-Davis, and the University of Minnesota:

'Where are you from?'

'Where were you born?'

'You are so articulate.'

'There is only one race, the human race.'

'I believe the most qualified person should get the job.'

It is also horrible to 'ask an Asian person to help with a Math or Science problem' because this sends the (apparently incredibly racist) message that 'All Asians are intelligent and good in Math/Sciences'. (I hope your math professor isn't Asian!)

Everyone, everywhere needs to ask an honest question right now: Do you truly want to live in a place where asking questions like 'Where are you from?' is considered a subtly aggressive form of racism? Where you aren't allowed to make non-racist statements about everyone being equal or that you want the best person to get the job? Because if we follow the guidelines of American universities, that's exactly what we are going to get.[28]

It isn't hard from a social psychological perspective to see where this comes from. It comes from single-minded authoritarianism. Liberal authoritarians are obsessed with a single-issue approach to life, and their formula for everything is basically 'conservative whites are racist'. So if a white person asks an Asian person 'Where are you from?' it must be a racist, exclusionary effort to say 'You are not American'.

Life provides a more nuanced lesson. No doubt, sometimes each of those phrases *has* been used in a racist fashion. Almost *anything* can be. But there is no reason to assume hostile motives all the time. The truth is, sometimes people ask others 'Where are you from?' because they are trying to express genuine warmth and welcome. Sometimes they ask because it is the polite thing to say and they don't actually mean to express welcome at all, like asking 'How's the weather?' Sometimes it is because there is an awkward pause and it's the first thing they think of. My point is, there are many varied motives, good or bad, someone might have for asking that question. Simplistically assuming it is racist or aggressive is not only wrong, it is destructive to society because it makes it harder and harder for people of different groups to connect. Maybe our hypothetical *SNL* skit from earlier is closer to the truth than we realize: Maybe white people are actually becoming afraid to talk about race – or talk *to* people of different races – because every time they do, someone assumes they are micro-aggressing. This is inherently divisive.

This attitude is seeping down into popular culture as well. The entertainment arm of the left-wing authoritarians – also known as *Disney* – put out a video series in the summer of 2022 called *Rise Up, Sing Out*. It is designed to teach children how to talk to each other. No responsible parent should allow their child to watch this video without reasonable commentary. In the video, a white child says to another kid with darker skin: 'I didn't know that was your mom. Your skin is so much darker than hers.'

The white kid is subsequently chastised for asking this question by another kid. Why? In the words of the chastiser: 'A micro-aggression is when someone says or does something that makes you feel bad, sometimes just because of your race ... you should be proud of your skin, it's what makes you you!'[29]

So a white kid asks an honest question. The kid didn't say anything criticizing the color of anyone else's skin. He was just curious, as kids often are. In the video, there's no hint that the kid had any malicious intent. And in spite of that, he was told, in essence, *don't ask questions because that is racist. You engaged in micro-aggressions!*

I could write an entire book on how bad it is developmentally to induce false guilt in children. But here I want to focus on something different. This single-mindedness is going to have a disastrous *societal* result. The sum total of it is that, if we really raise our kids this way, we'll never solve any problems. We'll never connect with people who are different than us. My wife and I were involved years ago with a group that tried to help poor children. One of the places we went had a few children who, until we arrived, had never seen a white person. One of the young children could not figure out why we looked different and kept trying to 'brush' the white color off us, asking repeatedly 'What do you have on your skin?' If we were going to do micro-aggressions in reverse, we would have chastised the kid for this perfectly innocent question, bringing him aside and telling him, 'I'm allowed to be proud of my skin, it makes me *me*! Stop micro-aggressing.'

That would of course be ridiculous. And that's my point. The net result of the liberal authoritarian mindset is that we're going to berate children for simply doing something they can't help doing – innocently noticing differences in their environment.

I honestly don't believe this is what most people in America want.

Single-Variable Thinking in Economics: Literally Everything Is About Race

Ibram X. Kendi's single-variable obsession is sinking in deep with liberals across the country. In July 2022, there was a lot of concern about a possible recession in the US economy. These concerns were widespread due to record-high inflation, baby formula shortages, stock market downturns, among many other poor economic indicators. Now, a recession is a complex thing, and there is no clear and easy determinant. As a result, a lot of complicated calculations go into deciding whether or not we're in one. But Nicole Goodkind of CNN wasn't worried about any of that. What was Nicole Goodkind worried about? To quote from the title of her report, she was worried about the fact that 'Eight White Economists' will decide if the US is in a recession.[30]

No, I'm serious. The whole article is dedicated to the horrible fact that the people on the 'Business Cycle Dating Committee' – part of a private nonprofit organization known as the National Bureau of Economic Research (NBER) – are all white. The article never explains why they chose a name that sounds like they invented a new kind of on-the-job speed-dating service instead of a serious economic think-tank. In fact, the article really doesn't explain anything at all. Instead, the author spends a lot of time saying things like this:

> There is a clear lack of racial diversity amongst the eight members, and NBER has never had a member who has been a racial minority.

In recent years, however, critics have said the NBER's recession and expansion determinations fail to consider the economic state of many underrepresented Americans.

I think the economics profession is notorious for being one of the least-diverse professions or disciplines along a number of lines: racial, gender and diversity in schools of thought.

It's difficult to break through and get people to consider new frameworks for how we understand disparity and inequality.

All those things are true and I'm not disputing their value. What I'd simply like to know more about is what they have to do with *whether or not we are actually in a recession*. I'll grant that race may have something to do with my taste in ice cream, but it's still a long way from that fact to an argument that my preference for rainbow sherbet is an indication of white privilege and systemic racism that ought to make me reconsider the ice cream I eat.

But the argument didn't specifically tie anything directly about racist white people to the recession. The closest thing it got to an argument was this statement: 'More diversity on the committee will bring in perspectives and other ideas about how we understand the health of the economy.' I actually agree with that as a general idea, and that's why I've long argued for diversity myself – everybody should be represented at the table. But the article didn't specify how, exactly, this was relevant to the specific idea of 'are we in a recession or not?' or even coherently suggest a plausible mechanism whereby biased decision-making would occur. What motive would the white people have for declaring or withholding the awful 'recession' status? The statistics it showed to back up its case were actually about poor people, but not specifically about blacks or whites. (Contrary to popular belief, there are actually a *lot* of poor white people in the US.) And even at that, those statistics just showed that poor people did worse in a recession than rich people. (File that one away under my favorite category of 'Did we really need a study for *that?*' Next up: Groundbreaking research showing that humans like food.) It is undeniably true almost by definition that poor people suffer more, but what relevance does it have, exactly, to the fact that eight *white* people make the decision of whether we *are* in a recession? And the article leaves a lot of obvious questions completely unanswered.

I wondered things like: Is there some reason that eight white people would be especially prone to want to call something a recession in a way that hurts poor people? How would declaring a recession too early or too late actually accomplish that goal? Or, for that matter, how can you use statistics showing that past recessions hurt poor people more when those recessions were only called recessions by ... rich white people? Or what is the solution to having rich people specifically on the committee? Since almost all economists with PhDs are extremely rich, is the author suggesting a randomly selected group of poor laypeople decide when we are in a recession? Newsflash: They'll almost certainly vote 'recession' much more quickly. Will that be good for everyone, rich or poor, given that public perception of a recession is itself one of the psychological drivers of a recession?

Look, I get that no single article can solve every problem. As an editor, I commonly reassure authors that it isn't their job to deal with every variable, because that's simply impossible. I get that. And I'm actually on the author's side here in the bigger sense – I think it is important to have as many people represented on this kind of committee as possible, including (but not limited to) race. That's why I like the American jury system, for all its flaws. It's also why I supported affirmative action programs in the 1990s. To be honest, I could probably have made a better argument for this specific position than the CNN writer did.

(I feel that way a lot reading or watching CNN. The downfall of CNN as a reliable, intelligent, and centrist network is one of the saddest things that's ever happened in my lifetime. But hey, they got what they wanted – Trump lost the election in 2020. I didn't like Trump either, but I *like truth* a whole lot more than I *dislike Trump*. So now I watch Fox News's *The Five*. Happy, CNN?)

But my point isn't that we should ignore the racial composition of this committee. My point rather is this: We should care about a *lot* more than *just* the racial composition of the committee. A recession is a complicated thing, and rather than integrate race effectively into that complicated morass, instead this author chose the new path of the left: To vaguely accuse something of being racist without making clear arguments for anything specific. I'm not sure the modern 'economy' cares whether you are black or white, although certainly there have been historical discrepancies and there are still problems.

But this simple-minded kind of thinking is dominating the American progressive movements: Without a really serious argument, they just paint everything about race. You can find an example of this almost every day. Biden's Transportation Secretary Pete Buttigieg puts forward a one billion dollar plan to address racist roads.[31] Biden's Treasury Secretary Janet Yellen has made 'racial equity the centerpiece of our economic agenda'.[32]

Biden's Agriculture Secretary Tom Vilsack forms an equity commission that he said would 'identify and root out any systemic racism that may exist'.[33]

What do these things have in common? Not one of them is about roads, or money, or farming. Those are the things people with those job titles are supposed to be working on. No; instead, all of them seem to be focused on ... racism. That's what happens when left-wing authoritarians start running things. Not only do complicated issues get reduced to simple ones, but those simple issues keep poking their heads into every nook and cranny of the world.

Critical Race Theory

In a book called *Just Practice: A Social Justice Approach to Social Work* by Janet Finn, students at the University of Montana were asked to read checklists essentially acknowledging the various ways that it was wrong to be white, to apologize for it, and ultimately to be tested over it. I had a student email me expressing concern about this book and the professor who taught it. The student was worried, wondering if maybe white people were not welcome in the Social Work program. They noted that they had talked to the program director, who assured them this was not the case, but in the end the student still felt confused. Their concern after talking to the director was in part this: The idea that they were welcome didn't seem consistent with the teachings in the book and the class. How does one reconcile those two things?

It's easy to see why the student would be frustrated. It turns out that the issues involved here are a lot more complex than a checklist proclaiming that one race is solely responsible for all these ills. And this isn't an isolated incident – it's happening all over the country under the guise of a highly authoritarian spectrum of ideas that coalesced under the umbrella known as Critical Race Theory (CRT).

CRT has an interesting history. For example, after months of mocking Republicans for merely suggesting that CRT is being taught in schools,[34] the largest and most powerful teachers' union in the country suddenly announced in the summer of 2021 that – surprise! – they support the teaching of CRT in schools.[35]

This and other charades just mask the real issues, however. The real issues involve the authoritarian simplicity often propagated by proponents of CRT. CRT is a broad set of social justice-relevant ideas that intersect with accepted social psychology research.[36] In other words, it hits pretty close to my own social psychology wheelhouse.

When I dig into it, I find that a lot of what CRT scholars say is fine as far as it goes. For example, CRT says that America has systemic racism built in,[37] and social psychological research suggests that's true.[38] America – like every nation before or since – has systemic biases that favor groups in power.

But that's not what makes CRT unique, and there have long been better social psychological theories out there to help us understand systemic racism. Instead, the distinguishing feature of CRT is that it argues, with alarming simplicity, that white people are uniquely and hopelessly racist, so much so that even apparently good social change – such as white support for non-racist policies – happens because of selfish motives in white people. In the words of CRT scholar India Thusi: 'An appeal to morality and equality is simply inadequate to achieve racial equity. White elites must experience some material benefit from supporting causes that would advance the position of Blacks in this country.'[39] According to CRT, the reason we've made apparent 'progress' isn't that people of all races wanted to make the world a better place, but because selfish white people decided they could benefit from the change. Those aren't my words, but CRT scholars' words. Consider this essay on the *Harvard Law Review Blog*: 'What has changed is not the legal, or even social status of Black people, but rather the social (media) acceptability of anti-Black racism. Said another way, it is now popular and financially advantageous to be anti-racist.'[40]

The implications of this surprisingly simplistic claim are staggering. White men voluntarily ceding voting rights to women? Selfish white people. Whites voting for Constitutional amendments to ensure civil rights for groups they don't belong to? Selfish white people. Whites running the Underground Railroad? Selfish white people.

But is this claim plausible? Taken in a less extreme fashion, there is of course some real truth to what CRT says. Whites are people, and all people are a mixed motivational bag. But CRT doesn't want me to believe that whites are a mixed motivational bag. Rather, CRT orders me, with cult-like enthusiasm, to accept on faith that there are no positive motives behind white people's actions ... because they are white. History teaches a more complex and nuanced lesson about human psychology. The whites who fought in the Civil War for the North had many mixed motives, and some of them were bad. But historical records strongly suggest that some of their motives were good. Consider highly respected Princeton professor James McPherson's book *For Cause and Comrades: Why Men Fought in the Civil War*.[41] This book suggests the whites who fought in the Civil War for the North had many mixed motives, and some of them were bad. But some of them were good. They gave up their livelihoods and many of them died for racial equality – are we really going to say, with no hint of nuance, that they only did so because of selfish motivations? That is the very height of psychological simplicity.

This has huge implications for Western societies. First, if you want positive cultural change, CRT is psychologically self-defeating. If white people actually believed CRT was true, what's to stop those same white people from saying, 'Well, if even our very best efforts are categorized as selfish, then why should we keep trying to make positive social change?' There may be a real cost of relegating 50 years of civil rights progress to the psychological trash bin with authoritarian simplicity.

Second, CRT judges individuals without context. CRT would tell an 11-year-old poor white child who was just beaten by his drunk white father that he is an 'oppressor', and tell an 11-year-old rich black child from a loving family that he is a 'victim'. In contrast, consider the American Psychological Association's more nuanced principle that says: 'Psychologists respect the dignity and worth of all people, and the rights of individuals to privacy, confidentiality, and self-determination.'[42] I challenge anyone to read that statement and tell me how those principles are facilitated by arbitrarily dividing individuals up by race, judging them as either oppressor or victim, and predetermining their story before you ask them about it?

Because of its authoritarian simplicity, Critical Race Theory is an enemy to the meaningful discussions we actually need to have about our nation's horrible history of racial injustice. If authoritarian democrats would stop pushing for CRT, maybe we could actually get back to trying to solve those (very real) problems. But I fear if we don't reject CRT soon, we're going to undo all the (also very real) progress we've made in the last 50 years.

Conclusion: If You Can't Stand Irony, Stop Reading

CRT and left-wing authoritarians believe that racism is simple: It comes from white conservatives.

But does it *actually?*

The truth turns out to be a lot more complex than that simple story. For example, a well-known study showed almost ten years ago that liberals' positive attitudes towards racial minority groups is dependent largely on the fact that they believe that those groups agree with them politically. What happens when they don't? Liberals turn on them. Liberals have negative attitudes towards African Americans when they believe they possess conservative attitudes.[43] In fact, research suggests that if white conservatives meet a conservative black person, they like that person just fine – but liberals don't. Thus, the perception that liberals are less racist than conservatives is in part based on a political mirage. Remove the mirage, and it is clear that both groups are equally capable of bias.

A few years later, our lab also showed that the relationship between politics and prejudice depends on the *target* of the prejudice. In particular, we rewrote a common prejudice scale to focus on religious (instead of ethnic) minorities. When we did that – when we made the target groups minorities that liberals don't jive with – liberals showed high prejudice scores. And that was particularly true for liberal *authoritarians*, who are (as we've discussed) especially likely to make group-based distinctions.[44]

What happened next is a curious academic tale. After we published our paper, some of our colleagues accused us of having 'selected targets of prejudice that are rarely victims of prejudice in the US'.[45] In other words, they were saying that prejudice against those religious people didn't matter because they weren't often targeted. When we debated with those colleagues at the SPSP conference, I tried to point out that many of those people they were dismissing actually had been pushed into a small box by liberals – religious people were being forced into silence, categorized, and demonized – and that by implication it is wrong to do that no matter the group who was doing the pushing, or the group who ended up in the metaphorical box. My colleague's response was essentially to say religious people's box was plenty big enough anyway because they had all the power. Quite a few people in the audience cheered at this remark.

I didn't say then what I wish now that I had said: The size of the box is relative to the context. In that room of 200 people at the symposium, religious people's box was awfully small. At the SPSP conference more broadly, where 4,000 people attend, religious people's box is awfully small. In academia, religious people's box is awfully small. In these contexts, people are vilified consistently just for *being religious*. They can be publicly humiliated just for *being religious*. They can lose their jobs, their livelihoods, just for *being religious*. They feel like they cannot speak out about who they are or what they believe. They are forced to live in a small box.

And the people responsible for most of their loss, responsible for most of this prejudice, are left-wing authoritarians. Liberal bullies. I hardly think it is justifiable for the people holding all the power in *these* contexts to dismiss research showing prejudice against these groups. To do so is not unlike people in the South in the 1950s dismissing prejudice against African Americans because they could not understand what it felt like in that context to live in a small box.

But that isn't the ironic thing that inspired the title of this concluding chapter section, nor is that the last twist in this academic tale. It turns out that left-wing authoritarians actually *do* exhibit a lot of bias against groups that have 'historically been the target of prejudice'. All that talk of right-wing authoritarians hating racial minority groups – and left-wing authoritarians can hate those groups just as much. In response to our colleagues' criticisms of our work, we ran two studies that demonstrated why this matters.[46] In particular, we looked at two groups that have historically been the target of prejudice: African Americans and Jews. We took a trait from each group that is strongly empirically associated with the group in the real world and asked people what they thought about the resulting representative set of group members. So, for African Americans, we asked participants what they thought of 'African American women/men who believe in the Bible'. This is a trait highly representative of African Americans: In the modern US, Pew Data reveal that 77% of African Americans believe that 'the Bible is the Word of God'.[47] For Jews, we asked participants how they felt about 'Jewish women/men who are strong supporters of the nation of Israel's interests'. This is a trait highly representative of American Jews, with Gallup survey estimates suggesting that 90% of Jews in the US show support for Israel.[48]

So what happens if you ask people to rate their perceptions of representative members of African Americans and Jews? What happens when you ask them about prototypical members of each group, based in real facts?

Liberal authoritarians really don't like either group very much.

This fact is strange on multiple levels – not the least of which is that African Americans and Jews are the two most reliable liberal voting blocks in the US.[49] And yet, when faced with a real trait indicative of those groups, liberal authoritarians turn on them.

The point of this work isn't to suddenly say that liberals are worse than conservatives. Obviously, conservatives have a long history of prejudice too, and if we changed our study to highlight more liberal traits that Jews and African Americans possess – such as their voting records – I've no doubt we'd get the opposite result.

My point is different: The accusation from many on the left that this is 'all a right-wing thing' is not empirically justifiable. Our work helps explain a lot of what's currently happening in the real world. One can see examples of liberal authoritarian prejudice almost every day. Conservative blacks in the US frequently note the amount of racist rhetoric they have to deal with – from the *left*. Consider that the incredibly racist 'Uncle Tim' trend – propagated by liberals and directed at African American senator Tim Scott – had to be shut down by Twitter.[50] Many American Jews are so tired of anti-Semitism from liberal authoritarians that they are immigrating to Israel.[51]

This follows from everything we've said so far. Authoritarians in general have a hard time with complexities. Their explanations for race are entirely one-sided. And yet that same simplicity causes them to toss aside members of the groups they say they are defending, the moment they no longer fit into their narrow vision of a racial category. And that is the final outcome of left-wing authoritarian simplicity: A world in which authoritarians bludgeon anyone who doesn't hold their simple views on race – even if that person isn't white.

CHAPTER 6

SELF-IGNORANCE: THE LEFT-WING AUTHORITARIANISM BLIND SPOT

I have yet to find ... a living, breathing, scientifically certifiable authoritarian on the left.

– Bob Altemeyer, social psychologist, in *The Authoritarian Specter*

Social psychologists have long denied that authoritarianism on the left was a topic worthy of study. Indeed, as recently as 2020, the very *existence* of *any* left-wing authoritarians was called 'largely mythical, like the Loch Ness Monster'.[1]

It often surprises outsiders to my field when I tell them that many social psychologists deny the *existence* of a meaningful number of left-wing authoritarians. Those outsiders immediately gravitate to obvious examples of left-wing authoritarians either in their own lives (that one mean uncle who keeps going on about Marxism) or in the political landscape (clear leftist authoritarian regimes such as Communist China or Cuba). This gap between academic psychologists and the public was apparent when we collected national samples to examine how many left-wing authoritarians normal Americans can identify in their own lives.[2] Before we looked at the data, I and one of my social psychology colleagues made guesses about the average number of liberal authoritarians in people's lives. I guessed one; my colleague guessed two. On a lark, I also asked a non-academic outside of our bubble to estimate how many left-wing authoritarians the average American knew. She said 15. I laughed and said: 'That can't be right!' But she was very nearly right. The actual number was not quite 15, but well over ten, and nowhere near the guesses that two social psychologists – two social psychologists who have championed the idea of left-wing authoritarianism, mind you – made. It was clear that I and my social psychology colleagues had no clue what was happening in the real world.

You may wonder how it is possible for academics to completely miss such an obvious truth, and the answer is important in helping us understand the nature of modern left-wing authoritarianism in the US – and why it is especially difficult to eradicate. The answer is that liberals are highly motivated not to see left-wing authoritarianism. And the more left-wing authoritarian they are, quite ironically, the less they want to believe in authoritarianism on the left. They have a kind of curious *self-ignorance* of their own authoritarian motives. In this chapter, we illuminate this liberal authoritarian blind spot.

Up until this point, we've talked about traits of left-wing authoritarians that more or less apply to *all* kinds of authoritarians. Authoritarians of every ilk tend to be intellectually apathetic, show an obsession with misinformation, trade in principles for groups, and exhibit cognitive simplicity. The specific domains attached to those traits do change, of course – for example, liberal authoritarians are especially simple about race, conservative authoritarians less so – and there are always exceptions we could make to those rules. But in general one would expect authoritarians everywhere to demonstrate the traits discussed in Chapters 2–5.

The topic of this chapter – the authoritarian motivational blind spot – is something that is unique to left-wing authoritarians. And this blind spot makes liberal authoritarianism uniquely dangerous.

As an academic psychologist who has taught prejudice for over 20 years, I've often said in my classes that one of the most dangerous people in society is the person who thinks they aren't racist. Why? Because everyone has the potential for racism, and the person who denies that potential will never address their own problems and thus will spend their life engaging in racist actions. By parallel, a political party is particularly dangerous when it claims the loudest that it is not authoritarian. Why? Because that party has potential authoritarians. Every party has potential authoritarians – but a party that *denies* the problem also won't *address* the problem.

Right now that party is the American Democrats. We've tacitly raised a generation of liberals who think that it's normal to fire Gina Carano for having a political opinion that some people don't like,[3] and yet also think they aren't authoritarian for doing so.

Psychologically speaking, such apparent contradictions are actually quite commonplace. For example, as anyone who has objectively observed a Nike commercial can tell you, it is well known that Americans are quite collectivistic about their individualism;[4] and it is certainly the case that conservatives hold seemingly contradictory beliefs in multiple domains.[5] The kind of psychological hypocrisy involved in the left-wing authoritarian is thus an instance of a common phenomenon: Just as it is psychologically quite possible to limit freedoms in the name of freedom or to exhibit collectivism in the name of individualism, it is possible to exhibit authoritarianism in the name of anti-authoritarian ideology.

How? When strongly held group norms go against individual motivational goals, you can get what appears to be a psychological contradiction. Conservatives have norms that suggest their group desires freedom; and yet sometimes they are individually motivated to set aside those beliefs.[6] To resolve the tension, conservatives may engage in the forbidden freedom-restricting behaviors but recast them as freedom-loving. They have a motivational blind spot for acknowledging that any of their behaviors could go against freedom.

Liberals have that same problem with the idea of authoritarianism. Liberals have norms that tell them their group *should* oppose authoritarianism. But often their individual members have motives towards authoritarianism – and the net result is that liberals have a *motivational blind spot* for believing that their own authoritarian behaviors are authoritarian. They simply don't *want* to believe it.

Scientific Data on Authoritarian Self-Ignorance

This isn't mere speculation. Our scientific data demonstrate this very clearly. In a national survey of over 5,000 Americans, we gave people a standard authoritarianism questionnaire and then afterwards asked them a simple question: 'Do you view yourself as a dogmatic and authoritarian person?'

Conservative Americans who scored high on the

LIBERAL BULLIES

authoritarianism questionnaire had no problem saying 'Yes, I am authoritarian'. But liberals were a different thing entirely. Not only were liberal authoritarians less likely than conservatives to accurately identify themselves as authoritarians (when they were, in fact, authoritarian), but there was actually a negative correlation between left-wing authoritarianism (the reality) and liberals' willingness to identify as authoritarian (their own perception). That means that the more authoritarian liberals are, the *less* they believe they are authoritarian!

The results of this survey were one of the most astonishing things I've seen in all my years conducting research. It is important to keep in mind that liberals who score high on the authoritarianism scale agree that (italicized words are direct quotes from the scale) *our country needs a mighty leader*; that the leader should *destroy* opponents; that people should *trust the judgment of the proper authorities*, avoid listening to *noisy rabble-rousers in our society who are trying to create doubts in people's minds, put some tough leaders in power who oppose those values and silence the troublemakers*, and *smash* the beliefs of opponents; that *what our country really needs is a strong, determined leader who will crush the evil*; that society should *strongly punish those* they disagree with. They also deny that an opponent has a right to *be wherever he or she wants to be*, and support the statement that the country would be better off if certain groups *would just shut up and accept their group's proper place in society*. These items hit all of the hallmarks of the consensus conceptualization of the authoritarian person. When conservatives agree with those items, they subsequently admit (accurately) that they are authoritarian. When liberals agree with those items, they actually are more likely to say they are not authoritarian.

Why is this? It is because American liberals have a

160

psychological dilemma about authoritarianism that conservatives don't have. Liberals, unlike conservatives, believe their group's norms are anti-authoritarian. Thus, they have a motivational blind spot for admitting they are authoritarian. And the more they actually *are* authoritarian, the more they are motivated to adhere to their group's anti-authoritarian norms, and thus the more motivated they are to deny their own authoritarian nature. Our data show this very clearly. The negative relationship between liberals' actual authoritarianism and their self-identification as authoritarian is reduced to essentially zero when we account for their perception of their own group's norms.[7] In non-statistical terms, this means that a large part of the reason that liberal authoritarians disavow their true authoritarian nature is that liberals believe that their group officially opposes authoritarianism.

My Whole Group Is Good: When Simplicity Is Actually Complexity

People often see what they want or expect to see. And what people see tells us as much about the inner mental workings of the observer as it does about the external political workings of the world.[8]

– Phil Tetlock, University of Pennsylvania professor

The above work shows that individual liberals don't want to consider themselves authoritarian and thus won't admit it when they are. But liberals likely have this authoritarian blind spot for *other* liberals, too.

Consider one of the defining traits of authoritarianism that we discussed in the last chapter: Simplicity. In one study, we wondered whether liberals and conservatives would mistakenly imagine that their party's political candidates were more complex than they were in reality.[9] To illustrate, think about which of the following two paragraphs you believe is more complex:

PARAGRAPH 1: Artificial intelligence and so much more is changing and we're falling behind the competition with the rest of the world. Decades ago we used to invest 2% of our gross domestic product in America, 2% of our gross domestic product in research and development today. Mr. Secretary, that's less than 1%. China and other countries are closing in fast. We have to develop and dominate the products and technologies of the future.

PARAGRAPH 2: The Senate will be voting on an immigration reform package in recent months. My administration has met extensively with both Democrats and Republicans to craft a bipartisan approach to immigration reform based on these discussions. We presented the Congress with a detailed proposal that should be supported by both parties as a fair compromise, one where nobody gets everything they want, but where our country gets the critical reforms it needs. Here are the four pillars.

The answer is that paragraph 2 is appreciably more complex than paragraph 1. Paragraph 1 offers a simple, straightforward idea: We're starting to fall behind in technology and we need to get ahead. No alternative perspectives are considered – no competing ideas about the costs and benefits of pursuing AI technology. Instead, paragraph 1 just argues that we should try to dominate the AI industry. It's bad if we don't, and it's good if we do. Paragraph 2, on the other hand, acknowledges two sides to a debate and provides a solution for both sides to work together to produce a new outcome (in complexity terms, a 'synthesis'). There is an acknowledged inherent tension and a proposed plan to resolve that tension. In fact, in numerical terms, the first paragraph was scored a 1 (the lowest possible complexity score) and the second was scored a 4 (much higher than the typical paragraph).

Now, here's the catch: What if I told you that one of the paragraphs was spoken by Biden and the other by Trump. Which paragraph do you think was spoken by which person? The reality is that the high-complexity paragraph (#2) was spoken by Trump and the low-complexity paragraph (#1) was spoken by Biden.

It turns out that liberals *really* want their candidates to be complex, and they *really* want their opponents' candidates to be simple. In our research, we found that if you tell liberal partici-pants 'You are about to read a paragraph from one of your own candidates' and then ask them to estimate its complexity, they overestimate it – they see more complexity than there really is. So if liberals read the low-complexity paragraph from Biden above, they'd say it was complex even though it isn't. On the flip side, if they read the high-complexity paragraph and they knew it was from Trump, they'd underestimate how complex it was. They wouldn't give it full credit for its complexity.

This is a uniquely liberal thing. Conservatives don't care very much about the issue at all, and they generally showed much smaller misestimation effects.

Why? The authoritarian blind spot. Liberals want to believe *their* group is the open-minded, complex bearer of the non-authoritarian flag. They want to believe conservatives are those nasty authoritarians. Simplicity is an authoritarian marker. So when presented with simple rhetoric from one of their own candidates, they don't want to see it as simplicity. Easy to fix – presto-whammo! – suddenly they've decided that authoritarian simplicity is actually open-minded complexity. And that apparent conservative complexity? No problem, it's actually just authoritarian simplicity.

It's worth noting that this strong emphasis on their group being complex and anti-authoritarian has both negative and positive consequences. On the negative side, it makes it especially difficult for liberals to admit obvious examples of authoritarianism in themselves and in other liberals. But, on the positive side, this means that liberals in the US do still have a built-in aversion to authoritarianism. If one can tap into that aversion, it could make it easier to defeat authoritarian tendencies on the left side of the aisle. That's probably why a lot of long-time progressives and liberals have clearly turned on American Democrats[10] – the reckoning is harsh once the blind spot is removed. When comedian, long-time Democrat, and one-time Bernie Sanders supporter Sarah Silverman left the Democratic Party, this is what she said: 'It's the absolutist-ness of the party I am in that is such a turnoff to me. It's so f***** elitist.'[11] This provides reasons for hope in overcoming left-wing authoritarianism. It may be harder to get leftists to see the problem than we'd like – but if we *can* get them to see the problem, they are naturally inclined to really want to solve it.

The Frame Name Game

DARTH VADER:	Calrissian, take the princess and the Wookiee to my ship.
LANDO CALRISSIAN:	You said they'd be left at the city under my supervision!
DARTH VADER:	I am altering the deal. Pray I don't alter it any further.

– From *Star Wars, Episode V: The Empire Strikes Back*

Getting them to see it is challenging. This is partially because, like Darth Vader in *The Empire Strikes Back*, people often change the rules to meet their own selfish needs. In one of my favorite *Dilbert* cartoons, Dogbert can't seem to win at solitaire. So he randomly shuffles the cards and declares himself the winner. 'That was surprisingly satisfying,' he concludes.

An Outback Steakhouse commercial whimsically illustrated this same phenomenon. The owner offered a free steak to whoever could hit a bullseye on a dartboard. And this worked fine until someone hit the bullseye. At that point, the owner said, 'Wait, did I say bullseye? I meant a triple 20.' And then, after someone hit triple 20, the owner panned: 'Wait, did I say blindfolded?'[12]

In common parlance, this phenomenon is called 'moving the goalposts', but in my field, we sometimes call this 'reframing'.[13] When something isn't what you want it to be, you simply re-name it something else that better suits your fancy. Don't want to let Princess Leia go? You simply reframe what the 'deal' you made means. If you can't win at solitaire, you simply reframe what 'winning' means. If you don't want to give away a free steak, you simply reframe what 'hitting the target' entails. And a lot of research suggests that this kind of reframing is indeed 'surprisingly satisfying' to us. We do it all the time.

When it comes to left-wing authoritarianism, liberals are especially prone to this kind of reframing. Liberals don't *want* themselves or other liberals to be authoritarian. That's what those darn *conservatives* are. So, like Dogbert reframing 'winning' at solitaire, liberals just reframe their own authoritarianism as something more positive. The simplicity of Joe Biden is reframed as complexity. The complexity of Donald Trump is reframed as authoritarian simplicity. They shuffle those cards and declare themselves the winner.

This can easily be seen by evaluating the history of political measurement in my own field. We have discussed right-wing authoritarian measurement in Chapter 1. One thing worth noting, however, is that sometimes right-wing authoritarianism measurements are not used to measure authoritarianism. Rather, like dogmatism measurements, authoritarianism measurements are often used to measure – you guessed it – conservatism. In fact, in arguably the most influential political psychology paper of all time, the authors used right-wing authoritarianism as a measurement of conservatism.[14] They then argued from that evidence that conservatives were more dogmatic, more simple-minded, and more racist, among other things.

This is classic reframing. Imagine that I wanted to write a scale that could determine if you were a jerk. And suppose I hated ice cream and, as a result of some childhood ice cream truck trauma, I believed that all people who like ice cream are jerks. So I wrote a 'Jerk Evaluation Scale' that looks like the five-item scale in Figure 1.

Now, if you are the sensible, ice-cream-loving person I take you to be, you'd probably score pretty high on that measure.

But remember – to me, it isn't a measurement of ice cream. I've reframed your love of ice cream as your being a jerk.

From a larger population perspective, if my questionnaire became the standard questionnaire for measuring *jerkishness*, that means that it is literally not possible for anyone who loves ice cream to be considered a nice person. By definition, your love of ice cream *makes* you a jerk. Only ice cream haters can be nice people in this world. We have predetermined the conclusion by the way we asked the questions. I've shuffled the cards and declared my group of ice cream haters the winner.

FIGURE 1: JERK EVALUATION SCALE

For each item, enter a number between 1 and 5 that indicates your level of agreement, where 1 = I completely disagree, 3 = I neither agree nor disagree, and 5 = I completely agree.

1. Ice cream tastes great.
2. I think eating ice cream in moderation is enjoyable.
3. I eat ice cream as much as I reasonably can.
4. I love ice cream.
5. Eating ice cream is a pleasurable experience.

Our Jerk Evaluation Scale is not as far from what happened with authoritarian research as you'd think. What actually happened is a bit more subtle – but functionally identical. That more complicated reality is captured by Figure 2. Imagine that I really had it in for ice cream lovers. I might try the obvious reframing that I used in the Jerk Evaluation Scale. But I could also start at the other end and try to write a scale that measured ice cream lovers in such a way that all ice cream lovers would *look* like jerks. In a sense, instead of directly calling those who eat ice cream jerks, I've written every item to *preclude the possibility* of a nice ice cream lover.

FIGURE 2: ICE CREAM EVALUATION SCALE

For each item, enter a number between 1 and 5 that indicates your level of agreement, where 1 = I completely disagree, 3 = I neither agree nor disagree, and 5 = I completely agree.

1. I think we should pass laws to hurt people who think ice cream is bad.
2. I think eating ice cream in moderation is enjoyable, and I'm a total racist.
3. I love ice cream so much that I force puppies, kittens, and small children to eat it even when they don't want to.
4. I love ice cream and I believe torturing innocent people is good.
5. Eating ice cream is a pleasurable experience and you are simply inhuman if you can't see that.

In this questionnaire, I've perfectly conflated eating ice cream and being a jerk. Imagine four kinds of people in the world. There are those who love ice cream and are jerks. There are those who hate ice cream and are jerks. There are those who love ice cream and are nice. There are those who hate ice cream and are nice. Now, how would each of those people score on the above scale?

Only one of our four types of persons can possibly score high on that questionnaire: People who love ice cream *and* people who are total jerks. Obviously people who hate ice cream will score low right out of the gate, because every item has something relevant to liking ice cream. But here's the key point: What if you like ice cream and you are a really nice person? How will you score on the Ice Cream Evaluation Scale?

You'll score as someone who doesn't really like ice cream. Because you're not a jerk, you will not say 'you are inhuman' if you disagree with other people. Even though you like ice cream, you won't want to force puppies and children to eat it. You won't want to pass laws to force your love of ice cream on others. So you'll actually score – on the ice cream lover's scale – as someone who *doesn't like ice cream*. Even though you really like ice cream.

Note that this functionally reframes ice cream lovers as jerks in exactly the same way as our original Jerk Evaluation Scale does. It is just more subtle. It essentially reframes all nice ice cream lovers as ice cream haters – nice ice cream lovers have no choice but to say they won't be mean – because they are nice. So the only people who score high on our Ice Cream Evaluation Scale are going to be complete jerks. And then, when we run studies on whether or not ice cream lovers look like bad people, guess what? If we use our scale as the measurement, they'll look like terrible people. The ice cream literature will be replete with studies showing how ice cream lovers hate puppies, or children, desire mean-spirited laws, show discrimination against minority groups, and refuse to help elderly grandmothers. And they would show all this because we used a subtle – but impactful – kind of reframing. We are still shuffling the cards and declaring our anti-ice cream group the winner.

The Ice Cream Evaluation Scale is a perfect analogy for what's happened with the history of authoritarianism. Consider that the

RWA scale – a scale used to measure conservatism – is chock-full of items like this: 'Our country desperately needs a mighty leader who will do what has to be done to destroy the radical new ways and sinfulness that are ruining us.' Does this pick up on conservatism? Sure. Conservatives are more likely than liberals to dislike radical new ways. Our Ice Cream Evaluation Scale does actually pick up on ice cream loving, too. But, just like our Ice Cream Scale picks up on jerkishness, this conservatism scale (RWA) also picks up on *authoritarianism*: In fact, you have to be pretty mean in order to score high on it. You have to really want to *destroy people*. A nice person doesn't typically want to destroy their fellow citizens.

The result of this is obvious: You will only score high on the RWA scale if you are *both* mean *and* conservative. Nice liberals will score low. Mean liberals will score low. But also – and here is the key point – *nice conservatives will score low*. On a measurement often used to capture who is a *conservative*. That means it is literally not possible on this scale for a nice conservative to exist. In fact, all nice conservatives will be scored as liberals.

If you never again think hard about any measurement issue, think about this one. In fact, I encourage you to put down this book and contemplate this for two minutes: For the last 50 years, every time the RWA scale has been used to measure conservatism, it recategorizes a *nice conservative* as a *liberal*. That is truly incredible. It is very hard for liberals to admit that conservatives *aren't* authoritarian.

And it is equally hard for them to admit that liberals *are* authoritarian. Used as an authoritarianism measure, the RWA scale essentially ensures that mean liberals will be classified as non-authoritarians because the scale only measures *conservative* authoritarians. Indeed, this kind of reframing has become a staple of the left both inside and outside academia. In August 2021, a Salon piece's title read: 'Republicans claim to fear left-wing authoritarianism – but there is no such thing'.[15] Now, the average person may wonder: Well, what do liberals make of clearly left-wing tyrannical leaders? How do they explain away obvious left-wing authoritarians like Stalin or Castro? The subtitle to the article gives away the hypocrisy: 'Yes, dictators sometimes cloak themselves in "socialism". But tyranny, here and elsewhere, is always right-wing.'

Do you see what is happening here? Anytime someone seems to be a left-wing authoritarian, it turns out that (fortunately for liberals!) they are actually a right-wing authoritarian. We just reframe Stalin as right-wing and *ta-da!* We've got ourselves a clearly right-wing authoritarian problem. Oh, those pesky right-wing communists! Oh, those pesky right-wing Marxists! Oh, those pesky right-wing socialists! The moment Bernie Sanders truly looks like a dictator, I suppose he'll be considered right-wing too.

Don't laugh – it could actually happen.

Now, let me hasten to add this: Part of the problem is that liberals do *partially* have a point. Sometimes what seems like liberal authoritarianism actually *is* conservatism. We've made a similar point ourselves in academic articles in at least two different places,[16] and I've also noted this on my own (what used to be known as) Twitter account. Take work on Russian authoritarianism. In a lot of that work, communists – an entirely left-wing political ideology – are more authoritarian, a tendency that extends from at least the 1990s into the last couple of years.[17] While that does suggest that authoritarians can be more liberal, Russian authoritarianism is also correlated with a lot of positions clearly more *socially* conservative, such as opposition to gay marriage.[18] This means that as evidence for left-wing authoritarianism, it's a mixed bag.

While that is an important thing to consider, it should not undermine the large amount of evidence showing that left-wing authoritarianism is a real problem. In fact, it was partially to clarify this state of things that we developed our parallel test of LWA directly from the most-used RWA questionnaire while substituting explicitly left-wing causes. That LWA questionnaire cannot be misinterpreted to mean authoritarianism to right-wing causes, and anyone who scores high on it clearly is authoritarian – by any reasonable standard – to liberal causes, and liberal causes alone. And as we've already documented, in both our work and other well-respected academic work, *that* kind of liberal authoritarianism is running rampant all over the world.

This means that the efforts of the left to *simply* reframe communist dictators as conservatives ought to be met with some suspicion. After all, it is Marxism and communism that most left-wing authoritarians *here* want us to embrace. And the practical outcome of that communism in every part of the world where it has been tried so far is … an authoritarian dictatorship. Should we simply allow liberals to move that goalpost every time and in every way, so much that Salon could say: 'Yes, dictators sometimes cloak themselves in "socialism". But tyranny, here and elsewhere, is always right-wing'? Really, Salon? *Every* part of *every* tyranny is *always and completely* right-wing? Honestly, that sounds an awful lot like shuffling solitaire cards and declaring yourself the winner.

The Motivational Blind Spot Is Alive and Well

You can see this self-ignorance all the time amongst liberal authoritarians. Consider, for example, a special issue in January 2022 of the journal *The Annals of the American Academy of Political and Social Science* devoted to 'Democratic Vulnerabilities'.[19] There were 14 papers in the issue. Quite incredibly, every single paper focused on threats to democracy from those evil right-wingers. An entire issue devoted to vulnerabilities to democracy in a world populated by millions of left-wing authoritarian people and dozens of left-wing authoritarian governments, and not *one* paper, not *one* mention, of threats to democracy from the *left*?

The really shocking thing is that the papers in the issue consistently focused on a lack of institutional trust as a driver for the loss of democracy – and yet the entire issue was nothing except an attempt to undermine institutional trust. If you think that institutional trust is key to sustaining democracy, then maybe you ought not go around telling everyone on your side that the other side is evil and you can't trust any of our institutions? And not one paper that I could find seemed self-aware enough to note that maybe *they* were the ones undermining institutional trust, that maybe *they* were threats to democracy. That's what happens when you have a blind spot to authoritarians on your own side.

Beyond academia the situation is hardly better. Whatever else you think about the US Supreme Court overturning *Roe v. Wade*, it was a decision rendered legally within the confines of the Constitution. It is a hallmark of authoritarianism to want strong leaders to bypass laws and subvert the system. For example, remember that one of the three items on the well-respected

World Values Survey's authoritarianism questionnaire is 'Having a strong leader who does not have to bother with parliament and elections'. If you want to bypass the normal legal systems, if you don't care about that, if you don't want to bother with elections, or laws, or ... the Supreme Court ... or the Constitution ... then you've really crossed a line. In light of this, if you really want to talk about threats to democracy, any reasonable person should be concerned by the Democrats' response to the *Roe* overturn. Keith Olbermann, one of the most prominent Democratic personalities, said that American states should ignore the Supreme Court's edicts.[20] The chairman of the Democratic National Committee called the Supreme Court 'illegitimate'.[21] And what were they responding to? Were they responding to the tyrannical over-turning of democracy? No. They were responding to a decision that literally gave the people in each state the democratic right to pass laws.

Similarly, liberal US congresswoman Rashida Tlaib called the Supreme Court 'fascist'.[22] Why? Did the Supreme Court decide to take away the rights of US citizens? Did the Supreme Court give more power to the executive branch to engage in authoritarian behavior? Not at all. The reason this prominent Democrat said the Supreme Court was fascist was ... because they *restricted the power of the executive branch* to make decisions on the environment and *required Congress* instead to make laws. So it is now 'fascist' to take away the unbridled power of the executive and force democracy to work? That makes zero sense, and yet I haven't seen a single Democrat point out how obviously authoritarian it is to prefer the executive branch to have unbridled power. They seem blind to their own authoritarianism.

From where I sit, Democrats have done more to undermine

democracy in their statements about recent Supreme Court decisions than any Republican has ever done in my lifetime. Many Democrats want to abolish the Supreme Court.[23] They want to abolish one of the institutions designed to protect Constitutional rights. Designed to protect the balance of power. They want to do this so that their leaders can impose their will on their enemies. And were they aware of how authoritarian this is? Did they think they were being authoritarian when they wanted their leaders to burn the institution down? When they said Democratic leaders should defy the Constitution to institute their own political whims? No. In fact, they were so self-ignorant that they actually raged and raged about how other people were the *real* threats to democracy.

Authoritarian Projection: The Gaslighting of America

> Here again though I think is another example of projection. Because the president sits there and calls his political opponents Bull Connor or George Wallace while pushing for literal segregation in terms of vaccination status. Hoping to have Americans use their race as their primary identifying factor, and in fact embrace concepts that would segregate our classrooms. I think what we're watching once again is the president project his own sins onto the American people.[24]
>
> – Will Cain, Fox News analyst

One of the things we've seen in these examples is that left-wing authoritarians are especially prone to deny authoritarianism in themselves and other liberals, and especially prone to simultaneously accuse their enemies of engaging in the very authoritarianism they are imposing. Both sides do this, but this *authoritarian projection* is far more common among left-wing authoritarians than right-wing authoritarians.

In fact, historically, right-wing authoritarians are pretty straightforward about their authoritarian intentions and don't spend a lot of time denying them. As Hitler said at Nuremberg in 1935: 'Nothing is possible unless one will commands, a will which has to be obeyed by others, beginning at the top and ending only at the very bottom. This is the expression of an authoritarian state – not of a weak, babbling democracy – of an authoritarian state where everyone is proud to obey, because he knows: I will likewise be obeyed when I must take command.'[25]

Modern liberal authoritarians are of a different kind entirely. Consider the following exchange on CNN's show *Erin Burnett OutFront*.[26] Asra Nomani, a Muslim woman born in India, made several substantive points about how it is wrong to use modern academic theory to divide children by race. One of her points was the following:

> Just look at this idea that is in [the children's book] *Not My Idea*. It literally says here 'Whiteness is a bad deal' and it has a symbol of Satan. And this is the contract they say whiteness brings and children are getting this book. And so there is a direct correlation from these ideas [holds up Critical Race Theory book] to these dangerous principles [holds up *Not My Idea*]. And I fit into the intersectional world. I'm a Muslim, I'm an immigrant, I'm a mom of color, I'm a single mom, but yet I deny all of these 'privileges' in the new paradigm of the oppression matrix – because we're all human beings. And that's what we need to teach our children. Of course race is an important issue. Our racial history

is important. But right now, Critical Race Theory is bringing into our schools racism, bigotry, and separation. Affinity circles, segregation, it's not OK and it's not healthy for our kids.

Now hit the pause button here. Whatever you think about the larger debate, it is a serious point worth considering whether we are all OK with schools teaching a book that defines *being white* as *making a deal with the devil*. If an academic had tried to teach a book that equated being African American or being from India with making a deal with the devil, that academic would rightly be questioned seriously about that decision. So it is a reasonable, substantive question, deserving of a reasonable, substantive answer, why one would be in favor of a book that seems to make such a racist claim. And the answer from liberal respondent Kazique Prince to this statement is telling:

> What I say is that, you know, one of the big problems that we have today – and we've learned this during the pandemic situation that we're in today – that we have too many people who know little or nothing about education trying to tell professionals who are in this industry who have been working hard, if anything we've learned that their jobs are much harder than we think they are, and we're coming in as weekend warriors trying to tell them what education should look like. And what I would say is that we need to put a little more trust in our educators. We need to put a little more trust in people who have actually researched this issue and who are actually better informed because they actually spent the time and energy necessary to really understand some of the nuances that are being just kind of blown over here in this conversation … Basically, the response

is, let's not have this conversation, so we can keep them quiet
and silent and really make no real change in society.

This reply is astonishing. If someone says to you that your teachers are requiring a book that is racist, it is not an argument at all
to suggest that you should just be quiet and trust the teachers. If
a black parent had questioned white teachers in the 1960s about
the racism being taught in schools, it would not be an argument
to say 'You don't understand the issue; trust the teachers'. No, it
is not an argument; it is obviously authoritarianism.

As we've seen, one of the hallmarks of authoritarianism is that
it doesn't try to persuade; it thoughtlessly bludgeons. It responds
to debate by claiming that authority figures understand and we
should just trust them. 'We have too many people who know
little or nothing about education trying to tell professionals
who are in this industry what to do' could be an item on any
authoritarian measure.

But notice something else; it is that something that makes
modern liberal authoritarians somewhat unique. Liberal authoritarians tend to deny their own authoritarianism while projecting
it on other people. Kazique Prince didn't say: 'I believe in authoritarianism, and therefore I want to silence you because you should
not talk.' Rather, after saying he did not believe his opponent
should be talking about this issue because she should leave it to
the authorities – one of the hallmarks of authoritarianism – he
then accused his opponent of authoritarian silencing: '[your]
response is, let's not have this conversation, so we can keep them
quiet and silent and really make no real change in society.'

In other words, he gaslit his opponent. He engaged in
authoritarian silencing, but projected his own behavior onto his

opponent – and thus acted like he was the victim of his own crimes.

This gaslighting is ubiquitous. It can be seen at ground zero of the political fight over schools in the US as a case study: Loudoun County, Virginia.[27] What we see there is a microcosm of what is happening across the country: (1) Democrats push a radical educational agenda on American parents, while (2) simultaneously claiming they are not pushing an authoritarian agenda, and (3) calling all resistance to the agenda authoritarian silencing. Democrats' own efforts to silence Virginia parents got so intense that they called parents 'domestic terrorists' and enlisted the FBI to issue a memorandum against them[28] – and yet, somehow, many Democrats do not see this overtly authoritarian behavior as abnormal at all. In fact, they see it as a normal, non-authoritarian response to the authoritarian behavior of their opponents. They think parents angry about being left out of their kids' education are the 'real authoritarians'.

Importantly, this has absolutely nothing to do with whether what the curriculum liberals want in schools is in fact a good curriculum. Doubtless, like all such curricula, it has many positive elements. Rather, it is about the authoritarian projection process that was used to enact the curriculum. In a democracy, public schools are a part of the public sphere. When you tell people that 'I don't think parents should be telling schools what they should teach', as former governor and 2022 Democratic gubernatorial candidate Terry McAuliffe did, you're substituting authoritarianism for debate in the public sphere.[29] In a functioning democracy, people rightly believe they *do* have a collective voice in what their children learn at the schools they pay taxes to support. In a democracy, if you want to change a school's curriculum, you don't dictate it from the top down, pretend you aren't dictating it from the top down, blame your opponents for authoritarianism because they resist, and then intimidate anyone who dares disagree.

This gaslighting phenomenon highlights that left-wing authoritarians seem uniquely prone to engage in authoritarian silencing while projecting their very behavior onto their opponents. While no doubt a fair bit of this is just political posturing, part of it is a kind of other-blindness that conveniently assumes ill intentions in one's opponents (whether they have those ill intentions or not). This is a natural psychological extension of their motivations for self-ignorance. They are motivated to believe they are not authoritarian and their opponents are – and the end result is they project their own authoritarian behaviors onto their opponents.

If Liberal Authoritarians Shuffle the Cards Enough, They Might Actually Win

Liberals have been reshuffling the cards and declaring themselves the winners; but, unlike Dogbert, they aren't playing solitaire. They are playing a cut-throat game of poker against traditional Western civilization. And as we've seen, this motivational blind spot causes them to reframe many things in themselves that are authoritarian and project it onto their opponents.

But there is a real danger that they might win, if we don't do something about it. Perhaps the most telling example of this involves disinformation boards. The *New York Times* published an article about how 'disinformation boards' had become kind of untouchable in Washington due to pushback from the American people.[30] Although they don't use the actual term 'tragedy', the article's tone nonetheless suggests what a tragedy it is that the US government is afraid to regulate the speech of its citizens, saying things like this:

> There is wide agreement across the federal government that coordinated disinformation campaigns threaten to exacerbate public health emergencies, stoke ethnic and racial divisions and even undermine democracy itself. The board's fate, however, has underscored how deeply partisan the issue has become in Washington, making it nearly impossible to consider addressing the threat.
>
> The failure to act, according to experts, has left openings for new waves of disinformation ahead of November's midterm elections – and even for violence like the racist massacre at a Buffalo supermarket in May, which was motivated by a baseless conspiracy theory that global forces aimed to 'replace' white Americans with immigrants.
>
> A prominent author and researcher in the field of disinformation, who once advised Ukraine's government, Ms. Jankowicz became a focus of the furor, targeted online by false or misleading information about her role in what critics denounced as a Ministry of Truth.
>
> The threats from disinformation today involve issues that not long ago might have transcended partisan politics. Instead, disinformation has become mired in the country's deepening partisan and geographical divides over issues like abortion, guns and climate change.

Its roots began in Russia's interference in the 2016 election of President Donald J. Trump, which he and his allies repeatedly denounced as fake despite evidence compiled by federal investigators about Russian complicity.

Disinformation that continues to swirl around Covid-19 and the 2020 election of President Biden – which Mr. Trump continues to insist, against all evidence, was a fraud – has made many Republicans view the very fight against disinformation as a partisan assault.

By all accounts, the department failed to anticipate the furor that the creation of the advisory panel would cause – as well as the ease with which critics would tar it with the very kind of campaigns it was meant to monitor.

'The right recognizes it is a way to whip up people in a furor,' Ms. Jankowicz said. 'The problem is there are very real national security issues here, and not being able to talk about this in a mature way is a real disservice to the country.'

'We're basically at this point unable to have a calm discussion about this problem,' said Paul Barrett, the deputy director of the Stern Center for Business and Human Rights at New York University. 'And there's a weird, circular, looping-around effect. The problem itself is helping make us unable to talk about the problem.'

What is remarkable about these statements isn't that many of them are brazenly false (apparently the *New York Times* missed the part about the Russian collusion hoax, ummm, being a hoax?[31]) and most of them are at a minimum hyperbolic (it is honestly hard to consider Ms Jankowicz a serious candidate given her own obvious misinformation issues[32] and lack of relevant experience). After all, some of the claims are no doubt true – I certainly see little evidence that the election in 2020 was illegitimate. (I also did not see the *New York Times* crying foul when Hillary Clinton consistently claimed – even as late as 2020 – that the 2016 election was illegitimate, an equally false claim as far as I can tell.[33] See Chapter 4 on groups over principles). So while the mixture of false arguments and true arguments is important, that's not what I want to focus on here. Rather, what is remarkable is that these statements are completely ignorant of their own authoritarianism while projecting it on their opponents. They implicitly attack conservatives as being the political authoritarians. But the backdrop of all these statements is an underpinning desire to curb free speech – a desire that the authors want to normalize in their audience. They don't want themselves or their audience to deeply ponder the degree that these violations of free speech are authoritarian.[34] To illustrate, let's dive into just a few of these statements in more depth.

> There is wide agreement across the federal government that coordinated disinformation campaigns threaten to exacerbate public health emergencies, stoke ethnic and racial divisions and even undermine democracy itself. The board's fate, however, has underscored how deeply partisan the issue has become in Washington, making it nearly impossible to consider addressing the threat.

This is incredibly insidious and yet, without analyzing what it says deeply, it could appear almost benign. 'There is wide agreement that disinformation campaigns have tried to undermine democracy,' the article says, while bemoaning that we can't stop the disinformation because the issue is deeply partisan now. But what does that mean, exactly? It isn't ambiguous at all. It means *conservatives didn't like the disinformation board*. All the examples of disinformation are right-wing examples. The implication throughout is that the issue is partisan because conservatives are wrong. So all these misinforming conservatives are a threat to democracy – that's the takeaway message here. But in reality, by far the biggest threat to democracy is … the disinformation board itself. In other words, while tacitly supporting censoring much of the population of the US, the article claims that it is *that* part of the population – the population they want to censor – that is the threat to democracy. 'Stop hitting me,' the bully cries as he bludgeons the small kid who tries in vain to punch back.

'The right recognizes it is a way to whip up people in a furor,' Ms. Jankowicz said. 'The problem is there are very real national security issues here, and not being able to talk about this in a mature way is a real disservice to the country.'

Note what she says here: Those darn conservatives don't want their rights taken away and *that's* the problem. Not the fact that *you are taking their rights away*. They just need to be more mature about losing free speech and we'd all be fine. Apparently the authors of the article didn't see anything hypocritical about this – they were self-ignorant.

Let's take these last two comments together.

By all accounts, the department failed to anticipate the furor that the creation of the advisory panel would cause – as well as the ease with which critics would tar it with the very kind of campaigns it was meant to monitor.

The problem itself is helping make us unable to talk about the problem.

Of course misinformation *can* make it tough to talk about misinformation. It's hard to talk to liars about their lying problem because they might lie about *that* too. But the actual and very clear implication here is that we can't talk about censoring people because people are mad about being censored. In other words, those darn deplorable conservatives are the problem. The conservative 'critics' are always the ones spreading misinformation for nefarious purposes. Despite all the evidence that we've already documented in this book that a lot of misinformation comes from the left – and despite the fact that Jankowicz herself argued for the censoring of conservative talking points that everyone now agrees are true – the problem is all those darn conservatives are spreading misinformation to stop us from censoring them.

The most disturbing part of this is that this left-wing article, so completely ignorant of its own authoritarian vibe, clearly wasn't authoritarian enough for a lot of the left. In fact, one of my own colleagues in the field of political psychology, University of Minnesota professor Chris Federico, said this about the *New York Times* article: 'Right-wing commentators and politicians are always going to demagogue on stuff like this. They will never be brought on board in the present environment. The relevant agencies should ignore them and proceed rather than throwing up their hands.'[35]

Dr Federico is well-respected in my field, and in fact I've always loved his work. I used to think of him as a relatively moderate and open-minded researcher. And *that* person, that respected colleague, on the issue of forming boards to censor political conservatives, said that those conservatives will 'never be brought on board' and the agencies should 'ignore them and proceed rather than throwing up their hands'. Oh, how far we've fallen. A respected academic, someone I've always thought of as looking at issues on both sides, someone who has actually done research showing the legitimacy of left-wing authoritarianism – *that* academic believes that government agencies should just ignore free speech and 'proceed' with their censorship of conservatives because, hey, those conservatives will 'never be brought on board'. I wonder if it ever occurred to him that maybe, just maybe, the problem is that few people will easily be brought on board having their rights to free speech taken away? I wonder if it occurred to him that he was actively endorsing authoritarian censorship as he wrote that tweet? There is no evidence of that. And that's the really alarming thing. This kind of person on the left can argue for authoritarianism while imagining that it is all those ruffian demagogues on the other side who are really the problem.

If you aren't alarmed yet – you should be. When we arrive at a point that decent people think it's normal to claim their opponents are authoritarian censors while censoring them, then we've come close to the edge of a precipice that I fear we may never come back from. Eventually, if the Democrats shuffle those cards enough, their authoritarian projections might actually *be* the winner.

Given this then – given the very real threat of left-wing authoritarianism – it is worth pursuing the question: How do we stop it? Psychology teaches us a lot about that question. And in the last three chapters, having diagnosed the disease, I talk about the cure.

CHAPTER 7

WE'RE DOING THIS WRONG

War must be, while we defend our lives against a destroyer who would devour all; but I do not love the bright sword for its sharpness, nor the arrow for its swiftness, nor the warrior for his glory. I love only that which they defend: the city of Númenor; and I would have her loved for her memory, her ancientry, her beauty, and her present wisdom. Not feared, save as men may fear the dignity of a man old and wise.

– Faramir, in J. R. R. Tolkien's *The Lord of the Rings: The Two Towers*

If we could create the perfect anti-authoritarian soldier, what would that person look like?

In the quote above, Faramir considers the *purpose* of war. What is the point of the soldier? And he comes to a conclusion that will guide much of our discussion in this chapter: The point of the sword is to defend something beautiful. Faramir doesn't value aggression for aggression's sake. He only values it as a tool to a larger end. But the end – the aim – is the important thing.

With respect to authoritarianism, understanding the broader aims is especially important, because the natural tendencies we have for dealing with authoritarianism go wrong in a lot of different directions. Thus, we need to take a step back and evaluate broader, big-picture questions, like: What is the perfect anti-authoritarian soldier like? Why should that soldier fight at all?

The answer is not quite what we might expect.

The Inherent Tensions in Fighting Authoritarianism

Most people can see the tension between having the courage to stand up to bullies and being kind to them. Most people recognize that it is difficult to stop a bully without becoming a bully. But the natural tendency of everyday decent people when they note tensions between two opposing ideas is to find the middle of them. That won't work here.

This natural tendency is often perfectly reasonable. When our family tries to decide on a time to eat, one person inevitably says 5:30 and the next person says 6:30. So we all agree on 6:00. That's going in the middle. Taking the moderate path.

That works for some kinds of things. But it fails miserably at others. If one person wants pizza and another person wants an ice cream smoothie, the moderate path won't work. You can't mix up the pizza with the smoothie and call it good. Something else is required. If you want to keep the smoothie and the pizza, you'll have to preserve them in their original form without moderating either one of them at all.

We cannot fight authoritarianism by accepting a moderate position. We cannot fight authoritarianism by taking the average of extreme kindness and extreme courage. That leads to a person who is only sort of nice and only sort of courageous. That perfectly reasonable moderate person has a lot of common sense and will be really good at dinner parties – but he or she will not be very successful at fighting authoritarianism. That person basically does nothing meaningful towards authoritarianism, either good or bad. And if we do nothing, authoritarianism wins.

No, what we need instead – what ideal anti-authoritarian soldiers are like – are people who are both extremely courageous *and* extremely nice. We need *Faramirs* who know that freedom comes with a price. People who are motivated by a passion to defend something beautiful. That price includes both extreme courage and extreme niceness. You need courage to be called a racist by mean people. You need boldness to stand up to the bullies who would tear you down. But it also requires something else: Goodness. Niceness. Kindness. You have to care more about dignity and wisdom than about winning. You have to care, not about the bright sword, but about the thing it defends: Freedom. And that means you have to care about your neighbor's freedom as well as your own.

Thus, this clearly requires more than merely being *kind of courageous* and *kind of nice*. It requires changing our ideal to be *very courageous* and *very nice* at the same time. Now, before you panic and think 'I can't do that!', don't worry – you don't have to be perfect to make a difference. None of us are the ideal solider. As we'll see, you can make a difference even in little things. But what I want you to see here is the goal. If we don't even aim for the right goal to stop authoritarianism, then we're doomed to fail for sure. If you bring your golf clubs to the course, you will still hit a few bad shots. You may have a bad round. But if you bring a hammer instead because you think the goal is to drive the ball downward, you are certainly going to fail. So it helps to first get the right idea of what we are *trying* to do in your head.

In one sense, the antidote to left-wing authoritarianism is obvious. We have diagnosed the disease and the cure ought to be the opposite of all those things. If left-wing authoritarianism involves simplicity, then we need complexity. If left-wing authoritarianism involves a lack of equally applied principle, then we need more equally applied principle. We can counter intellectual apathy with a tolerance for vigorous debate. We can counter a misinformation obsession by voting for laws that don't allow government entities to suppress things they deem incorrect.

But obvious though it is, it actually isn't that easy in practice. And below, I offer two broad categories of reasons why authoritarianism is currently winning. The first reason is that people who don't like authoritarianism simply don't care enough about it to do something. They are being too passive. There are millions of moderate, average, everyday people right now who simply tolerate authoritarianism. The first order of business is to wake them up – to wake up their courage. The second is our tendency, once woken, to use the sword to merely punish our enemies.

As we'll see, we're doing a lot of this wrong. But we can use these case studies in how we're doing this wrong to illustrate what we should be doing instead. So let's take each of these issues in turn as a means of highlighting the ultimate aim of the anti-authoritarian soldier.

Tolerance for Authoritarianism in the Gray Area

From a leader's perspective, authoritarianism is an all-or-none gamble. If you succeed in gaining total control, you can then – from a position of top-down power – use all your influence to create only one narrative. That's what's happened in China. Evaluating how China's authoritarian government has succeeded, political scientists Daniela Stockmann and Mary E. Gallagher note: 'The state is able to achieve its political goal because of the lack of conflicting sources of information and the lack of previous experience with the reformed legal system among citizens.'[1] China's authoritarian state has controlled a narrative and, given the lack of a conflicting narrative, the authoritarians stay in power. Thus, authoritarianism can overcome many of its own psychological obstacles with countermanding strengths.

But that doesn't mean the Chinese populace is completely OK with authoritarianism. Actually, the truth turns out to be much more complicated. Although China holds much higher levels of authoritarian followers than most countries, nonetheless there are a lot of Chinese who do not like the current authoritarian regime.[2] Similarly, lots of Germans really didn't like the Nazis.[3] And yet most of those people in China and Germany didn't do anything. Why? What causes the inaction of those people? And particularly in the formative stages of authoritarianism – which is where we are in America right now – why do people tolerate authoritarianism? Why don't average people speak out?

While some of those answers are obvious, some of them are not obvious at all.

In this book, I've largely been talking like we can divide the world up into authoritarians and non-authoritarians. As if there are two, and only two, categorically different kinds of people.

Of course, the reality is much more complex. Authoritarianism is a dimension more than a category. That means that people can score high or low, or sort of low, or sort of high, or anywhere in between. This truth is important if we want to understand how authoritarianism thrives. There is a lot of room between 'I refuse to follow authoritarian bullies on both sides of the political aisle' and 'I want an authoritarian to silence and imprison all my enemies'. There are millions of sensible, average, moderate people who are not especially mean nor especially bold. What is it that makes people in the 'middle' – people who aren't especially authoritarian – tolerate their own authoritarian leaders? What stops them from stopping authoritarianism? We will turn now to discuss several reasons why average citizens don't do anything.

Working Within the System Versus Challenging It

[You] have to change with the times or you die.

– American comedian Jay Leno, discussing cancel culture[4]

Imagine your boss supports Political Cause X, and the boss uses half of every business meeting to discuss the glories of his pet political cause. Would you try to do something to stop his incessant rambling? What if instead of merely wasting time during work hours, your boss orders you to go to a political rally to march in favor of the cause. Would you do it?

Now imagine that your boss doesn't just order you to go to a political rally, but says you will be fired if you do not allow him to mail in your own private ballot, on which you *will* vote for Political Cause X. Would you stand up to your boss even then?

What if the boss orders you to steal other people's ballots so he can forge your friends' votes in favor of the cause?

These questions help highlight that there is a cost–benefit analysis that guides much of our behavior relevant to authoritarianism. If a boss rambles in a meeting, you probably just endure the waste of time and roll your eyes. If the boss orders you to march at a political rally, you will likely spend more time evaluating the costs and benefits. How much do you need the job? Do you agree with the political cause? If you agree with the cause and can't live without the job, you almost certainly would just march at the rally. If you hate the cause and could get another job, you might refuse to go. However, if your boss asks you to do something totally illegal – as authoritarians often do – then that makes the costs of doing nothing about authoritarianism even higher, and increases the odds that you would do something.

This means that, often, average people will simply work within the growing authoritarian system rather than challenge it. Average people need to eat. They need their jobs. The cost of challenging authoritarianism can be very high. Thus, unless the costs of *following* authoritarian dictates or *tolerating* authoritarian people become higher than the costs of *fighting* them, often average people will avoid the conflict, keep their heads down, and obey. Sometimes, like Jay Leno, they come to believe that they have to just accept the authoritarianism or they die.

The importance of this cost–benefit psychology can be seen in a rather remarkable study run by British researchers.

The BBC Prison Study

An entire generation of Psychology 101 students grew up reading about the weird nastiness that occurred in Phil Zimbardo's now-infamous Stanford Prison Experiment (1971). In their classes, they watched scratchy VHS videos with horrified fascination, cringing as apparently normal college students who had been randomly assigned to be 'guards' stripped their fellow student 'prisoners' naked and punished them in horrible and mean-spirited ways. All this happened even though they were all just part of a psychology study!

The long-taught conclusion from the Zimbardo study is that social roles are all-consuming. If average people are assigned to be prison guards, they will start stripping people naked and starving them because that's what prison guards do. If average people are assigned to be prisoners, they will accept being stripped and starved because that's what prisoners do. Authoritarianism thus comes from role assignment – stop assigning people to authoritarian roles and you'll stop authoritarianism.

Only it turns out that this explanation is not that compelling. For one thing, it isn't clear that this group of participants was all that 'average'. In 2007, two researchers did a very simple thing: They advertised for a study using *either* the exact same wording used by Zimbardo for recruitment – 'the psychological study of prison life' – or some neutral wording that didn't involve prison life.[5] They found that people responding to the prison wording were more authoritarian, more socially dominant, and more aggressive than those responding to the neutral wording. We don't know for sure that this was true of the Zimbardo study, but it suggests that maybe the methods used by Zimbardo were tilted to get authoritarian people into the study in the first place – and that might partially explain what happened.

As a result, we didn't really learn a whole lot about where authoritarianism comes from in the *Stanford Prison Experiment*. However, years later, in 2001, two researchers performed a more carefully controlled version of the experiment in England that has come to be known as the BBC Prison Study.[6] In that study, 15 men were randomly assigned to prisoner or guard roles for eight days. Ten were assigned to be prisoners and five to be guards. They were selected from a pool of 332 people – the selection criteria were that they wanted people who had no clinical problems (e.g., depression) or anti-social behavior problems (e.g., authoritarianism, social dominance, and modern racism), so they took people who had low levels of these issues. Even so, there was still individual variability – some of the men were more authoritarian than others. As a result, researchers further ensured that these persons were 'matched' in terms of prisoners and guards, using a randomized matching procedure, so that there were roughly equal levels of (say) authoritarian traits in both prisoner and guard camps.

The guards were told they needed to draw up a set of prison rules. They could not use violence but other than that could use any means they chose. Guards had access to rewards (snacks) and punishments (an isolation cell, bread-and-water diets). They also had superior living conditions. Prisoners were escorted to their cells by the guards. They were given almost no directions except a loudspeaker announcement by the experimenters which contained a statement prohibiting violence. They had a set of 'prisoners' rights' posted on the walls. Other than this, they were basically at the whim of the guards.

In the beginning, the guards' authoritarian regime was quite successful. In fact, in the first few days, the authoritarian guards were much happier and felt much more confident about their group, while the prisoners were less happy and confident. All seemed to be going well for the guards. However, only six days into the experiment, the tide had turned and the prisoners had completely overthrown the authoritarian guards: On that day, some of the prisoners broke out of the cell and occupied the guards' quarters. At that point, everyone agreed that the guards' regime was at an end.

So the original authoritarian regime failed after six days. What caused it to fail? What changed that led the early success of authoritarianism to ultimately collapse?

One of the factors that changed was something researchers call 'permeability'. Permeability in this context means the degree that it's possible for people at the bottom end of the authoritarian hierarchy to work their way to the top of the hierarchy. If you think that maybe you can one day become a boss, you live in a permeable environment. If you think you will always be subject to your current boss, then you live in a non-permeable environment.

The BBC Prison Study manipulated permeability. In particular, all the participants were told that the guards had been selected for their role because of pre-testing, but that some of the prisoners may also make good guards.[7] This meant that for the first three days, prisoners thought they might have 'upward mobility' in this world. And one prisoner was in fact promoted to guard. However, after three days, it was announced that no further promotions would occur. Would this matter?

It mattered a lot. After the permeability was removed – after it was clear that no one was going to move up within the system – the prisoners started to become more determined as a group to overthrow the regime. Three days later, they did so.

Permeability is one factor in the cost–benefit analysis. Part of the problem is that average people *accept* authoritarianism even when they don't like it. And part of the reason they accept it is that, in a cost–benefit analysis, they may gain more by working within the existing system than by fighting it. Thus, to stop authoritarianism, we have to get people to the point where they see the cost–benefit analysis more in favor of fighting it than of working with it.

So what specifically is causing the modern Western world to sleepwalk its way to authoritarianism? How did we get here? To understand that, we turn to an unlikely source: Bureaucracy.

Tolerance for Unnecessary Bureaucracy Is a Clue to Our Problem

CAPT. VASILI BORODIN: And I will have a pickup truck … maybe even a 'recreational vehicle'. And drive from state to state. Do they let you do that?

CAPTAIN RAMIUS: I suppose.

CAPT. VASILI BORODIN: No papers?

CAPTAIN RAMIUS: No papers, state to state.

– *The Hunt for Red October*

In this iconic movie from my childhood, Soviet submarine captain Marko Ramius and his second in command Vasili defect to the US. Every time I watched this scene, where the defining difference between Soviet tyranny and American freedom is that you could move from state to state with 'no papers', I always thought how incredible it would be to feel grateful for such an obvious freedom. I just took that kind of thing for granted.

Except that now I'm not so sure.

We recently moved from Montana to Pennsylvania. This required us to spend two weeks of our lives wading through bureaucracy in order to get all the 'papers' necessary for us to live in a new state – such as a new driver's license. It's important to note that a driver's license doesn't just let you drive; in the modern US, it is essential to your rights as a citizen. So this is a vital piece of paper to get.

I am an American citizen. On my person that first day, I had an American passport; I had a valid American driver's license from an American state; I had evidence that I had paid American taxes for years; I had the title to my Pennsylvania house; and multiple other forms of identification that showed I was a valid American resident who was currently residing in Pennsylvania. And yet, I was forced to go back multiple times and spend hours gathering additional documents, carrying on long arguments, among other indignities, just to get the Pennsylvania driver's license that I would need to essentially *live* in the state of Pennsylvania. Without that license, I could not drive; I could not fly; I could not *vote*. I could not have most of the basic rights that I – as an American citizen – am essentially guaranteed.

State to state, no papers?

I'm beginning to wonder. The title to my Pennsylvania house was denied as proof of residency, even though Pennsylvania listed it as one of the acceptable documents for that purpose, and despite the fact that the document itself was *issued by the state of Pennsylvania through official channels*. My printed tax forms from the US government weren't considered evidence of

my citizenship, even though that was again specifically listed as an acceptable document for that purpose by the state of Pennsylvania. In each case the reasons given for the rejection were both small and bizarrely illogical.

I did eventually get my license, and the point of this story isn't to complain about Pennsylvania specifically. I have loved my time in this beautiful state so far and I don't hold this experience against it. I understand that there are legitimate reasons why states want to ensure the people they grant licenses to are residents. What I want you to take from this is different. These are just representative examples of a long list of problems that not only I, but also my family and countless other people in the country, had in simply *transferring our legally earned proof of US citizenship* from one state to another. What should have been a brief afternoon turned into a weeks-long hassle, where we had to fight and scratch and argue and provide proof after proof of our citizenship as legal Americans and our residency in Pennsylvania. At multiple points during this agonizingly difficult process, I began to wonder why this felt more like my visions of the Soviet Union than my beloved America. Why was it so difficult to move from 'state to state' without the right 'papers'? And it isn't just this issue and it isn't just us – Americans generally report being fed up with government bureaucracy.[8]

Which leads to the question – why do we all put up with it? If, as Albert Einstein said, 'bureaucracy is the death of any achievement,' why do we let it slow us down? And the answer is that we've become inured to minor levels of authoritarianism. We've increasingly tolerated small but unnecessary invasions of our freedom. We've become tolerant of unnecessary bureaucracy.

Look at this picture I took at the airport in Rochester, New York. The sign says 'No Standing' and yet you can see people clearly standing in the background. Why are they standing? Are they horrible rule-breakers? Not likely. They are standing because these signs are posted in the arrival area where people pick up their friends and families after their flights. Now I don't know what was going on in the minds of the people who decided to make the no-standing rule. I don't know why they decided to spend quite a bit of taxpayer money to put up the many, many signs at the airport that say 'No Standing'. But what I want to point out is this: These signs are plastered all over a place whose sole function must, by necessity, *involve standing*. It is almost not possible for people who are waiting for their relatives to pick them up – as the people in this photo are doing – to do so without standing. There are no chairs; there are no yoga mats; there is literally nothing for them to do but stand while they wait. And what of the people – like we were that day – waiting for their relatives to arrive? We needed to get out of our car and stand there, looking for our relatives so they could see us. Were we supposed to sit, and if we needed to move about, crawl? Should we have constantly been jumping so we technically were never just standing?

My point is, there may be legitimate reasons for the 'No Standing' sign. Perhaps they really meant 'don't just stand here for an hour'. (If so, they should have said that.) But whatever those reasons are, they aren't obvious or meaningful to most people. And yet – people are standing there next to those signs. No one thinks the signs are meaningful – but no one cares enough to try to change the rule. We've become completely tolerant of rules that everyone can see aren't very functional. We try to find a way around the rules; we try to find a way to work within the system; but we tolerate the invasive and authoritarian rules.

Now I try to point out these and thousands of other examples, and people just roll their eyes. 'Who cares?' you say. 'It's just a sign. People are ignoring it anyway.' I think the tendency to roll our eyes at minor violations of freedom is one of our biggest problems. I have two words to say in response.

Broken windows.

The Psychology of Broken Windows

Academic scholars James Wilson and George Kelling introduced the now-famous 'broken windows' theory of criminal reform in a piece in *The Atlantic* in the early 1980s.[9] They summarized it like this: 'Social psychologists and police officers tend to agree that if a window in a building is broken and is left unrepaired, all the rest of the windows will soon be broken. This is as true in nice neighborhoods as in rundown ones.'

Functionally, the theory meant that police should focus more on the enforcement of small crimes. On the surface, it is counterintuitive. If you are facing a high murder rate, wouldn't it make more sense to focus efforts specifically on stopping murders instead of stopping petty thefts? But the broken windows theory says the opposite. It says that if you want to stop murders, you have to fix *all* the windows. You have to stop *all* crime, or else eventually people just stop caring about windows altogether.

Facing record murder rates with no end in sight, New York City embraced the broken windows idea in the 1990s. The most famous example was their radical police focus on 'squeegee' people.[10] These folks were annoying – they would clean your windows while you were stopped at a light without your permission, then aggressively seek payment from you afterwards. This was against the law, and New York had let it go for years, even though it made people feel unsafe and they didn't like it. And suddenly, cops all over the place stopped the squeegee people from doing their thing. They focused on small crimes like *that*. And guess what happened?

Murders went down dramatically. By the end of the decade, murder rates in New York had plummeted.[11] While there is some debate over how much of this is due to the broken windows policy, there is a lot of psychology that would show why this approach to policing would reduce crime.

To better understand why broken windows policies work, let me ask you a question. Imagine someone came to your house today and asked if they could put up a very large billboard in your front yard that read 'Drive Carefully'. They showed you a picture of what it would look like, a picture that revealed the billboard was poorly lettered and quite ugly, and would visually block much of your house. Would you say yes to this request?

If you were like most of the control participants in a famous study by Freedman and Fraser from the 1960s, you would flatly deny this request.[12] Participants in that study were, according to the researchers, 'shown a picture of a very large sign reading "Drive Carefully" placed in front of an attractive house. The picture was taken so that the sign obscured much of the front of the house and completely concealed the doorway.' Participants were then asked if they'd be OK with that billboard being installed at *their* house. Predictably, only 17% of them agreed.

However, for a different group of people, a couple of weeks prior, they had been asked to comply with a much smaller request: To accept a three-inch sticker that said 'Be a Safe Driver'. Almost everyone complied with this tiny request. There was little cost to simply taking a small sticker and agreeing to put it up somewhere.

But the really important thing is what happened next to the sticker group. Like the control group, they were also eventually asked if they would put up the giant billboard. Of those people who had been randomly assigned to the condition that asked them to take a small sticker, an incredible 76% of them subsequently agreed two weeks later to have a giant ugly billboard put up in their yard. So a request that most people turned down became a request that most people said yes to. What on earth happened?

The answer is a clue to the psychology of broken windows. One of the most powerful techniques for persuasion is called the 'foot-in-the-door' technique. This technique takes advantage of people's desire for *consistency*. People don't like change. If you can get them to lean in a particular direction, it is hard for them to stop leaning. The foot-in-the-door technique capitalizes on this psychological inertia. So when people have previously put up a small sticker saying 'Be a Safe Driver', it seems inconsistent for them to later deny a request to put up a huge 'Drive Carefully' billboard – even though under normal circumstances the second request is quite ridiculous.

That's part of the reason that broken windows policies work. Small things lead to big things. If people get used to broken windows, they think their neighborhood is the kind of place where crime happens. That consistency is a powerful force. People tolerate a small thing (like a nuisance sticker) and then later it's easy for them to tolerate a big thing (like a giant billboard that blocks their house). People tolerate comparatively small crimes (like squeegee people) and then later it's easy for them to tolerate big crimes (like muggings).

And that brings us back to unnecessary bureaucracy. The broken windows theory has a lot to teach us if we want to truly stop authoritarianism on both sides of the political aisle.

The Broken Windows Theory of Authoritarian Tolerance

Why is authoritarianism on both sides rampant? Part of the reason involves fear. But part of the reason is that a lot of people who don't like authoritarianism have learned to tolerate it. Let's translate the broken windows theory to authoritarianism.

From this lens, what is happening to us is that we've become so inured to unnecessary laws that we've started to accept actual tyranny. We've started to accept the government taking away our freedom as if that is what governments do. We've started to accept that a poor person on the Florida coast can have her land taken away by the government working with private business to *force her to move*.[13] We've started to accept that the government has the right to force kids to take a vaccine, even when scientists agree those kids aren't in danger of the disease[14] *and* there are legitimate questions about the long-term (and largely unknown) safety of the vaccine.[15] We've started to accept that the government can work with information companies to censor what people are allowed to say. We've started to accept that the government can directly tell doctors what medical information they are and are not allowed to give to their patients.[16] Thirty years ago, almost every single one of these things would have been shockingly unrealistic. And now? There has been pushback on each of those things, sure, but that kind of thing is so commonplace that most Americans just accept it. Why?

Broken windows.

Because we've accepted so many small authoritarian violations, we've become accustomed to them. Like participants in Freedman and Fraser's study, we've allowed small 'authoritarianism is OK' stickers in our rooms. We've allowed the government to force a lot of unnecessary bureaucracy on us. It's small, like a single broken window. But it only starts small. Psychologically, that small thing grows and grows until … we allow large-scale violations of freedoms. One day, I'm tolerating an absurdly unnecessary bureaucratic headache to get my 'papers' from the state of Pennsylvania. The next year, I'm tolerating the federal government telling me that I can't safely remove bats from my own house, because they've declared that bats have more rights in my own home than I do.[17] Years later, I'm tolerating the federal government telling me I can't post a political opinion on the internet.

This sounds horrible, but the broken windows theory offers us a lot of hope. *You* can do something where *you* are. Maybe you can't fix government censorship, but you can try to fix whatever broken window is in your metaphorical neighborhood. Maybe it involves a school board. Maybe it just involves a conversation in an internet chat room. Maybe it involves starting a petition to get rid of useless bureaucracy in your own town or state. Maybe it involves filing a complaint with your workplace that they won't let you install items you need for your job on your own computer. But whatever it is, the hopeful message is that everything can matter. It might not have seemed like much to each cop that stopped a squeegee guy, but the cumulative effect changed New York City. If a lot of us work to stop small authoritarian injustices in our own lives, it can add up to … saving the country.

So it is clear that part of the problem is that average people are, right now, keeping their heads down and working within the authoritarian system. They haven't yet taken up the sword at all, because they don't see the need for it yet. Their cost–benefit analyses haven't led to that outcome. So part of what we need to do – part of what I'm hoping to get you to do – is to wake up to the fact that the cost of this slow decline into authoritarianism is ultimately huge. You don't actually have to be a hero or the perfect authoritarian soldier described earlier. But you have to do something. You have to be willing to take a stand of some kind, where you are. And often that will start with the small things you see around you. There really *isn't* a reason in a democracy that you should simply tolerate a million small violations of your freedom.

On the other hand, there is a danger in the other direction also. We can do this wrong by failing to care enough to fight; but we can also do this wrong by fighting authoritarianism with methods doomed to produce more authoritarianism. We can take up the sword for the wrong reasons.

The Seductive Temptation of the Bright Sword: The Authoritarian Threat Cycle

When children feel frightened at night, they generally cry out for an adult to comfort them.

There is nothing wrong with that instinct. But that simple psychological fact turns out to play a huge role in understanding the psychological origins of authoritarianism.

What turns people into authoritarians? The overwhelming answer from my own field suggests very clearly the primary causal factor that leads to authoritarianism: Fear. When people feel afraid, they turn to authoritarians to help solve their problems. Like a child scared at night, we want an adult to take our fears away.

Thus, it is not surprising that every major theory of the origins of authoritarianism has *fear* at the center. Altemeyer's RWA Model shows that people who believe the world is dangerous – who live with chronic fear – are more likely to be authoritarian.[18] Feldman's Social Conformity Model shows that authoritarianism lies at the intersection of threat and social conformity.[19] In probably the most influential model of the origins of authoritarianism,

Duckitt's Dual Process Model, authoritarianism primarily comes from threat.[20]

These models differ in various ways, but they all agree that a primary cause of authoritarianism is people's fear. Like children, we reach out for authoritarian leaders to solve our problems when we are worried about what might be in the dark.

This is true for authoritarianism on both the right *and* the left. For example, in our own work, we evaluated the degree that authoritarianism comes from fears of ecological disasters.[21] We asked people across the US simple questions about the existence of various threats in the area where they lived – threats such as disease, hurricanes, earthquakes, and the like. And we found that people who thought they lived in regions that were more dangerous were more likely to be authoritarians – an effect that was roughly equal for both liberals and conservatives. This fact is quite remarkable when one considers that none of our ecological threats had any mention of authority figures – or anything remotely related to authoritarianism – at all. It isn't like people in our studies thought 'authoritarians can stop earthquakes'. But just living in a place you think is dangerous predisposes people to reach out, like children in the dark, for an authoritarian to make them feel safer.

Thus, fear can serve as a background that makes authoritarianism of any kind more likely, even when (as in our study) there is no necessary connection between the authoritarian and the threat. However, often the authoritarianism appears as a direct solution to a particular threat. We discuss two of those kinds of fear next.

Authoritarianism and Fear of System Collapse

Although in the BBC Prison Study, the original authoritarian regime ended after six days, the study itself kept going for two more. And what happened in those two days teaches us something important about authoritarianism.

You'd think that authoritarianism was over in the study when the guards lost power. And, in fact, all but two participants wanted to continue the study by forming a non-authoritarian commune. So that's exactly what they did. They met with experimenters and drew up plans for the self-governing commune.

Many of the people who had been at odds as guards/prisoners now had a shared identity in the commune and got along great. However, some of the people who had been the strongest opponents of the old authoritarian guard regime did not like the new commune, and in fact started rebelling against it by violating commune rules (such as refusing to do work). After a single day of the anti-authoritarian commune, they were plotting to overthrow the new democracy, and it was obvious that the new social order was in crisis.

Four commune members (one ex-guard and three ex-prisoners) started a plan to create a new dictatorial regime that was even harsher than before – one where the people in charge had more authority over the commune. They called a meeting, where the supporters of the commune were largely passive in response to this plan, even though the new regime would be run by the people proposing the plan! A number of the commune supporters later acknowledged that, even though they were opposed to the authoritarian regime, the failure of their own system had made them more likely to accept the possibility of putting someone back in charge.

Interestingly, the people who were more likely to want to be guards at the end (who proposed the new regime) were also likely to be more authoritarian *at the beginning*. This suggests a personality factor at play in determining which persons were happiest with the egalitarian system. However – and this is important – people who were less authoritarian at the beginning became more so at the end. There was a general shift towards authoritarianism.

The proposed new authoritarian regime seemed like it might indeed be implemented, but it was so harsh that the experimenters had to stop the study on Day 8. (In a strange quirk, the study was terminated two days early – just like the Stanford Prison Experiment.)

So what led to the sudden reversal back to authoritarianism? That seems clear. What led to it was that people feared their own system was failing. When they fear disorder, people become more open to the authoritarian leaders who want to take control. In the words of the authors of the study:

> [B]ased on the present data, we would argue that failing groups almost inevitably create a host of problems for their own members and for others. These problems have a deleterious impact on organization, on individuals' clinical state, and – most relevant here – on society. For it is when people cannot create a social system for themselves that they will more readily accept extreme solutions proposed by others. It is when groups lack the power to exercise choice that an authoritarian ideology that promises to create order for them appears more seductive. In short, it is the breakdown of groups and powerlessness that creates the conditions under which tyranny can triumph.[22]

When uncertainty and fear become paramount, authoritarianism often steps in to fill the void. It is under these conditions of fear and threat of group collapse that the authoritarian virus can spread most quickly.

Social Threats: Why Authoritarianism Is Self-Perpetuating

Authoritarianism in response to threats isn't entirely illogical. In fact, it partially makes sense to reach out to a strong authority figure when you are frightened, because that authority figure might in fact be able to help. The problem with authoritarianism is that one of the most important kinds of threat tends to produce a cycle of authoritarianism that is, in one sense, artificial and avoidable.

We are a social species, and often our biggest perceived threats are ... people. By their nature, authoritarians are divisive and threatening. They punish, they cheat, they steal, they use an unfair standard – they harm.

This is especially troubling if one 'does the authoritarian psychological math'. (1) Authoritarians are especially threatening people. (2) Authoritarianism comes from threats. If you put those two things together, this means that *authoritarianism begets authoritarianism*. Right-wing authoritarians make left-wingers afraid and thus create left-wing authoritarians; but that same knife cuts both ways, and left-wing authoritarians may create a new generation of right-wing authoritarians for the exact same reason.

Left-wingers often justify authoritarianism on their side as a necessary response to the authoritarianism inspired by

Donald Trump and other conservative leaders. However, is it possible that, before that, the election of Donald Trump itself was a response to *left*-wing authoritarianism? There certainly was reason to think left-wingers had authoritarian censorship tendencies. In fact, researchers had long noted the authoritarian proclivity of left-wingers towards censorship, especially in North America. Commenting on a Canadian sample, for example, Peter Suedfeld and colleagues said way back in 1994: 'Supporters of Canada's most left-wing (social democratic) major federal party were most favorable to censorship ... the least support for censorship was indicated by the adherents of the federal Progressive Conservative party, whose position is that of moderate conservatism.'[23]

Did this left-wing authoritarianism ultimately produce a backlash? In the US it did. Our lab's research shows how Donald Trump won, in part, as a reactionary response to left-wing authoritarian communication norms.[24] In the run-up to the 2016 election, we asked a group of people to tell us whether they were going to vote for Clinton or Trump. Now, our group of participants was on average slightly liberal, and left to their own devices they tended to support Clinton. But there was a catch: for some of the participants, we randomly assigned them to a condition where they had to think about restrictive communication norms – political correctness or 'woke' norms – that censor what people can say. So what happens when you make people think about authoritarian liberal communication norms?

You might imagine that thinking of *liberal* communication norms would make a *left-leaning* sample more likely to vote for *liberal* candidate Hillary Clinton. You'd be wrong about that.

Thinking about liberal communication norms made people more likely to vote for Donald Trump. Why?

Because people were afraid their right to say what they want was being whittled away by liberals, and reminding them of 'woke' communication norms made both conservatives *and* liberals want to reach out to someone they believed would restore that right. Even someone they might think was authoritarian, like Donald Trump. And it wasn't just our lab that noticed this – polling data suggested that one of the appeals of Donald Trump was that he represented a voice to stand up against authoritarian bullies.[25] In fact, 'feeling voiceless' was one of the best predictors of support for Trump, eclipsing variables such as age, race, and attitudes towards Muslims or illegal immigrants.[26] So when the left tried to suppress speech in an authoritarian manner via 'cancel culture' or 'political correctness', the result was clear:

Authoritarianism begat authoritarianism.

The same processes apply to the rise of left-wing authoritarianism. If you have a great deal of courage and a strong stomach for foul language, you can see this yourself by simply reading the comments people post below almost any political article in the US these days. To name just one example, this is a comment on an article for *New York* magazine's Intelligencer blog on the possibility of Republicans winning power in the 2022 or 2024 elections:

> The Democrats *can't and shouldn't* hand power back. If the Republicans 'win' back the house or Senate in 2022 or 2024, or Trump 'wins' in 2024, I won't believe it. Unless the Army and Democratic poll watchers are present at every polling place, I won't believe or accept for a second if Republicans 'win' in any but

the most red counties. I'll be chanting stop the steal and agitating right back at the GOP freaks, and I hope the Dems will be right there with me. Otherwise, this country and our way of life will be over thanks to these suckers following basically a con man.[27]

When another commenter suggested that Democrats needed to win in fair elections or not at all, this same commenter replied: 'I'm not handing them power when they cheat. Anyway, I'd rather live under the Soviets than the Taliban.' This commenter represents a growing percentage of Democrats these days. They'll throw the whole democratic system away because the other side is so bad, so threatening, that they'll refuse to accept any election results. As long as the authority figure who keeps power is on *their* side, the rule of law doesn't matter. Why? Because the other side – the Republican side – is the 'Taliban'. It's because they are threatening. Give us the authoritarian Soviets because we don't want the authoritarian Taliban. The threat of authoritarianism begets authoritarianism.

This is probably why the country is spiraling into an authoritarian abyss. Consider this fact: Joe Biden and Donald Trump are two of the most simple-minded presidents of all time. This isn't speculation: Our lab scored the complexity of all presidential State of the Union speeches, presidential debates, and inaugural speeches for a recent paper. We found that Joe Biden and Donald Trump were both historically low in complexity.[28]

Why is that? There is a tendency to assume that, well, they are both simple-minded guys. It's something about their personalities that causes them to be simple. Maybe Trump's just a jerk and maybe Biden's just not cognitively capable. And our data reveals that part of it *is* unique to them. But that's not most of the story. The majority of the reason they are simple is not about them at all. It's about *us*. Indeed, our data show something quite remarkable: We can predict both presidents' low complexity from a long, slow decline in complexity that has been occurring across all presidents in both parties. These two men didn't just come out of nowhere. There is a historical trend of downward complexity of US presidents – and they are largely just a continuation of that trend. It may be that they have personalities that are simple, but they were elected by us. And we *wanted* that. They *are* us.

It is probably not a coincidence that this downward trend in complexity coincides with a historical rise in political polarization. The more opposing political groups in the US hate each other, the simpler their politicians become. Authoritarianism begets authoritarian simplicity. Hatred reproduces itself.

And what is happening in my country is clear – and has lessons that reverberate around the globe for all people at all times in all places. Having gotten mired in this punitive authoritarianism cycle, we are having a hard time finding a road pointing away from it. At this point, it hardly matters who started it. The real question is: Can we get out of it?

The answer is yes. We *can* get out of it. But one of the things that follows from the authoritarian threat cycle is that solving our problem inevitably means we have to deal with *both* conservative and liberal authoritarianism *together*. It will hardly do us any good to stop the bear that's attacking us if the equally dangerous tiger eventually kills us. If we stop left-wing authoritarianism by creating right-wing authoritarianism, we're just as doomed as we would be if the left-wing authoritarians win. If we stop right-wing authoritarians only to fall prey to a left-wing authoritarian nightmare, our world will still be a bad place. Because this bear and this tiger come out largely in response to each other, we have to deal with them at the same time.

As we'll see in the next two chapters, I'm going to talk about exactly what we can do to make that happen. The road is difficult; but a difficult road is not an impossible one.

CHAPTER 8

THE PARADOX OF THE AUTHORITARIAN DETERRENCE SYSTEM

A bully is nothing more than a bunch of bull with a Y attached to its rear.

> – Lorin Morgan-Richards, American author

Bullying is about judging. It's about establishing who is more worthy or important. The more powerful kids judge the less powerful kids. They judge them to be less valuable human beings, and they rub their faces in it on a daily basis.

> – Carol Dweck, psychologist

Bullies do not just wake up and decide to be one. They are people who have or are experiencing emotional or verbal abuse. All you can do is not retaliate but show them love. Doing so, allows them see what they are missing and need.

> – Kemi Sogunle, author of *Beyond the Pain: A Return to Love*

The bullies literally cram their will down the throats of those who are weaker.

> – James Dobson, founder of conservative Christian
> organization Focus on the Family

Each of us deserves the freedom to pursue our own version of happiness. No one deserves to be bullied.

> – Barack Obama, former US president

Bullies are always to be found where there are cowards.

> – Mahatma Gandhi

People have no end of things to say about bullies.

A quick internet search reveals varying theories about where they come from, what drives their behavior, whether they have a self-esteem problem, and how best to deal with them. In many cases, there is very little agreement on any of these issues. But there is absolutely one thing that *everyone* agrees about.

Bullies are terrible. No one likes bullies at all.

The above set of representative quotes come from a psychologist, two popular authors, a former Democratic American president, a conservative Christian, and a Hindu spiritual leader. There are many varied things said about bullies from these many varied people, but one thing is clear: None of them like bullies very much.

You see, as humans, we have a natural aversion to mean people who want to bully us. And this fact turns out to be very important in understanding how best to stop authoritarianism. Because the problem with trying to stop bullies is that, sometimes, other people may think that *we're* the bully – even when that isn't what we want. We have a natural authoritarian deterrence system that kicks in when we perceive bullies are around, and it doesn't always work just right.

Thus, before we can fully grasp how best to accomplish our perfect soldier ideal from the last chapter – before we can talk about the best way to use our bright sword without creating more authoritarians – we need to better understand the mechanisms by which average people resist authoritarianism. We need to understand the *natural authoritarian deterrence system*.

The Authoritarian Pressure Paradox

Imagine you attended a talk with 20 other people, and the speaker opened his talk like this: 'I think Rocky Road ice cream is the best kind of ice cream ever! And I know everyone agrees with me. In fact, before I begin, I want every single one of you to come up here and take the "Rocky Road Ice Cream" pledge. In front of everyone, I want you to state that you really like Rocky Road ice cream. If you don't do this, you won't be allowed to stay and there will be serious repercussions for you. Don't mess with me.' And then you are called up in front of the room and ordered to avow the glories of Rocky Road ice cream. What would be the result?

Psychological research provides a clear answer. Three things would happen. First, to a surprising degree, you and everyone else would publicly comply with the order and state that you loved Rocky Road ice cream. This fact is important. People are generally bad at predicting what they would do in these kinds of situations, because most people imagine they would not give in to such an obvious authoritarian pressure. But it turns out that overwhelming evidence suggests you and nearly everyone else would comply. Decades of research using the famous Milgram 'shock the learner' paradigm – and related offshoots – shows the quite alarming degree to which people will obey authoritarian pressures no matter how absurd they seem.[1]

So one of the effects of authoritarian pressures is short-term compliance. However, these pressures also invoke a kind of psychological paradox. The very thing that makes them effective in the short term also undermines their long-term survival potential. Because while simultaneously increasing short-term compliance, authoritarian pressures invoke two processes that act as a long-term deterrence system against the ultimate success of those pressures. Psychologists call the first response 'reactance' and the second response 'informational contamination', and together they comprise our natural deterrence to authoritarianism.

To understand both their potential and their danger, we need to dig a little deeper into the psychology behind these responses.

Psychological Reactance

The first response is the obvious one. Even if you complied, you'd be pretty angry at being forced to state an opinion against your will. People don't like their freedom to say what they want to say being taken away, and it makes them mad. So even if you didn't express your anger at the meeting – and evidence suggests you wouldn't – you'd be super-ticked off behind the scenes at having been made to do something against your will. Psychologists call this *reactance*. *Reactance* occurs when people think their freedom has been taken away. They naturally feel angry because they want their freedom back.

Surprisingly, it doesn't matter how you feel about the thing you are ordered to do. You may actually agree with that thing. But it turns out that reactance will occur anyway, if you are *forced* to do it. The founder of reactance theory, Jack Brehm, noted this long ago.[2] He asked the reader to imagine Mr. Smith choosing a candy bar at a vending machine. Mr. Smith wants a Snickers bar. He walks up to choose, but before he can push the button, his favorite Snickers candy bar drops out. You think he'd be happy, right? Without having to do anything, the Snickers bar he wanted appeared like magic for him. But Brehm notes that what actually would happen is the opposite. Mr. Smith would instead use his money to purchase a *Mars* bar. The Snickers bar becomes less appealing. That's because he would have reactance against having his choice taken away and subsequently his favorite candy would become less favored. He'd thumb his nose at the universe by picking something other than what he was forced to take.

Research bears out his analogy. For example, in an interesting study, researchers had participants walk down an aisle to choose a candy bar from a vending machine three times.[3] In one condition, the aisle was very narrow, but in another it was very wide. Left to their own devices, most people just pick their favorite candy bar three times. That's what people in the wide aisle did. But people in the narrow aisle felt a loss of freedom. They felt constrained in their movements by the narrowness of the corridor. And when we feel a loss of freedom, we often try to re-establish that freedom by showing we can choose. Thus, when faced with a narrow aisle, people were more likely to choose different candy bars each time. They did this even though the source of their reactance was unrelated to their candy bar choice, and even though this meant they were often choosing something they liked less.

Thus, in our hypothetical example, the key issue isn't whether you like Rocky Road ice cream or not. You may agree with the authoritarian speaker that Rocky Road ice cream is the best, or you may disagree. Either way, you are going to feel reactance. Either way, you are going to be ticked off that your freedom to choose was taken away. Either way, you are going to feel those walls closing in and want to re-establish your own right to choose. You might comply with the request in the short term; but the reactance seed has been planted. Your initial compliance is paired with a lasting sense that you'd stop that stupid speaker from ordering you about if you could. The seed merely waits for the right opportunity, a moment when the speaker seems to no longer be in charge, to reassert its freedom.

Indeed, reactance is even more powerful when it is authoritarian in nature. In our research, for example, we presented people with business scenarios where we asked them to imagine being at an office. We found that when a boss at the office gave a nice suggestion, it didn't cause much reactance. But when that boss used authoritarian orders to bludgeon his employees into submission, it invoked a *lot* of reactance. And it did so regardless of whether or not participants took his 'side' on the issue in question.[4]

Thus, authoritarianism tends to invoke strong reactance – that's why reactance is a natural defense against it. It is the fairly routine consequence of authoritarian bullying.

Informational Contamination

Nothing is written in stone.

> – Sign on a walkway outside a coffee shop in
> Manchester, Vermont … written in stone[5]

223

The second psychological deterrent to authoritarianism is more subtle, but no less important. You would not only be irritated at being forced to do something (reactance), you'd also be unlikely to think that anything that happened in the meeting represented anyone's real opinion. The whole thing would seem *artificial* to you.

Consider the hypocritical signs that are a part of everyday life. If you search the internet, you can see signs next to a swimming pool that say 'Diving is Fun' right next to a 'No Diving' sign.[6] Or a man hanging a 'Safety First' sign while straddling dangerously a 10-foot high ladder. You can see signs that abandon even the pretense of logic and literally say 'No posting of signs'. *Nothing is written in stone* ... except for this sign written in stone.

Often, of course, these signs are merely attempts at humor or click-bait. (My personal favorite is the bumper sticker that says 'Hypocrites Against Bumper Stickers'.) However, whether humorous or otherwise, they illustrate an important psychological point. All else being equal, a 'Diving is Fun' sign might actually make us consider that diving *actually is* fun. Research bears that out: Repeated exposure to messages makes us more likely to believe those messages.[7] However, when that message is paired with a restriction telling us we can't dive – it makes us question whether or not the powers that be really *do* believe diving is fun. It undermines the value of the sign.

Our lab calls this phenomenon 'informational contamination'. The informational value you might otherwise have received from the 'Diving is Fun' message is *contaminated* by the prohibition on diving. You lose trust that the people posting the sign about the glories of diving *really* meant it. After all, if they thought so highly of diving, why completely prohibit it?

Sometimes informational contamination is more subtle. For example, consider the fitness center that has an escalator carrying its would-be exercisers up the stairs.[8] At some point, one wonders if the center is *really* serious about the importance of fitness. Why build an escalator to bypass a set of stairs if you really want people to get exercise?

Authoritarian pressures put metaphorical escalators in our cultural fitness centers. They put 'No Diving' signs next to their messages about how great driving is. Their very nature makes us distrust their messages. We think it is driven by some kind of ulterior motive that isn't related to fitness or diving at all.

To see how, let's go back to our Rocky Road ice cream example. Imagine that after the speaker ordered everyone to take the 'I love Rocky Road' pledge, every single person in the room, one at a time, came up and publicly endorsed the speaker's position and said they loved Rocky Road ice cream. That would mean that the speaker had succeeded in getting complete agreement. Authoritarianism had won – right?

Yes, but only temporarily. That's because one of the effects of that strategy is that you'd distrust what you watched. You'd view the fact that everyone loved Rocky Road with skepticism. Why? Because of informational contamination. I see that everyone 'took the pledge', but I think it was artificially manufactured. As a result, I don't trust it.

This is important because one of the biggest factors in psychological and cultural change involves our perception of how many other people hold a particular belief, or how many people practice a particular behavior. In my field, we call this the 'psychology of consensus'. Consensus says that we're far more influenced when we think a lot of people agree on something than when only a few people agree. This isn't irrational. It's actually quite sensible to assume the crowd has a point. There is a reason that most of the world likes ice cream and most of the world does not eat glass shards. Ice cream is generally delicious and glass shards are not. Thus, consensus provides a useful piece of information. It isn't perfect, but the odds are that if most people really like ice cream, you will too. If most people don't like glass shards, you won't either. We generally value knowing what lots of other people think because it gives us information about the thing they are thinking about.

Informational contamination undermines the value of consensus information by making it seem falsely manufactured. We can't trust it as much. And that is true even if everyone really does like Rocky Road ice cream. After all, it may well have been that everyone would take the Rocky Road pledge on their own, without coercion. But now I don't know, because – thanks to the authoritarian command – I'm inclined to distrust the information that I *do* know.

As a result, the very command that produces the pro-Rocky Road consensus simultaneously psychologically undermines it in the long term. In the short term, the command produces its desired effect. But in the long term, I'm much more likely to obey the pledge if I really believe that Rocky Road is great, and I'm much more likely to believe it is great if I truly believe everyone else thinks it is great. But I don't, because I attribute the fact that everyone said they liked it to the authoritarian bully. That consensus information is contaminated.

Consequences of the Authoritarian Deterrence System

Both reactance and informational contamination contribute to why authoritarianism often backfires. For example, in one set of studies, we placed participants in a fictitious business scenario.[9] Participants were randomly assigned to one of two conditions. In one condition, their boss in the scenario demanded that everyone on the participants' committee vote in a particular way on a crucial business decision. In the other scenario, he told them to vote how they wanted. Contrary to decades of research on obedience, the authoritarian command actually backfired and caused more deviance instead. The reasons this happened were simple: The authoritarian command invoked participants' *authoritarian deterrence system* – it caused them to feel reactance and experience informational contamination. Importantly, this backfiring effect didn't happen all the time in our studies. For example, it did *not* occur when participants believed they would still be under the power of the authoritarian boss moving forward. In that case, they still felt reactance and perceived informational contamination, but they were much more likely just to 'go along' with whatever he said. This shows that as long as the authoritarian wields immediate power in a situation, people will do what they are told. But once that veil is removed, there will be a rebound effect. Authoritarian commands work in the short term when the pressure can't be avoided. But it sows the seeds of its own undoing.

We've found similar results with respect to authoritarian stereotype messaging. For example, in one study we asked participants to imagine that an authoritarian professor ordered students to talk positively about a particular group. Compared to a control condition, participants who had been under the thumb of the authoritarian professor later wrote more negatively about the group in a 'letter' to a friend. Why? Because of reactance and informational contamination. Although they would of course comply with the professor's request in the short term, underneath the surface they felt annoyed at being forced to talk in a certain way and didn't trust the information they received about the groups. Authoritarianism backfired.

These kinds of processes have implications for real-world beliefs, too. For example, have you ever wondered why a subset of the population doesn't believe in human-caused climate change despite 97% consensus from scientists that the climate is changing due to human causes? There has historically been a tendency to blame uneducated conservatives. But, while conservatives do believe less in human-caused climate change than liberals, our data suggest a completely different process altogether: Both liberals and conservatives often don't believe in climate change because they think the 97% consensus results from authoritarian pressures.[10] They believe it is manufactured for an authoritarian cause. They believe it exists due to ideological pressures and not scientific analysis. As a result, across partisan lines, people don't trust the 97% consensus – they think the information it represents is contaminated. (They are, in my experience, at least partly right to believe that. As we've seen in this book, a lot of modern academia is indeed driven by authoritarian left-wing ideology. I don't trust that 97% consensus nearly as much as I used to because of exposure to repeated left-wing authoritarian pressures.)

Similarly, in the previous chapter, I discussed how Trump won in part because people didn't like the authoritarian messaging on the left. In that study, we specifically tied this to the authoritarian deterrence system. The primary reasons that both liberals and conservatives said they voted for Trump involved reactance (and, to a lesser degree, informational contamination). People didn't like being told what they could say – and they liked that Trump stood for them. Their vote for him was, in part, a vote from reactance. It was their natural authoritarian deterrence system that caused left-wing authoritarianism to backfire.[11]

You can see this authoritarian deterrence system in action outside of laboratory experiments, too. What is the consequence of authoritarian mandates? They cause initial short-term compliance; but in the long term, they sow the seeds of discord. Consider the issue of vaccines during the pandemic. Did vaccine mandates increase vaccination rates? Of course. Listen to star basketball player Andrew Wiggins, who had to get the vaccine to keep his job playing for the Golden State Warriors:

The only options were to get vaccinated or not play in the NBA. It was a tough decision. Hopefully, it works out in the long run and in 10 years I'm still healthy. It feels good to play, but getting vaccinated, that's going to be something that stays in my mind for a long time. It's not something I wanted to do, but I was forced to … I guess to do certain stuff to work, I guess you don't own your body. That's what it comes down to. If you want to work in society today, then I guess they made the rules of what goes in your body and what you do. Hopefully, there's a lot of people out there that are stronger than me and keep fighting, stand for what they believe, and hopefully, it works out for them.[12]

Andrew Wiggins *got* vaccinated. But he certainly doesn't sound like someone who felt good about it. And in fact, almost a year later – even after his team won a championship that season and he was named an All-Star for the first time – Wiggins still expressed frustration that he was forced to get the vaccine and still said he didn't want it.[13] Well, if you force someone to do something, they often do it. So that's one consequence. But people still hate it.

And you can see that by asking those people who, in Wiggins's words, keep fighting why they weren't vaccinated. A group of researchers from Rutgers, Northwestern, and other prestigious universities did just that: They ran an excellent set of surveys asking the unvaccinated why they were not vaccinated.[14] One of the central reasons? They didn't trust the information sources. In the words of the researchers: 'Underlying many of the concerns regarding the Covid-19 vaccines is a lack of trust in the institutions that oversee and vouch for their safety.'

Authoritarian shaming was the engine that drove this informational contamination. Headlines like the following were commonplace: 'The Unvaccinated Are Not Oppressed – They're Dangerous'.[15] Among the reasons stated in this medical outlet for hating the unvaccinated is that 'the fact that anti-vaxxers and anti-maskers can protest proves that they are not oppressed'. So does the fact that George Floyd protestors protest prove that they also are not oppressed? The whole article reads like a wild, illogical, vindictive attack on people who turn out to be mostly reasonable folk who just don't like having their medical decisions made by political authoritarians who hate them. This article, incredibly, was claimed to be 'fact checked' by a credible source, even though it is a shockingly vitriolic diatribe, the vast majority of which could be proven false quite easily.

And academics spend countless hours wondering why all those unvaccinated people are hesitant? The answer is clear: This was always about a lack of trust, and at the heart of that lack of trust was – and is – partisan authoritarianism. It's informational contamination. People believe the information they receive is 'contaminated' by partisan motives. I know people myself who *wanted* to take a vaccine for Covid, but when they asked questions about vaccine safety – reasonable questions – they were shut down and basically told to get the shot or else. They were treated like idiots for asking an honest and perfectly reasonable question. Those vaccine-hesitant people basically said, 'Well, I can't trust the system, so I better wait until more information comes out.'

Thus, it is hardly surprising that, although authoritarian vaccine mandates inevitably produce a short-term increase in vaccination rates, they also undermine public trust in the health system and might cause lower *future* vaccine rates. Dr Susy Hota – the medical director of infection control and prevention at Toronto's University Health Network – said it this way: 'The best way is instilling in people the importance of getting the vaccine while still making it a voluntary thing. Because if you were to make it mandatory you're really undermining confidence and trust, and that's going to have an effect in future vaccines and uptake as well.'[16]

Similarly, the importing of the American antiracist protest of 'taking a knee' before English football games accomplished a unified outward expression of consensus in the short term – showing that England was united against racism. But it also caused people to question the already-existing English programs against racism, and further provoked a lot of reactance-based booing in England. One fan expressed his frustration this way: 'Booing is a way football fans can communicate dissatisfaction,' noting that he was expressing objection to 'an identity politics agenda that focuses on black people and skin colour, when as far as I am concerned we are all England fans regardless of colour. Some seem to genuinely believe booing is an act of racism – I reject that.' Another fan said: 'If I want to watch politics, I'd switch on Westminster Live.'[17] Thus, while successful in the short term, in the long term this authoritarian tactic that falsely gives the impression that all players support the practice (when some players do not like it at all, with one calling it 'degrading'[18]) is clearly already showing signs of backfiring long-term.

Along the same lines, we noted in Chapter 6 that parents had been gaslighted in Virginia with authoritarian tactics. While that worked in the short term in bludgeoning through an unpopular curriculum, the authoritarianism ultimately backfired: Running on a 'take back the schools for parents' campaign that essentially focused on capturing the spirit of reactance, the Republican gubernatorial candidate won a state that Republicans had lost by 10 percentage points only a year earlier.

In all these cases, you can see the backfire-inducing authoritarian deterrence system at work. Authoritarians try to bludgeon the populace. The populace generally complies superficially, but behind the scenes, the seeds are planted for the ultimate overthrow of the authoritarian mandates. People experience reactance and informational contamination – they are buffered against the authoritarianism – and often, eventually, those things take out the authoritarianism itself.

Why Not Just Let Authoritarianism Fail?

As we've illustrated, humanity has a kind of psychological deterrence system that helps us fight authoritarianism. When authoritarianism appears, so inevitably do reactance and informational contamination. This means that authoritarian tactics, as primary tools for producing a stable society, are seductive – but ultimately self-defeating.[19] There is a sense that every specific authoritarian movement is doomed to fail in the long term. Reactance and informational contamination are, from this point of view, our allies in this fight. It is healthy to want to take your freedom back. It is good to distrust sources who are trying to mislead you for their own gain. These things serve as safeguards against totalitarianism.

Given that seemingly good news, you may think: Well, what have we to worry about then? If authoritarianism is doomed to fail, why not just sit back and wait for it to fail?

There are two primary reasons why *merely waiting* is a bad plan. First, the deterrence system is just one factor in the spread of authoritarianism. Sometimes these psychological deterrents are overwhelmed by other factors. We've already talked about some of these factors in Chapter 7 – factors such as fear and permeability. To return to our virus metaphor, fear is like a super-spreader event that provides the perfect environment for massive quick dispersal of the authoritarian virus. Permeability basically weakens the immune deterrence system of the people in the path of the disease. So we can't just count on psychological reactance and informational contamination to do the whole thing; sometimes people may feel those things, but the cost–benefit analysis will lead them to keep accepting authoritarianism longer than they otherwise would. History is replete with long-standing authoritarian regimes, and democracy by comparison is much rarer. So just because authoritarianism has a proclivity towards being psychologically self-defeating, that doesn't mean it can't ultimately win for long periods of time. We need to be more proactive.

A second reason is even more important. Authoritarian pressures succeed in building an artificial consensus. They can very quickly change civilizations. Authoritarians aren't successful by accident. Fear is a powerful motivator. So authoritarians can definitely build societies. But what they produce is ultimately very destructive for *everyone*.

The structure produced by authoritarian pressures is like a building made of glass. The process of constructing the building, however, produces small but indistinguishable cracks in the glass panes. The structure may seem fine on the surface, but those cracks – reactance and informational contamination – mean that certain kinds of pressure, applied at just the right points, can cause the glass structure to break. When that happens, the whole structure comes crashing down. If the authority figure loses power, or the laws change, or the cost–benefit ratio of the population changes, or any number of winds cause the people to angrily rise up, then the artificially built glass structure will completely collapse.

And here's why we should not just sit back and wait for authoritarianism to fail on its own: Because when authoritarianism breaks like *that*, it destroys everything. Authoritarianism doesn't break into democracy; it breaks into chaos. And as we've seen, fear and chaos are simply a formula for a *new* authoritarian to rise in its place. We can't merely let authoritarians build buildings that will eventually break to pieces, because we all go down with them. If we don't have something better in its place, other authoritarians will build other buildings out of the same glass formula.

This provides an important lesson for us. The authoritarian structures currently being put in place by left-wing authoritarians are, in one sense, very fragile. They have used fear-mongering to produce a large artifice that has cracks in it. And we can break those cracks. We're going to talk about some success stories in doing so in the next chapter.

But there's a catch. If we destroy that authoritarian building only to create a new authoritarian building, *our* building will also be just as fragile. We're going to have to punch back. We're going to have to use the sword. That means our building will have some scratches in it too. That means that every time we use tactics that require pressure – and we will have to use such tactics – there is the potential to invoke reactance and informational contamination. When we do that, we are in danger of ruining our own structure.

Our building metaphor suggests two different metaphorical solutions. First, it means that we need to minimize the number of psychological scratches in our own structure by not overdoing our use of high-pressure tactics. And second, it means that we need to build the structure, not out of panes of glass, but out of bricks and mortar, stone and steel. We need better building blocks. It is fine to live with a few scratches – in fact, it is necessary. Beating authoritarianism will not always be pretty. But if our whole house is made of authoritarian panes of glass, it *will* fall eventually. To ultimately beat authoritarianism, we have not just to deal with the authoritarians at the moment, but also to think of the potential future authoritarians, the ones that we might create down the road, the ones who will show backfiring to our pressure tactics.

Building a Free Society That *Lasts*

The challenge here is great. When we punch back at authoritarians, we often use tactics that – like authoritarian pressures – can create informational contamination and reactance. The punch may work, but it also has side effects. Now, we know that informational contamination and reactance aren't bad on their own. In fact, they are generally a healthy response to bad authoritarianism. As we've said, they are as much our allies against tyranny as they are dangers. They are what motivate us to stand up to bullies in the first place.

But our deterrence system often can't tell the difference between someone *implementing* authoritarianism and someone *resisting* authoritarianism. A lot of evidence shows that we tend to overestimate the threat from other people – especially when we are scared.[20] We're not always good at telling the difference. Thus, when you create a law to constrain your enemies from engaging in bullying, it may well appear to a non-bully on the other side as if you are being an authoritarian. And even decent people may then experience reactance and informational contamination to your metaphorical punch, even though you don't want that. Like an auto-immune system gone bad, it is possible that the disease will simply cause us to collectively kill our own society. Despite your best intentions, you may end up creating a structure with so many cracks that it won't stand the test of time. We need to build a stronger building made of sterner stuff.

Our authoritarian deterrence system thus provides a clue for how we should approach this thorny problem. In the last chapter, I'm going to specifically tell you what psychological research says we can do to solve it. We're going to first cover some practical advice about what the punch looks like – and then we're going to discuss six psychological principles that, in a sense, serve as bricks and mortar for building a democratic city that can *last*.

CHAPTER 9

HOW TO FIGHT FIRE WITH FIRE WITHOUT BURNING EVERYTHING DOWN

Fighting Obama's fire with fire of our own

– Title of an op-ed written by Ben Shapiro, 2010[1]

When people say 'let's fight fire with fire' it usually conveys the following message: If *they* are going to do something dirty, then *we* have to do something equally dirty to win.

As a metaphor applied to our current case, that would be a disaster. Authoritarianism begets authoritarianism. This particular fire will simply self-perpetuate until everything burns down. If our only method of fighting authoritarianism is another cycle of authoritarianism on the other side, the most logical outcome of fighting fire with fire is that the whole of Western civilization is going to burn.

It is natural to fight that way. It is understandable human nature to say, 'Well, they did that to us and so I want an authoritarian to do that to them, too.' So while people often prefer to keep their head down and work within the system, just as often, when they *do* decide they want to stop bullies on the other side, they often root for authoritarian bullies on their side. They are primed by the bullies who beat them up to want a bully to beat up the bullies.

Avoiding that outcome requires us to fight, not just liberal authoritarian bullies, but also that natural tendency in ourselves to become a bully. It requires us to use our sword, but to use it only to defend freedom – and no more. This requires a fundamental shift in all of us, right now, from caring about sticking our sword in someone else, to being willing to use our sword to defend something worth defending. We need lots of passion and courage, we have to be willing to fight – but we have to resist the urge to love fighting for its own sake.

The immediate practical difference between those two things is not noticeable. The immediate result of the person who uses their sword for authoritarian revenge and the person who uses their sword to defend that which is beautiful is that something gets stuck. But the long-term difference is literally the difference between creating a healthy and stable society and ... civil war.

So, as you read this, the real question you need to ask about our collective response to authoritarianism is this: Do you want the temporary satisfaction of crushing your enemies or do you want your children to grow up in a free society? Because ultimately, you cannot have both. Eventually, the freedoms you deny your enemies will be the freedoms your enemies deny your children. That is true whether you are currently fighting right-wing authoritarians, left-wing authoritarians, or both.

In this concluding chapter, we first offer basic advice for how to punch back, and reveal why there is hope that these methods can work. In the second part of the chapter, we talk about how these temporary victories will only produce a stable society if we use them in the right way.

Reasons for Hope: Evidence the Bright Sword Can Curb Left-Wing Authoritarianism

In his excellent book *The Authoritarian Moment*, Ben Shapiro offers three specific recommendations for fighting back at left-wing authoritarians.[2] He suggests that we need to (1) fight back with legal action to stop authoritarian bullies, (2) expand anti-discrimination laws to include political views so it is easier to stop bullies from winning, and (3) build alternative institutions so that large liberal companies aren't the only game in town.

Evidence suggests that people have heeded his advice. And it's working. This war can be won. There is reason for hope. Given what we've said about the psychological fragility of authoritarianism, this isn't entirely surprising.

Indeed, victories against left-wing authoritarianism are mounting. For example, Robert Fellner was a law student at George Mason University who didn't want to take a booster shot for Covid. So he was alarmed to learn that his university was going to require a third booster shot for students, or else students would face repercussions. In his words: 'It's very ironic. It was in my torts class where I learned the importance of having free and voluntary choice and informed consent. So when I got this letter from the president, I thought it was a pop quiz.'[3] But Fellner decided to do something about it. He started a petition opposing the mandates that was signed by over 1,000 students.[4] Then a national organization took up his cause, and very shortly afterwards, the mandate was quietly lifted.[5] Note that he likely wouldn't have won without growing institutional support and without the recent election of a new governor in Virginia. But those things, too, come from people financing organizations and voting for elected officials who don't like mandates. And the point is – he won. He could have done what almost all students across the country did during Covid, and simply endure the mandates. But he stood up to authoritarian bullies, got connected with other students and organizations who felt similarly, and beat them.

In Lowell High School in San Francisco, merit admissions were dropped because of 'white supremacy'.[6] However, these and other extreme measures caused super-liberal San Francisco to overwhelmingly recall and then replace its school board. Those school board members overturned the no-merit policy and went back to merit admissions. This was a victory over the authoritarian bullies on the left. But it wasn't easy. Wesley Yang said it this way: 'Thousands of normal parents, many of them Asian-American, had to endure being called white supremacists every day by unhinged activists for more than a year to reach this outcome.'[7] Yet, this group of parents endured long enough to beat the liberal bullies.

This battle isn't just being fought in the US, of course. As we noted in Chapter 1, one of the most authoritarian places during Covid was Canada. In fact, one news reporter (accurately, in my view) wrote that 'Canada had some of the most stringent coronavirus mandates in the world, including making vaccinations mandatory in federally regulated workplaces, shutting down businesses for months, and arresting citizens if they were found violating lockdown protocols.'[8]

But some Canadians fought back. They didn't just take it from the bullies. Truckers rather famously peacefully protested throughout the country. In Alberta, Danielle Smith, the premier of the province, announced that the days of such mandates were over – and even went so far as to apologize for the discriminatory behavior that happened to the unvaccinated during the pandemic. She also suggested that she would consider pardoning unvaccinated people who had been arrested or fined. In her words: 'I'm deeply sorry for anyone who was inappropriately subjected to discrimination as a result of their vaccine status. I am deeply sorry for any government employee that was fired from their job because of their vaccine status, and I welcome them back if they want to come back.'[9] This change in policy away from authoritarian mandates never would have happened if individual people in Alberta and across Canada had not stood up against these mandates.

Authoritarianism is alive and well in our southern neighbor, Mexico, as well. Christian Cortez Pérez had earned a psychology degree and license from a large public Mexican university, the Autonomous University of Baja California (which, Americans may be surprised to find out, is in Mexico, not the American state of California). In fact, he was the valedictorian of his class, and as such, gave the speech at his graduation ceremony. In his speech, he espoused some conservative values, such as saying: 'Today we are deep into a real anthropological struggle to redefine the human being, the human person, man, through the implementation of ideologies and fashions of thought that always end up undermining dignity and freedom.' The backlash was swift, and many in the cancel culture crowd – mostly students and professors – released a 'manifesto' that called on the university to remove his merit award and scold him to larger psychological organizations. But he fought back – and the university sided with him. He said in response: 'I am overjoyed that the University has recognized that I committed no wrong in exercising my free speech rights to speak about issues of profound moral concern from the graduation podium. What happened to me shows how dangerous it is when professors with agendas try to punish students with whom they disagree.'[10]

These are just a few examples of how left-wing authoritarians are starting to lose their grip all over the world. But simply winning back power from them is not enough. We need to establish something better to avoid another round of authoritarian threat. It's not enough to punch; we need to punch well, and for the right reasons. We can't merely tear down our enemies' building, only to build our own building out of another big pane of glass; we have to build it back with better stuff. So next we discuss how we can fight authoritarianism without ultimately descending into chaos.

Fighting Fire with Fire the Right Way: Principles for *Truly* Overcoming Authoritarianism

We have seen that *fighting fire with fire* is disastrous if we view it as a license to indiscriminately use the same dirty authoritarian tactics of our opponents. But the *fight fire with fire* metaphor is helpful if we trace the expression back to its earliest known usage.[11] Originally, the expression didn't mean 'fight a fire by shooting a flamethrower at the fire itself'. In fact, at its root, it meant fighting a fire by pre-emptively burning an area in a carefully controlled way, to stop the spread of a larger fire from getting out of control. Forest service agencies use this method all the time – they burn areas selectively that might be prone to fire in order to provide a barrier that stops the whole forest from burning down.

This metaphor applies to our present case. It is going to take some vigorous fighting to stop left-wing authoritarianism. Some of that fighting may well look like fire itself. But the ultimate goal of fighting fire with fire is to get rid of fire. Some of the things that combat authoritarianism effectively might, on the surface, have the potential to lead to more authoritarianism. They are firm. They involve laws. They involve fighting back. They even involve dictates. I am not suggesting we just lie down, sing 'Kumbaya', and hope everything gets better. We need to act and act vigorously.

Ben Shapiro is aware of the dangers of this strategy, which is one of the many reasons I like his book. In fact, in the article about fighting fire with fire cited earlier, he wasn't actually talking about setting fire to Democrats. He was actually talking about lighting a fire under Republicans. In his book, he further notes many of the dangers of applying the strategies he recommends. He reluctantly argues for anti-discrimination laws because the idea of creating such extreme laws can be 'ugly'. He worries that creating alternative institutions could undermine the country's identity and backfire.

He's right to worry. If the ultimate aim is simply to replace one authoritarianism with another, then the whole forest will eventually burn. If we want to save this beautiful forest, we're going to have to explicitly use such methods in such a way that doesn't let that authoritarian fire get out of control.

Is that even possible? It's all well and good to say 'Fight back against the bully without becoming a bully yourself,' but practically speaking, what does this look like? It's probably occurred to you that some of our divisions are based on very serious disagreements about what we ought to do. Abortion, war, disease, racism – these and other issues are incredibly important. And they are deep issues on which people have very real and deep feelings. Research doesn't suggest we should just stop putting public pressure on everyone, have no laws, and hope we can 'all just get along'! Sometimes, pressure is necessary and you may have to risk divisions to accomplish some greater goal. Sometimes, you may have to pass laws to curb authoritarians or to see your own side through. Sometimes, top-down pressures are necessary. As we've seen, those laws will inevitably cause a few scratches in your structure. There is no magic pill to cure all that ails us.

However, the work we've discussed so far suggests a few principles about how best to fight authoritarianism in order to build a stable, non-authoritarian society. If you think abortion is so bad that it is murder, you shouldn't give up on your goal. But you *should* approach it in as non-authoritarian a way as possible. If you think abortion is such a fundamental right that taking that right away is a violation of the Constitution, then you shouldn't give up on your goal. But you *should* approach it in as non-authoritarian a manner as possible. Because we know the psychological consequences of top-down pressures, because we know the psychological outcomes of metaphorical punches, we know how best to use them to maximize their value and minimize their consequences. Thus, in this closing section, we will discuss the psychology of how to build a society where people can disagree without devolving into authoritarianism. How can we practically fight authoritarianism in such a way that it doesn't create a new generation of authoritarians? What are the best methods for fighting authoritarianism vigorously – and yet doing so in a way that doesn't end in another authoritarian cycle? And in this final section, I'm going to offer six principles that should guide our fight against authoritarianism on both sides.

PRINCIPLE #1: PRESSURE ONLY AS MUCH AS YOU HAVE TO, PERSUADE AS MUCH AS YOU CAN

Realistically speaking, most movements use both top-down pressure and bottom-up, 'grass roots' persuasion. The present approach suggests, however, that top-down pressure should be used judiciously and with the full awareness of its long-term psychological cost. Metaphorically bludgeoning people with pressure, laws, authority dictates, or military force to achieve goals is sometimes necessary; but it always comes with a cost. Thus, agreement pressure should be treated like a powerful and expensive drug that may or may not cure a disease, but has guaranteed terrible side effects. Decisions to strategically use it to create large-scale public change should therefore be determined in part by the nature of the disease (do not attempt to use something divisive in the long term on something comparatively unimportant) and by how necessary the risks are for a possible cure (do not attempt to use something so divisive if other and better means might work).

– Conway et al. (2021). 'The agreement paradox: How pressures for agreement can ultimately divide us'[12]

We've seen that when you use authoritarian-like methods, it can produce new authoritarians.

This means that any kind of perceived pressure from the top down – even well-intended pressure – has potentially deadly side effects. As a result, as we have previously written in the book chapter quoted above, the use of such pressure should be viewed like a very powerful drug that may help cure a disease, but which has known side effects. Anytime we are going to curb authoritarianism with such tactics, it should be done with this cost in mind.

Consider the case of WePay, a subsidiary of America's largest bank, JPMorgan Chase. WePay removed the account of the conservative organization Defense of Liberty, saying it was engaging in 'hate, violence, racial intolerance, terrorism, or financial exploitation of a crime, or items or activities that encourage, promote, facilitate, or instruct others regarding the same'.[13] And what was Defense of Liberty's egregious crime? What was so hateful and terrorist-like? Holding a political rally that featured Donald Trump, Jr. So basically having a conservative political rally was, in fine authoritarian fashion, considered a hate crime and financially ostracized by the country's biggest bank.

What happened next is instructive. The state of Missouri said fine, if you want to exclude 60% of our citizens, then you can get out. And JPMorgan Chase quietly relented and reinstated the organization's account: 'After further review, we determined that this organization didn't violate the terms of service, and we are reaching out to the client to discuss reinstating the account. To be clear, we have never and would never close an account due to a client's political affiliation.'[14]

Note that, on the surface, this method of fighting back might seem to lead in an authoritarian direction. Conservative Missourians basically said, *If you are going to bully us, then we're going to bully you right back.* As most people who have been bullied on a playground know, sometimes it takes standing up to the bully to stop them.

Such fighting back is of course necessary. However, here is the key point. Tactics that could potentially lead to authoritarianism should be used like fire – with the full knowledge that they may actually burn the whole thing down. As we discussed earlier, such authoritarian tactics have known negative downstream consequences, as revealed by decades of social psychology research. Therefore, they should be purposefully minimized and only used in conjunction with other non-authority-based tactics. Creating laws banning Critical Race Theory or threatening to kick JPMorgan Chase out of your state may be useful to stop the authoritarian disease, but they are like a powerful drug that should be used with the knowledge of its potentially fatal side effects.

Only use such tactics in as much as they are necessary, and no more. The goal of threatening to remove JPMorgan Chase is to stop authoritarian bullying. But conservative Missourians shouldn't use their power beyond that. They shouldn't, for example, try to turn the tables on liberals and start banning liberal organizations that supported JPMorgan Chase's initial actions, or in other ways to exclude liberals from the financial public sphere. If the goal is to maintain a stable democratic society, then we must fight fire with fire only when necessary to stop direct attempts at authoritarianism; we must never use fire for any other purpose.

Equally as importantly, while such top-down tactics are often necessary, it is nonetheless vital to persuade as much as possible. We should never give up simply trying to convince people with rational argument. Decades of research on persuasion teaches us why. That research, often cast under the rubric of the Elaboration Likelihood Model of persuasion, reveals that although you can persuade people through top-down heuristics, the persuasion that *lasts* is done by getting people to think for themselves. In one study, for example, they used that old social psychology classic and tried to persuade college students that an 'exit exam' for all college seniors – a test that students would have to pass in order to graduate – was a good thing. In one condition, they gave people good arguments given by a credible authority, while in another they got bad arguments given by a non-credible authority.[15] But there was a catch: Some participants were told the exam was being considered for next year (so the students would have to take it) while others were told it was being considered ten years later (so the students – presumably! – would be long gone and it would not affect them). This manipulation of 'personal relevance' changes the likelihood that students will *think hard* about the arguments.

What happened in this study is instructive for our discussion. Immediately after the persuasion attempt, whether students thought hard about the arguments or not, they were persuaded more by the good arguments from the credible authority than the bad arguments from the less credible authority. But when the researchers measured the same participants two weeks later, those attitudes only persisted for one group – the group who had been told that the test might apply to them and thus had thought about the actual arguments. In fact, the seeming persuasion from the group that had not thought about the arguments had almost entirely evaporated in two weeks, so that they were essentially indistinguishable from a control condition that had gotten no arguments at all! As one group of researchers said in summarizing this study: 'This was expected because the low relevance subjects should have been influenced mostly by the favorable or unfavorable cues in the message and these peripheral route attitudes should decay over time.'[16]

This and other research shows that if you want to create attitude change that lasts, you have to get people to think hard about stuff. You can't just bludgeon them with how credible a source is – like trying to get people to believe in vaccines because 'the CDC said so'. You have to present good arguments to them and get them to think about those arguments. And the best way to get them to think about those arguments is to talk about something that *they* care about. That means you have to enter into their world, understand who they are, and rationally argue with them. If you don't, you might create a temporary blip in cultural change that looks like the real thing – but it is unlikely to last.

This means that you should never stop trying to win an argument in the public sphere, even if you have to punch hard as well. For years, I taught a class to incoming teachers at the University of Montana on how to teach. And one of the things I emphasized is that they should not tolerate a lot of bad behavior – but they should simultaneously explain to the class *why* they were willing to come down hard on class disruptors. If they tolerated students bullying and interrupting, their class would be a poor learning environment for everyone. So *explain* that. Don't ever stop giving reasons, debating, discussing, with other people. Persuade as much as you can. Many of my teachers found, as I did, that if you explain that to people, you actually have to use less power to control them. There is value to persuading people with real arguments. The more they understand, the less they feel the need to react against what you are doing, and the less informational contamination they feel.

PRINCIPLE #2: WIN GRACEFULLY

> But a great many of the hillmen had given themselves up; and they were afraid, and cried for mercy. The Men of the Mark took their weapons from them, and set them to work. 'Help now to repair the evil in which you have joined,' said Elkenbrand, 'and afterwards you shall take an oath never again to pass the Fords of Isen in arms, nor to march with the enemies of Men; and then you shall go free back to your land. For you have been deluded by Saruman. Many of you have got death as the reward of your trust in him; but had you conquered, little better would your wages have been.'
>
> The men of Dunland were amazed; for Saruman had told them that the men of Rohan were cruel and burned their captives alive.
>
> – J. R. R. Tolkien, *Lord of the Rings: The Two Towers*

Sometimes fighting is necessary. Sometimes you have to punch at the bully who is punching you. Punch hard; punch to win. Have courage. Be bold. Don't back down. But one of the clear implications of the psychology of authoritarianism we've discussed so far is this:

If you win, win gracefully.

The Men of Rohan had faced an authoritarian bully. They had fought their enemies and won. And when they won, they enacted rules with their power that would stop their enemies from doing that authoritarian thing again. They didn't just let things go back to the way they were. But note this: They also treated those enemies gracefully. They gave them their freedom back – in total – in their own lands. They didn't fight to bully. They fought to *stop* bullies. And the biggest difference between the bully and the good leader is this: When the good leader wins, they win gracefully.

It turns out that winning gracefully is actually necessary, not just for creating a stable society, but also for maintaining your own gains. Consider the case of Prohibition in the US. The Prohibitionists had gotten 75% of the states to pass a Constitutional amendment banning alcohol. I imagine that after they did that, they felt pretty secure that they'd won, and won permanently. It is extremely hard to get an amendment to the US Constitution passed, and it is extremely hard to undo once it is passed. So after a long fight to the top of the legal food chain, it certainly appeared that one side had one that debate.

But watch what happened next. The Prohibitionists didn't win gracefully. In fact, they bludgeoned their enemies.[17] They used the Ku Klux Klan to illegally seek out and punish violators. They engaged in a lot of authoritarian tactics. And behind the scenes, the predictable result grew. People began expressing reactance; lay juries tried to 'nullify' the law by judging violators as 'innocent'.

History is a funny thing, and we don't of course know for sure what would have happened if the Prohibitionists had been less authoritarian winners. Maybe their movement was doomed to fail on other grounds. But what we do know is this: Those people who were punitive winners, who sat high and mighty on their Constitutional victory, ultimately lost. Their amendment was overturned a mere 13 years later.

Prohibition is a cautionary tale for all of us. If you want to change things, no matter what thing you are changing, even if that thing is stopping bullies, then you may need to punch hard. You may need to change some laws from the top down. But if you win, win gracefully. Be thoughtful, not just of yourself, but of the people you beat. Yes, even if those people are authoritarians who attacked you, you ultimately gain more by being graceful than by being authoritarian in return.

History teaches what can happen both ways. For example, scholars have compared the victors' responses to their defeated enemies in World War I versus World War II. After World War I, the defeated Germans and her allies were treated very harshly. The victorious countries refused to end their blockade – a blockade that was starving millions of German citizens to death – until eight months after the fighting had ceased. Some estimates place the number of German citizens killed by this additional blockade as high as 250,000.[18] Further, the treaty they forced Germany to sign absolutely decimated the country, among other things demanding financial reparations to be paid to the victors.[19]

What was the result? The Nazis. More authoritarianism. World War II. The authoritarian threat cycle continued. Millions more lives lost on all sides.

After World War II, the allies took a different approach. Rather than merely sticking it to their enemies, the famed 'Marshall Plan' and other similar plans actually provided *for* the defeated nations. We sent over a million dollars to Germany.[20] We sent similarly large sums to Japan.[21] While historians have debated for decades exactly how much the revival of Germany and Japan can be attributed to this approach, it seems clear that it at least helped.[22] And the results are undeniable: Being gracious to our enemies in defeat changed our relations with those countries for the better. It helped them and it helped us.

Taken together, principles #1 and #2 suggest that not only should top-down tactics such as passing laws or making rules be minimized, but they should only be used rightly and in conjunction with other, clearly non-authoritarian tactics. Fire can and should be used; but that should not replace a healthy dose of water. You must sometimes risk cracks in your building; but build that structure with materials besides glass. Use really strong stuff.

Indeed, it is often what comes *after* the vigorous action that matters. What does Missouri do next? What does Virginia do next? That is the kind of question that ought to be on the mind of every anti-authoritarian. And everything we've said so far in *Liberal Bullies* provides a guide as to what should happen next: We should all put pressure for the next thing to be proverbial water to each of the five authoritarian traits discussed in this book.

So if conservative Missourians start harassing liberal citizens' banking status (inconsistent standard), or classifying liberal tweets as 'misinformation' (misinformation obsession), or demonizing liberals in a black-and-white way (simplicity), or refusing to listen to the legitimate concerns that liberals have with Trump authoritarianism (intellectual apathy), to name a few possibilities, then we are going to end up in another authoritarian cycle. Build with better stuff.

PRINCIPLE #3: PUSH THE COST-BENEFIT RATIO EARLY AND OFTEN

Information Technology Departments are the new authoritarians.
— Luke Conway, only half-jokingly

254

It's been years now, but I still remember when the first seemingly benign order came from my information technology department at my old job: Faculty would be required to perform routine updates on our computers. My personal work computer is the lifeblood of my job, so I didn't like this command. But it wasn't a huge deal and so I let it slide.

Over the years, these orders became incrementally more invasive. And I fell into a pattern: My response to all of these increasingly irritating orders was to write increasingly long and increasingly irritated response emails that illuminated the cost–benefit analysis of the policy in question. In all these emails, I would ask the IT persons to consider, not just the single-minded issue they solely used to justify their policies – 'network security' – but also the huge cost of the policies to faculty's ability to do their jobs. If the policies made it impossible for us to do our jobs, there would be little point in protecting our computers from outside influences to begin with.

But I never sent any of the emails. After writing each and every one of them, I decided that it just wasn't worth the fight and I took advantage of that useful feature on my computer known as the 'delete' key. I decided it was better to keep my head down and live to fight another day.

Now that I see the result (which I would have been able to predict if I had remembered the broken windows principle discussed in Chapter 7), I regret not sending those emails. Because, by the end of my time at my old job, IT had locked us out of our own computers by refusing us 'administrator' access. This meant, among other things, we could not even download things we needed to actually perform our jobs. To get anything downloaded, we had to get someone at IT to do it for us. That may not sound like much to you, but in a fluid field like mine where I have to download stuff for my job all the time, it was horrible. It was kind of like asking me to lead a basketball team to an NBA championship, but forcing me to spend half of every game putting in requests to continue wearing my shoes. Meanwhile, I miss half of each game and we keep losing.

This serves as a parable to our third principle: Don't be afraid to push the cost–benefit ratio in response to authoritarian dictates, even in small arenas – and do so early and often. Don't get sucked into the single-issue narrative that authoritarians often use. Remember that authoritarians use simplicity like a weapon. Thus, very little is more antithetical to authoritarianism than a complex cost–benefit analysis.

For example, as we've seen in this book, authoritarians tried to simplify discussions during Covid. Take lockdown strategies. What we should have been doing is presenting all the evidence of the pros and cons of various lockdown strategies. We should have been weighing the known costs, such as inevitable increases in child suicides, against the projected gains. But what we mostly *did* is lock people down and then tell them it was good for them. However, some brave scientists stood out against that simplistic background. One of them was highly cited researcher and pediatrician Ari Joffe, who early in the pandemic looked at the cost–benefit analysis of lockdown strategies as they pertained to public health. Note that he did not consider *political* costs such as freedom at all – his sole focus was on public health markers. The result? Here are his own words: 'Considering this information, a cost–benefit analysis of the response to Covid-19 finds that lockdowns are far more harmful to public health (at least 5–10 times so in terms of wellbeing years) than Covid-19 can be.'[23]

Focusing on the cost–benefit analysis has at least two advantages. First, cost–benefit ratios are more complex than single-issue analyses – and just as authoritarian simplicity begets more simplicity, so too can complex cost–benefit analyses help increase complexity (and in so doing, potentially decrease authoritarianism). Some subset of your 'authoritarian opponents' may actually be open to persuasion if you don't bludgeon them, but rather present them with a balanced cost–benefit ratio. Peter Suedfeld, Dana Leighton, and I once wrote a chapter designed to teach international negotiators how to best use the complexity or simplicity of their language to produce positive outcomes in stressful negotiations.[24] One of the things we emphasized is that it is important for negotiators to start with the complex picture, considering alternatives and looking at multiple variables. If they don't – if they start with a simple hammer – then they don't give the other side a chance to be persuaded.

Second, cost–benefit analyses force *us* to think through our own positions so that we can be fair to our opponents. Sometimes we might come to realize that our opponents have a point. In the Covid lockdown research noted above, Dr Joffe started out his project assuming lockdowns worked. But, as often happens with cost–benefit analyses, his own work made him reconsider his views. In his own words: 'I explained why I changed my mind about supporting lockdowns.'

There is value in thinking through more than one issue at a time, not just to help other people avoid authoritarian pitfalls, but also to help *us* avoid them.

At a broad level, one of the things this means is that all of us need to consider more thoughtfully the thresholds we have for restrictive laws and policies. For of course, we do actually need laws for the common good. We can't have people say, 'I'm cool with murder.' It's not authoritarianism to have laws that put people in jail for killing other people. Authoritarianism begins when you want to put other group's people in jail but not your own people. And yet, as we've pointed out in our own work, some laws may technically apply to all people but are actually quite targeted to small minority groups as applied in reality.[25]

Technically speaking, laws banning gay marriage apply to everyone: No one can engage in gay marriage. But practically, it only applies to a comparatively small group of people – people in a numerical minority group, that group of people who would marry same-sex partners if they were allowed. Similarly, Covid vaccine mandates technically apply to everyone. But practically, they disproportionately affect a small minority of people, that smaller group of people who do not want to get vaccinated.

This doesn't mean that all reasonable laws have to affect literally everybody. Most people aren't tempted to commit murder, and yet we still need laws prohibiting murder. What it *does* mean is that we need to have a thoughtful discussion about the costs and benefits of removing people's freedoms. In the case of gay marriage laws, there is no 'cost' that I can see to giving members of the LGBT+ community the same right as straight people to get married. And the benefits are clear – everyone gets the same level of freedom. It doesn't matter whether you agree with gay marriage or not, and I respect that there is diversity of opinion about the issue. But it doesn't seem to come close to any cost–benefit threshold for prohibiting it.

Vaccine mandates are more complicated because it is quite possible for the greater good to be served by enforcing them.

And yet in my country, we never had a serious conversation about what such strategies entail. There was some debate, as noted earlier, about the health benefits of lockdown strategies. But more importantly, that conversation should have weighed the importance of non-health variables like freedom. Public health officials have no more or no less expertise than average citizens in deciding the point at which public health concerns should override freedom. And yet we acted like those health officials were more qualified to speak about that complex issue and subsequently ceded them enormous power. But no one asked the rest of us. If they *had* asked me, I would have said: Let me take my chances with Covid, the risk isn't great enough to remove freedoms from us. I think we should generally accept more risk to live in a free society. I didn't like the Patriot Act because I thought I'd rather accept more risk of terrorism than cede that much power to the government. I didn't like vaccine mandates for the same reason.

My point isn't about those specific arguments for those specific policies; rather, I use them as exemplars to illustrate the bigger principle. We need to think a bit harder about the cost–benefit ratio for freedom versus safety in making our decisions on when to restrict freedoms. And if you are OK with your own freedoms being restricted on something you care about down the road – if you really don't mind the principle being applied to you and your group just the same as it will be applied to other groups – then that's good. Enact your restrictive laws. But if you wouldn't like it when others might do that to you in a parallel case, then voting for that law is voting for authoritarianism. Focus on the cost–benefit ratio for everyone, and we all benefit.

PRINCIPLE #4: STOP CARING ABOUT WHAT
PEOPLE *SAY* YOU ARE, AND START CARING
ABOUT WHAT YOU *ACTUALLY* ARE

Dr Timothy Wilson of the University of Virginia is one of the most respected, and in my view best, scientists in my field. And on December 21, 2021, he sent out a post to the SPSP listserv bemoaning the lack of NIH funding for behavioral research on Covid pertaining to vaccine hesitancy. And here's the key part of the post: 'Kudos to those of you who have nevertheless managed to investigate attitudes and persuasion, social norms, political partisanship, and other issues that speak directly to why some people are vaccine resistant.'

I'm a huge fan of Wilson's, but with all respect intended, this is the wrong way to go about doing things. We're treating vaccine resistance as if it were some kind of disease to eradicate or nuisance to destroy. The very term 'resistance' instead of 'hesitance' is a clue. These aren't rational people looking for evidence; they are terrorists in a resistance. If we have to ask why people are vaccine-resistant in the same way we ask 'Why can't I get rid of this pesky poison ivy?' or 'Why can't we overthrow this dictatorship?', then we'll never find a solution to the problem. So when Wilson compliments the people who try to understand vaccine resistance through persuasion, norms, and partisanship (translated: oh those pesky conservatives we don't like and their persuasive norms), he is actually complimenting the people who are doing it all wrong.

The right way is to ask a different question: Maybe they don't trust us *because we are untrustworthy?*

It does not often (or, at least, as often as I'd like) seem to occur to my colleagues that the populace at large thinks academics are partisans doing biased research because … academics actually *are* partisans doing biased research. That maybe the reason some people are vaccine-hesitant is that they reasonably do not believe the people producing the vaccine research are primarily interested in public health, but are instead tainted by political goals. That maybe those people distrust others who say they are *resistant* when in fact they are merely *hesitant*.

That should be a cautionary tale to anyone who wants to stop authoritarianism, left *or* right. If you want to deal with a problem, you should think less about the public perception issue (Why do they think that about us?) and more about the actual issue (Are we actually being biased scientists?). You should maybe think more about your own behavior and less about the way your behavior may or may not be perceived.

This has a specific application to those of us fighting left-wing authoritarianism. Namely: It's time to stop caring that liberal authoritarians call us racist – and start caring about actually not *being* racist.

In C. S. Lewis's famous book *The Screwtape Letters*, a seasoned devil writes letters of advice to a younger devil about how best to tempt a human to the dark side. In one of the letters, this elder devil (Screwtape) notes with some alarm that his young tempter's human 'patient' has developed a troubling tendency to become humble. (To a devil, humility is a terrible trait for a human to have because it is a path to virtue, and they don't want us to be virtuous.) Then Screwtape gives this advice about how best to handle the situation:

> I see only one thing to do at the moment. Your patient has become humble; have you drawn his attention to the fact? All

virtues are less formidable to us once the man is aware that he has them, but this is specially true of humility. Catch him at the moment when he is really poor in spirit and smuggle into his mind the gratifying reflection, 'By jove! I'm being humble', and almost immediately pride – pride at his own humility – will appear. If he awakes to the danger and tries to smother this new form of pride, make him proud of his attempt – and so on, through as many stages as you please. But don't try this too long, for fear you awake his sense of humour and proportion, in which case he will merely laugh at you and go to bed.

We are being hounded by devils telling us lies about ourselves, that our progress is actually not progress, that believing in a colorblind standard of judgment is actually racist. Although that term was not used, I was practically called a racist at a faculty meeting once. My crime? I had dared to point out that vaccine mandates disproportionately hurt African Americans. Think about that for a second. It was implied I was racist because … I expressed concern that our proposed mandates would negatively impact minority groups.

We need to stop caring about those lies. We need to laugh at ourselves and go to bed. In fact, I think we need a collective cultural reset. I think part of what we need to cure the devils that ail us is to laugh at them and go to bed, and then wake up the next morning and start over.

But – and here is the key thing – the point of doing that is to actually *focus on the racism problem itself.* If we decide to refuse the 'racist' label only to allow ourselves to actually *become* racists, then we'll start a whole new round of authoritarianism. It is reasonable to have reactance to claims that you are racist for believing that the best person should get the job. It is reasonable to show concern of informational contamination from sources that, frankly, *are* contaminated by political authoritarianism.

Let the immune system do its work. Let it target the right thing. Lay that fire down to protect the house. But if the end of all that is 'Heck, those people are wrong about me so I can do anything I want,' then the authoritarians win. In C. S. Lewis's parable, laughing at the devil didn't lead to less humility in the 'patient'. Quite the opposite: The devil was merely distracting the patient from true humility. If the patient would ignore the devil and laugh at him, the next day he would be more humble, not less.

The same is true here. The liberal authoritarians' race-baiting agenda actually distracts us from solving the very real problems we have in the country. We have a long and bad history of racism. We are still feeling the effects of that history right now. If we don't own that history honestly, then we will in fact become what they say we are. Their accusations of false racism merely serve to distract us from the real problems. So don't accept their labels. Stop caring what they say about you. It doesn't matter what they *say* you are. But it matters infinitely what you actually *are*. Just because they are wrong about you, that doesn't mean that racism isn't a real problem and that all of us don't need to work to overcome our biases.

This leads us into principle #5. It is important that we stop worrying what other people think about *us*. But it is vitally important that, in doing so, we still care what they think about *everything else*. It is important that we listen to people enough to try and find some common ground with them.

PRINCIPLE #5: ACTIVELY SEEK COMMON GROUND

> Liberals and conservatives actually share a lot more of their
> moral values than anybody thinks.
>
> – University of Utah professor Jesse Graham[26]

As we discussed at length in Chapter 5, authoritarianism thrives on group disagreement. Authoritarians want a black-and-white, us-versus-them world. And thus, one of the clear antidotes to the authoritarian disease is for us to try to find common ground. One of the building blocks of a truly sturdy structure are things we *share*. To seek out things we have in common – values we share, beliefs we hold dear, love of family, love of freedom, health, safety. Finding the things we share across political boundaries is like throwing water on the authoritarian fire. Or, to use our building metaphor, it is like constructing something out of bricks and mortar and not glass.

How realistic is that goal? Far more realistic than most people think. Conservatives and liberals have some real differences. But a lot of times, these ideological opponents are not as far apart as rumor makes them – and what actually separates them is more emotional than logical.

Researchers have known this for years. In 2012, prominent researchers Jesse Graham, Brian Nosek, and Jonathan Haidt compared the beliefs liberals and conservatives had about each other's moral values to liberals' and conservatives' *actual* moral values.[27] The result? Both sides get it wrong. Both sides imagine the other side is really different from them – but it turns out, they aren't really that different after all. More recent research from Northwestern University revealed a similar story: Liberals and conservatives think they are wildly different from each other, but they really aren't that different.[28] This is largely because they both imagine extreme examples of the other party, instead of the middle. Liberals think most conservatives are extreme, but actually, most of them are pretty moderate. Conservatives think liberals are extreme, but actually most liberals are pretty moderate. Both parties think the other party is comprised of people who talk politics all the time, but actually, most people from both parties don't talk a lot of politics. They're getting it all wrong. In the words of the researchers: 'The types of partisans who inspire the strongest animus actually constitute only a small minority of both parties.' It is thus unsurprising that other research shows Republicans believe roughly 44% of Democrats are labor union members when it is actually only 11%, or that Democrats believe that 44% of Republicans are very wealthy when it is actually only 2%.[29] It is also not surprising that both Republicans and Democrats believe the other party dislikes them a lot more than they do in reality.[30]

And even when there are differences, those differences can sometimes mask a hidden common ground. For example, affirmative action – the precursor to modern 'equity' movements – was a hot-button political issue in the 1990s and 2000s. Conservatives generally opposed it. Liberals generally supported it. However, DePaul University professor Christine Reyna and colleagues showed that this apparent ideological divide was actually hiding an ideological agreement.[31] When these researchers asked Chicago-area college students and residents about affirmative action, it turns out that both groups were largely using the same standard to judge it: Merit.

Affirmative action proponents thought that affirmative action programs allowed meritorious candidates from minority groups who otherwise would not get the chance at a job to be provided resources and opportunities. Affirmative action opponents thought that affirmative action programs caused meritorious candidates from majority groups to be excluded. But Reyna and colleagues did an interesting thing: They also presented items that were clearly merit-violating (such as hiring unqualified minorities) and those that were clearly merit-upholding (such as recruiting qualified minority candidates). And it turns out that *both* liberal and conservative groups actually support affirmative action more when it is merit-upholding, and they support it less when it is merit-violating. In the words of the researchers: '[B]oth supporters and opponents showed more support for merit-upholding rather than merit-violating manifestations of affirmative action.' Hidden beneath an apparent disagreement was a shared value. The disagreement wasn't about the value as much as it was about whether or not the policy was perceived as primarily enhancing or primarily degrading the value. That's a real disagreement – but there is a lot more shared common ground than one would expect.

This can be seen during the Covid era as well. Although in America our political divides are real, sometimes research might unintentionally exaggerate differences between liberals and conservatives. Indeed, it is possible that my own lab's research has done exactly that. We published a paper showing that 'Perceived Coronavirus Threat was negatively related to Political Conservatism, r = –0.33, p < .001'.[32] That means that American conservatives do (on average) show less concern with the disease than liberals. I wrote a blog piece about this paper for Heterodox Academy that got quite a bit of airplay, and it was based on explaining this difference.[33]

But does that mean that conservatives and liberals are all that different in their perceived threat of Covid? No. Actually, looked at another way, the data from the study show that conservatives and liberals generally viewed the disease as similarly threatening: On a 1–7 scale, where 4 is the midpoint, liberals scored an average of 5.3, while conservatives scored an average of 4.6. In other words, both groups took the disease moderately seriously – both groups scored roughly in the same category (above the midpoint, but not near the top, of the scale). Liberals scored slightly more so; but in fact, it was only seven-tenths of a point more so.

While of course the divide is real, it raises the question about whether or not as a society we are emphasizing and highlighting differences when, in fact, there might (sometimes) be more similarities between liberals and conservatives than differences. If liberals and conservatives are actually fairly similar on issues that have been as divisive as how threatening Covid is, maybe they are actually fairly similar on other seemingly divisive issues too?

And a litany of evidence suggests they are far more similar than rumor makes it. Take the issue of abortion. If you watched the news or read a few polls, you'd think Americans had completely irreconcilable differences about the issue. One poll found, for example, that only 39% of Republicans believe abortion should be legal in all or most cases, versus 89% of Democrats.[34] People see that and think, 'Wow, we're really far apart.'

But that poll belies a lot of hidden common ground. Looking deeper, you can see that most Americans on both sides actually support some elements of pro-choice and pro-life positions. One poll found 87% support for abortion when the woman's life is in danger and 84% support for exceptions in the case of rape or incest. Most Republicans supported these things too. On the flip side, another poll found that 81% of Americans believe abortion should be banned in the third trimester – that's plenty of Democrats. If you look behind the scenes, you can see that the majority of Americans actually want some abortion to be legal – and especially in tough cases involving the health and well-being of the mother – but they don't want unrestricted abortions all the time. There is probably more common ground than there is opposing ground.

All of this suggests that yes, it is possible to find common ground. And research also demonstrates how this can work. One study found that simply making people aware that the other group didn't dislike them as much as they thought reduced their own sense of dislike.[35] Another study found that just talking to people with different political views led to more agreement than people thought would happen when they imagined those discussions.[36] Much research also suggests that emphasizing a common identity helps reduce polarization.

For example, Stanford University recently ran a contest where they selected 25 of the most promising animosity-reducing interventions from several hundred candidates. They then ran those interventions simultaneously in a competition to see which ones were the best at reducing partisan animosity (among other things).[37] Many of the 'winners' were brief interventions that highlighted Americans' common identity around democracy. In fact, one of the very strongest interventions was an extremely brief description of how most Americans on all sides of the political spectrum had basic values that supported democracy. Just reminding Americans of all we have in common was enough to significantly reduce the animosity that Democrats and Republicans feel for one another.

In his book *The Authoritarian Moment,* Ben Shapiro notes that part of the problem with any strategy that separates people is that it undermines our common identity. 'We might patronize different coffee brands, wear different shoes, subscribe to different streaming services. Our points of commonality might disappear.' Thus, we have to carefully apply any strategy in such a way that it maximizes our common identities.

How? The studies discussed in this section have a lot of practical implications for how to approach our everyday lives in this regard. One of the most powerful antidotes to authoritarianism is a shared principle that is applied equally to both groups. Thus, one of the most important things you can do is to show you are willing to do that. It makes a powerful statement to people on the other side and cuts across all the things that create authoritarianism in the first place. Indeed, one of the things the world most needs are people who are willing to stand up to bullies in their own groups by applying common principles.

Few people have done as much good in our society as the liberals who have stood up to liberal bullies (like liberal Bill Maher has stood up to the Woke bullies[38]), or the conservatives who have stood up to conservative bullies (like conservative churches who have stood up to the God Hates Gays bullies[39]). It is often a balm to a wound to see that someone on the other side actually recognizes your pain and is willing to be fair-minded. If we believe in democracy, it is important that we show we believe in it for the other side as well as ours. If we want to stand up to bullies, it is important that we stand up to them on our side as well as the other side. A common principle provides common ground. And common ground is one of the most important things that stops authoritarianism.

So yes, stand up to the bullies on the other side, don't let those bullies push you around. But if you want to truly defeat authoritarianism, stand up to the bullies on your side too, using the same principles in each case. Nothing destroys authoritarianism like a common principle applied to all sides equally.

PRINCIPLE #6: AGREEMENT IS NOT LOVE

You have heard that it was said, 'Love your neighbor and hate your enemy.' But I tell you, love your enemies and pray for those who persecute you … If you love those who love you, what reward will you get? Are not even the tax collectors doing that? And if you greet only your own people, what are you doing more than others?

– Jesus, in Matthew 5:43–47

Somewhere along the way, we got it in our heads that *agreement = love*. Now, no one I know would phrase it like that. If you asked them if they believed that agreeing with someone meant that you loved them, they'd most likely say no. But that's not how we treat each other. That's not how we feel about each other. We think people love us when they agree with us, and they hate us when they don't. We love people when they agree with us, and we cease to love them when they don't.

This can be seen in the fact that one of the best predictors of who we are attracted to is how similar their beliefs are to ours. Our cultural milieu suggests that 'opposites attract', but empirical evidence generally reveals a different story. More so than in other places, in North America people are generally attracted to people who are similar to them, who validate their beliefs.[40] We are especially prone to loving those who agree with us.

So it is easy to see why we have come to increasingly act like agreement and love are exact partners. But the truth is of course exactly the opposite. Love does not equal agreement. Love actually begins where agreement ends. It is easy to love the person who completely endorses every one of your beliefs. That person feeds your ego. That person validates everything about you. If you just greet your own people, what are you doing more than others? But it is hard to love the person who disagrees with you. It is hard to love your philosophical enemy.

And yet, if we are going to function in a pluralistic democracy, we have to disentangle agreement from love. We have to realize that we can love people we disagree with. Disagreement is OK. We don't need every single one of our beliefs to be validated by every person around us.

Evidence suggests this is possible. One of the winners of Stanford's Strengthening Democracy Challenge in reducing partisan animosity was a simple video that showed people disagreeing over major political issues – things like climate change and transgender issues – and yet still being warmly disposed to each other.[41] They still got a beer together. They still hung out. They still talked like friends.

This simple video reduced partisan animosity more than any other intervention. Think about that for a second. The most impactful way of reducing partisan animosity wasn't showing facts, or graphs, or even making pleas for a common identity – it was simply showing a video of complete strangers talking to each other about politics, in such a way that they could disagree and still show love to each other. Another intervention that was also powerful at reducing polarization showed a similarly simple video of five people from different political backgrounds telling their stories. These people all discussed how democracy can handle differences of opinion.

The common theme of these successful interventions at reducing polarization was a focus on allowing for disagreement. It was disentangling the agreement = love equation.

Sometimes it seems like the fight is hopeless and we can't do anything about it. But that is a lie. There is a hunger in the country for healing. There is a strong desire amongst a lot of people to love people they disagree with. Most people prefer unity to division. They don't want to scream at their neighbors; they'd actually prefer to get along with them, even if they have different political signs than they do. They'd love to believe their neighbors respected their political views even though they didn't agree with them.

I've seen this when I talk about left-wing authoritarianism too. At our SPSP symposium discussed in the Introduction, we had a vigorous debate about whether left-wing authoritarianism is a valid construct. The two sides purposefully agreed up front to two principles: (1) We would not hold anything back and would argue vigorously, and (2) we would argue respectfully. I think we accomplished those goals. There were plenty of vigorous arguments. We didn't agree on very much. We pulled no punches. But we were nice to each other. We actually told the audience that we still liked each other. We purposefully, like the people in the Strengthening Democracy video, were warm to each other.

After the debate, one academic came up and said this to me: 'It was so nice to see people actually arguing respectfully. It gives me hope for the country.' I get the sense that a lot of people feel that way. Let's argue, let's debate, let's disagree, but – let's stop hating each other. There is a hunger for respectful disagreement. I think we can tap that hunger. People don't want their opinions shut down. They don't want *forced* agreement. But they do long for *respectful disagreement*.

The Conclusion of the Matter: We Can Win This Fight

Although this book may feel like it is directed at conservatives who want to fight left-wing authoritarianism, it is actually directed at all people on all sides who want to save Western civilization from devolving into an authoritarian dystopia. That means that I could have written a book that targeted right-wing authoritarians and documented the many egregious things done by them, and written principles that would have applied to them. While there are predictable differences between left-wing and right-wing authoritarians, nonetheless much of what works to stop one stops the other. In fact, we simply can't stop one without stopping the other. We have to stop them both at the same time.

No; this book isn't just for conservatives. This book is for all of us. If you want to stop authoritarianism, you have to stop it on both sides. There is no other way. If you are a liberal and you want to stop conservative authoritarianism, you are going to have to be willing to stop liberal authoritarianism too. If you are a conservative and you want to stop liberal authoritarianism, you are going to have to be willing to stop conservative authoritarianism too. We have to work together for that shared value.

That doesn't mean we stop arguing. In fact, it means the opposite of that. We should argue – and argue vigorously. We should passionately pursue what we believe. We should try to win those arguments in the public sphere. But when we lose, we shouldn't burn the place down, and when we win, we should win gracefully. Because the freedoms we enjoy in the fabric of stable society are ultimately more important than any one of those issues we care about.

And of course, nowhere in this book have I suggested that we just sing hymns to each other and hope for the best. Sometimes we have to stand up to the bullies on both sides. And evidence suggests we can win that, too.

I know there is a tendency to think, 'I am only one person and I can't do anything about it.' But that is a lie. Individuals matter. In fact, where you sit right now, you matter. I do not of course mean that you can change the fate of conservative Missouri by wishing it so. But you *can* purposefully try to argue on Instagram and Twitter (aka X) and in other forums in a way that stands up to bullies on both sides equally in the circles you travel in; you *can* vote for candidates that stand up to bullies, but make it clear that you will stop voting for them if they become bullies. You *can* reach out to your neighbor you disagree with to try to find common ground. You *can* make a choice to care more about the freedoms we all share than the opinions we don't. Little else has ever changed society except individual citizens deciding to take the better road.

Research suggests what that road is, what it means to fight fire with fire without burning the forest down. Yes, it means to bring lightning like Dr Martin Luther King Jr. But it also means to say, as Dr King said in arguing for a better world, 'Black supremacy is as dangerous as white supremacy, and God is not interested merely in the freedom of black men and brown men and yellow men. God is interested in the freedom of the whole human race and the creation of a society where all men will live together as brothers, and all men will respect the dignity and the worth of all human personality.' Because Dr King knew that lasting change requires water as well as fire – and he changed the world.

Maybe you can, too.

NOTES

Introduction

1. As you'll see throughout this book, I'm also a 'now-former' liberal. But at that time, I still considered myself a liberal independent.
2. Oster, E., Jack, R., Halloran, C., Schoof, J., and McLeod, D. (2021). 'Covid-19 mitigation practices and Covid-19 rates in schools: Report on data from Florida, New York and Massachusetts' [preprint]. medRxiv. https://doi.org/10.1101/2 021.05.19.21257467.
3. Abaluck, J., Kwong, L. H., Styczynski, A., Haque, A., Kabir, M. A., Bates-Jeffery, E., Crawford, E., Benjamin-Chun, J., Raihan, S., Rahman, S., Benhachmi, S., Bintee, N. Z., Winch, P. J., Hossain, M., Reza, H. M., Jaber, A. A., Momen, S. G., Rahman, A., Banti, F. L., ... Mobarak, A. M. (2022). 'Impact of community masking on Covid-19: A cluster-randomized trial in Bangladesh'. *Science*, 375(6577), [eabi9069]. https://doi.org/10.1126/science.abi9069.
4. O'Brien, C. (2021). 'Former Biden Covid adviser says cloth masks ineffective, suggests Americans start wearing N-95 Masks'. FoxNews.com. https://www.foxnews.com/media/biden-covid-adviser-americans-need-to-wear-n95-masks.
5. See: https://twitter.com/mattwalshblog/status/1359881212358238210.
6. While I cannot verify the exact date the tweet was no longer active with 100% accuracy, it was active throughout much of the writing of this book, and was at least active as of this article in February 2021: Ellis, M. B. (2021), 'Pedro Pascal's controversial social media posts under fire after Gina Carano "cancelled" from Lucasfilm'. monstersandcritics.com. https://www.monstersandcritics.com/tv/pedro-pascals-controversial-social-media-posts-under-fire-after-gina-carano-cancelled-from-lucasfilm/. I could find no evidence that anyone forced the tweet to be taken down.
7. Del Vecchio, G. (2021). 'Disney's firing of Gina Carano is confusing and

hypocritical – lacking sound management'. *Forbes*. https://www.forbes.com/sites/genedelvecchio/2021/03/11/disneys-cancel-culture-is-confused-hypocritical-and-dangerous--lacking-sound-management/?sh=20ad8c8065a4.

8. Ibid.

9. See: Kangadis, N. (2021). 'MSNBC guest: Mandates "as American as apple pie", Biden should use "iron fist"'. MRCTV. https://www.mrctv.org/blog/msnbc-guest-says-mandates-american-apple-pie-biden-should-approach-iron-fist.

10. Conway, L. G., III. (2020, February). Left-wing authoritarianism: Evidence on both sides of the debate. Symposium at the Society for Personality and Social Psychology, New Orleans, LA.

Chapter 1

1. See: https://fullmovietext.com/scene/1/avengers/17/always-men-like-you.

2. Duster, C. (2021). 'Waters calls for protesters to "get more confrontational" if no guilty verdict is reached in Derek Chauvin trial'. CNN. https://www.cnn.com/2021/04/19/politics/maxine-waters-derek-chauvin-trial/index.html.

3. Altemeyer, B. (1998). 'The other "authoritarian" personality'. *Advances in Experimental Social Psychology, 30*, 47–91; Feldman, S. (2003). 'Enforcing social conformity: A theory of authoritarianism'. *Political Psychology, 24*(1), 41–74; Conway, L. G., III, Houck, S. C., Gornick, L. J., and Repke, M. R. (2018). 'Finding the Loch Ness Monster: Left-wing authoritarianism in the United States'. *Political Psychology, 39*, 1049–1067.

4. Conway, L. G., III, Clements, S. M., and Tweed, R. G. (2006). 'Collectivism and governmentally initiated restrictions: A cross-sectional and longitudinal analysis across nations and within a nation'. *Journal of Cross-Cultural Psychology, 37*, 1–23.

5. Altemeyer (1998). 'The other "authoritarian" personality'.

6. Altemeyer, B., and Hunsberger, B. (2005). 'Fundamentalism and authoritarianism'. In R. F. Paloutzian and C. L. Park (eds.). *Handbook of the Psychology of Religion and Spirituality* (378–393). New York: Guilford Press.

7. Baumrind, D. (1991). 'The influence of parenting style on adolescent competence and substance use'. *Journal of Early Adolescence, 11*(1), 56–95.

8. Ibid.

9. See, for example: Altemeyer (1998). 'The other "authoritarian" personality'.

10. Bègue, L., and Vezirian, K. (2021). 'Sacrificing animals in the name of scientific authority: The relationship between pro-scientific mindset and the lethal use of animals in biomedical experimentation'. *Personality and Social Psychology Bulletin,*

48(10), 1483–1498. https://doi.org/10.1177/01461672211039413.

11. Interview on *Tucker Carlson Tonight*, Fox News, April 19, 2022.

12. https://twitter.com/ggreenwald/status/1495783680412897281.

13. From CBC News, November 9, 2013, quoted on *Hannity*, Fox News, February 16, 2022.

14. Quoted in Stack, L. (2016). 'Justin Trudeau criticized for praising Fidel Castro as "remarkable leader"'. *New York Times.* https://www.nytimes.com/2016/11/26/world/americas/justin-trudeau-fidel-castro.html.

15. Anisin, A. (2022). 'Pandemic surveillance capitalism: Authoritarian liberalism or democratic backsliding?' *Journal of Political Power, 15*(2), 262–278.

16. Real Clear Politics. April 22, 2022. https://www.realclearpolitics.com/video/2022/04/22/fauci_on_mask_mandates_a_cdc_issue_it_should_not_be_a_court_issue.html.

17. Quoted in Meek, A. (2021). 'Dr Fauci: If you attack me, you attack science'. MSN.com. https://www.msn.com/en-us/news/technology/dr-fauci-if-you-attack-me-you-re-attacking-science/ar-AARhoqn.

18. Quoted in Kilander, G. (2021). 'Fauci fires back at Republicans to "get over it" and get vaccinated'. Yahoo News. https://news.yahoo.com/fauci-fires-back-republicans-over-134119137.html.

19. Rothman, N. (2022, October 7). 'TGIF: War games'. Free Press. https://www.thefp.com/p/tgif-war-games.

20. https://twitter.com/TracyBethHoeg/status/1759428534802739316.

21. Jussim, L. (2024). 'SPSP Censorship 2.0: We Are Above the Rules'. *Unsafe Science.* https://unsafescience.substack.com/p/spsp-censorship-20-we-are-above-the

22. Jussim, L. (2022). 'Notes from a witch hunt'. *Unsafe Science.* https://unsafescience.substack.com/p/notes-from-a-witch-hunt#footnote-1-89030173

23. Høeg, T. B. (2024, February). Presentation at Heterodox Academy's Summit *Covid and the Academy: What Have We Learned?* Palo Alto, California.

24. O'Neill, J. (2023, October). 'Cornell University professor calls Hamas terror attack "exhilarating" and "exciting"'. *New York Post.*

25. Conway, L. G., III, Chan, L., and Woodard, S. R. (2020). 'Socio-ecological influences on political ideology'. *Current Opinion in Psychology, 32*, 76–80.

26. Hazony, Y. (2017, October 13). 'Is "classical liberalism" conservative?' *Wall Street Journal.* https://www.wsj.com/articles/is-classical-liberalism-conservative-1507931462.

27. Waller, J. G. (2023). 'Distinctions with a difference: Illiberalism and authoritarianism in scholarly study'. *Political Studies Review.* https://doi.org/10.1177/14789299231159253.

28. As just one example, see: Conway, L. G., III, Woodard, S. R., Zubrod, A., and

Chan, L. (2021). 'Why are conservatives less concerned about the coronavirus (Covid-19) than liberals? Comparing political, experiential, and partisan messaging explanations'. *Personality and Individual Differences, 183*, 111124.

29. Hazony (2017). 'Is "Classical Liberalism" Conservative?'

30. Quoted ibid.

31. See Economics Department, Grove City College. https://www.gcc.edu/Home/Academics/Majors-Departments/School-of-Business/Economics.

32. UBC Department of Psychology. (2019, July 4). 'Professor emeritus Peter Suedfeld receives one of Canada's highest civilian honours'. https://psych.ubc.ca/news/professor-emeritus-peter-suedfeld-receives-one-of-canadas-highest-civilian-honours/.

33. Jost, T., Glaser, J., Kruglanski, A. W., and Sulloway, F. J. (2003). 'Political conservatism as motivated social cognition'. *Psychological Bulletin, 129*(3), 339–375.

34. Van Hiel, A., Onraet, E., & De Pauw, S. (2010). 'The relationship between social-cultural attitudes and behavioral measures of cognitive style: A meta-analytic integration of studies'. *Journal of Personality, 78*(6), 1765–1800.

35. Conway, L. G., III, Gornick, L. J., Houck, S. C., Anderson, C., Stockert, J., Sessoms, D., and McCue, K. (2016). 'Are conservatives really more simple-minded than liberals? The domain specificity of complex thinking'. *Political Psychology, 37*(6), 777–798.

36. Conway et al. (2018). 'Finding the Loch Ness Monster'.

37. Ibid. This paper was featured in a virtual issue of *Political Psychology* containing Most-Cited Papers from 2016 to 2018: https://onlinelibrary.wiley.com/doi/toc/10.1111/(ISSN)1467-9221.top-cited-vi. The paper was separately awarded the *Top 20 Most Downloaded Articles 2017–2018* by Wiley for *Political Psychology*.

38. Van Hiel, A., Duriez, B., and Kossowska, M. (2006). 'The presence of left-wing authoritarianism in Western Europe and its relationship with conservative ideology'. *Political Psychology, 27*(5), 769–793.

39. Conway, L. G., III, Zubrod, A., Chan, L., McFarland, J. D., and Van de Vliert, E. (2022). 'Is the myth of left-wing authoritarianism itself a myth?' *Frontiers in Psychology, 8*(13), 1041391.

40. Proch, J., Elad-Strenger, J., and Kessler, T. (2018). 'Liberalism and conservatism, for a change!: Rethinking the association between political orientation and relation to societal change'. *Political Psychology, 40*(4), 877–903.

41. Fiagbenu, M. E., Proch, J., and Kessler, T. (2019). 'Of deadly beans and risky stocks: Political ideology and attitude formation via exploration depend on the nature of the attitude stimuli'. *British Journal of Psychology, 112*(1), 342–357. https://doi.org/10.1111/bjop.12430.

42. Newman, L. S., and Sargent, R. H. (2020). 'Liberals report lower levels of attitudinal ambivalence than conservatives'. *Social Psychological and Personality Science*, *12*(5). https://doi.org/10.1177/1948550620939798.

43. Ditto, P., Liu, B., Clark, C. J., Wojcik, S., Chen, E., Grady, R. H., Celniker, J. B., and Zinger, J. (2019). 'At least bias is bipartisan: A meta-analytic comparison of partisan bias in liberals and conservatives'. *Perspectives on Psychological Science*, *14*(2), 273–291.

44. Chambers, J. R., Schlenker, B. R., and Collisson, B. (2013). 'Ideology and prejudice: The role of value conflicts'. *Psychological Science*, *24*(2), 140–149.

45. Costello, T. H., Bowes, S. M., Stevens, S. T., Waldman, I. D., Tasimi, A., and Lilienfeld, S. O. (2022). 'Clarifying the structure and nature of left-wing authoritarianism'. *Journal of Personality and Social Psychology*, *122*(1), 135–170. https://doi.org/10.1037/pspp0000341.

46. Ibid.

47. From *The Story With Martha MacCallum*, Fox News, July 2, 2021.

48. De Regt, S., Mortelmans, D., and Smits, T. (2011). 'Left-wing authoritarianism is not a myth, but worrisome reality: Evidence from 13 Eastern European countries'. *Communist and Post-Communist Studies*, *44*(4), 299–308; Van Hiel, A., Duriez, B., and Kossowska, M. (2006). 'The presence of leftwing authoritarianism in Western Europe and its relationship with conservative ideology'. *Political Psychology*, *27*(5), 769–793.

49. Conway et al. (2022). 'Is the myth of left-wing authoritarianism itself a myth?'

Chapter 2

1. Ekins, E. (2020). 'Poll: 62% of Americans say they have political views they're afraid to share'. The Cato Institute. https://www.cato.org/survey-reports/poll-62-americans-say-they-have-political-views-theyre-afraid-share#introduction.

2. Parker, R., and Couch, A. (2021). '"The Mandalorian" star Gina Carano fired amid social media controversy'. *The Hollywood Reporter*. https://www.hollywoodreporter.com/tv/tv-news/the-mandalorian-star-gina-carano-fired-amid-social-media-controversy-4131168/.

3. Bianco, G. (2019). '"I got fired because I was conservative." Curt Schilling decries media bias at Penn event'. *The Daily Pennsylvanian*. https://www.thedp.com/article/2019/10/curt-schilling-upenn-baseball-pitcher-politics-philly-ivy-league.

4. Copeland, R. (2019). 'Fired by Google, a Republican engineer hits back: "There's been a lot of bullying".' *Wall Street Journal*. https://www.wsj.com/articles/fired-by-google-a-republican-engineer-hits-back-theres-been-a-lot-of-bullying-11564651801.

5. Ekins (2020). 'Poll: 62% of Americans say they have political views they're afraid to share'.

6. Pennycook, G., and Rand, D. G. (2019). 'Lazy, not biased: Susceptibility to partisan fake news is better explained by lack of reasoning than by motivated reasoning'. *Cognition*, *188*, 39–50.

7. Choma, B. L., Sumantry, D., and Hanoch, Y. (2019). 'Right-wing ideology and numeracy: A perception of greater ability, but poorer performance'. *Judgment and Decision-making*, *14*(4), 412.

8. Conway, L.G.III., Chan, L., and Zubrod, A. (2020). 'Authoritarianism and fake news endorsement'. Unpublished data.

9. Cacioppo, J. T., Petty, R. E., and Morris, K. J. (1983). 'Effects of need for cognition on message evaluation, recall, and persuasion.' *Journal of Personality and Social Psychology*, *45*(4), 805.

10. Wu, C. H., Parker, S. K., and De Jong, J. P. (2014). 'Need for cognition as an antecedent of individual innovation behavior'. *Journal of Management*, *40*(6), 1511–1534.

11. See Jost, T., Glaser, J., Kruglanski, A. W., and Sulloway, F. J. (2003). 'Political conservatism as motivated social cognition'. *Psychological Bulletin*, *129*(3), 339–375.

12. Conway, L. G., III, Zubrod, A., Chan, L., McFarland, J. D., and Van de Vliert, E. (2022). 'Is the myth of left-wing authoritarianism itself a myth?' *Frontiers in Psychology*, *8*(13), 1041391; Conway, L. G., III, Houck, S. C., Gornick, L. J., and Repke, M. R. (2018). 'Finding the Loch Ness Monster: Left-wing authoritarianism in the United States'. *Political Psychology*, *39*, 1049–1067.

13. Costello, T. H., Bowes, S. M., Stevens, S. T., Waldman, I. D., Tasimi, A., and Lilienfeld, S. O. (2022). 'Clarifying the structure and nature of left-wing authoritarianism'. *Journal of Personality and Social Psychology*, *122*(1), 135–170, https://doi.org/10.1037/pspp0000341

14. Conway, L. G., III, and Schaller, M. (2007). 'How communication shapes culture'. In K. Fiedler (ed.), *Frontiers of Social Psychology: Social Communication* (107–127). New York: Psychology Press.

15. Schaller, M., Conway, L. G., III, and Tanchuk, T. L. (2002). 'Selective pressures on the once and future contents of ethnic stereotypes: Effects of the communicability of traits'. *Journal of Personality and Social Psychology*, *82*(6), 861.

16. Rentfrow, P. J., Gosling, S. D., and Potter, J. (2008). 'A theory of the emergence, persistence, and expression of geographic variation in psychological characteristics'. *Perspectives on Psychological Science*, *3*(5), 339–369.

17. Conway et al. (2007). 'How communication shapes culture'.

18. Hatfield, E., Cacioppo, J. T., and Rapson, R. L. (1994). *Emotional Contagion.* Cambridge, England: Cambridge University Press.

19. Conway, L. G., III. (2004). 'Social contagion of time perception'. *Journal of Experimental Social Psychology, 40,* 113–120.

20. Tetlock, P. E. (1985). 'Integrative complexity of American and Soviet foreign policy rhetoric: A time-series analysis'. *Journal of Personality and Social Psychology, 49,* 1565–1585.

21. Dhont, K., Roets, A., and Van Hiel, A. (2013). 'The intergenerational transmission of need for closure underlies the transmission of authoritarianism and anti-immigrant prejudice'. *Personality and Individual Differences, 54*(6), 779–784.

22. See, for example: Prentice, D. A., and Miller, D. T. (1993). 'Pluralistic ignorance and alcohol use on campus: Some consequences of misperceiving the social norm'. *Journal of Personality and Social Psychology, 64*(2), 243.

23. Asch, S. E. (1956). 'Studies of independence and conformity: I. A minority of one against a unanimous majority'. *Psychological Monographs, 70,* 1–70.

24. Bond, R., and Smith, P. B. (1996). 'Culture and conformity: A meta-analysis of studies using Asch's (1952b, 1956) line judgment task'. *Psychological Bulletin, 119*(1), 111.

25. For a review, see: Gardikiotis, A. (2011). 'Minority influence'. *Social And Personality Psychology Compass, 5*(9), 679–693. https://doi.org/10.1111/j.1751-9004.2011.00377.x.

26. Interview on *Tucker Carlson Tonight,* Fox News, November 17, 2021. See also Atlas, S. (2021). *A Plague Upon Our House.* New York: Bombardier Books.

27. 'GRE requirement for PhD program application' (2020, May). Thread posted to Society of Personality and Social Psychology Open Forum.

28. Kuncel, N. R., Hezlett, S. A., and Ones, D. S. (2001). 'A comprehensive meta-analysis of the predictive validity of the Graduate Record Examinations: Implications for graduate student selection and performance'. *Psychological Bulletin, 127*(1), 162–181. https://doi.org/10.1037/0033-2909.127.1.162. As of this writing, this analysis has been cited almost 1,000 times. In case you are wondering: In scientific terms, that's a lot.

29. Lawrie, E. (2021). 'Free speech row prof Kathleen Stock: Protests like anxiety dream'. BBC News. https://www.bbc.com/news/education-59148324.

30. For more on the concept of groupthink, see Janis, I. L. (1972). *Victims of Groupthink: A Psychological Study of Foreign-Policy Decisions and Fiascoes.* Boston: Houghton Mifflin.

31. Mastrangelo, D. (2022, July 12). 'Berkeley professor to Hawley: "Your line of questioning is transphobic"'. *The Hill.* https://thehill.com/blogs/blog-briefing-

room/news/3555771-berkeley-professor-to-hawley-your-line-of-questioning-is-transphobic/.

32. Discussion on *The Five*, Fox News, July 13, 2022.

33. Woodhouse, L. (2022, June 22). 'They questioned gender-affirming care. Then their kids were kicked out of school'. Free Press. https://www.thefp.com/p/they-questioned-gender-affirming. All subsequent quotations in this section relating to Marin Country Day School and the Sinclairs are taken from this source.

34. Sullum, J. (2022, July 5). 'After a SCOTUS Rebuke, New York imposes oppressive new restrictions on the right to bear arms'. Reason.com. https://reason.com/2022/07/05/after-a-scotus-rebuke-new-york-imposes-oppressive-new-restrictions-on-the-right-to-bear-arms/printer/. All subsequent quotations in this section relating to the New York gun laws are taken from this source.

Chapter 3

1. Kalathil, S., and Boas, T. C. (2001). 'The Internet and state control in authoritarian regimes'. *First Monday*, 6(8). https://doi.org/10.5210/fm.v6i8.876.

2. Yes, I'm aware that, technically, misinformation means 'spreading false information without malicious intent' while disinformation means 'spreading false information purposefully to harm someone'. But the way we use the terms in actual reality – and their practical implications – is essentially identical, so in this book I will use them interchangeably. Which term Democrats decide is the flavor of the month seems to be a matter of faddishness rather than something decided via a reasoned approach.

3. When I point this out, liberals *these* days (oh, how the times change!) tend to note obvious restrictions to free speech like 'you can't shout fire in a public theater'. But even if the statements prove equally false, equating 'I think Covid vaccines are completely ineffective' with shouting fire in a public theater is not defensible from a free speech perspective. The reasonable limits to free speech involve purposefully false statements that pose immediate and obvious harm to others. As with most such things, there is some gray area, and the exact point we enter 'immediate and obvious' is often fuzzy. Nonetheless, larger debates about scientific/medical/political questions where people express their real (and thus not disingenuous) opinions – which is the kind of misinformation I discuss here – are not in the same category as shouting fire in a theater. If you can't see *that*, then we really are doomed.

4. Rutz, D. (2021, September 21). 'Politico confirmation of Hunter Biden laptop materials prompts criticism of earlier suppression of the story'. FoxNews.com.

https://www.foxnews.com/media/politico-confirmation-hunter-biden-laptop-materials-prompts-criticism-media.

5. Stephens, B. (2021, May 31). 'Media groupthink and the lab-leak theory'. *New York Times.* https://www.nytimes.com/2021/05/31/opinion/media-lab-leak-theory.html.

6. Quoted in Myers, S. L., and Sullivan, E. (2022, July 6). 'Disinformation has become another untouchable problem in Washington'. *New York Times.* https://www.nytimes.com/2022/07/06/business/disinformation-board-dc.html?smid=tw-share.

7. Arkes, H. R. (2003). 'The nonuse of psychological research at two federal agencies'. *Psychological Science, 14*(1), 1–6.

8. Kruglanski, A. W., Webster, D. M., and Klem, A. (1993). 'Motivated resistance and openness to persuasion in the presence or absence of prior information'. *Journal of Personality and Social Psychology, 65*(5), 861.

9. Jost, T., Glaser, J., Kruglanski, A. W., and Sulloway, F. J. (2003). 'Political conservatism as motivated social cognition'. *Psychological Bulletin 129*(3), 339–375.

10. van Baar, J. M., Halpern, D. J., and Feldman-Hall, O. (2021). 'Intolerance of uncertainty modulates brain-to-brain synchrony during politically polarized perception'. *Proceedings of the National Academy of Sciences, 118*(20), e2022491118.

11. Newman, L. S., and Sargent, R. H. (2021). 'Liberals report lower levels of attitudinal ambivalence than conservatives'. *Social Psychological and Personality Science, 12*(5), 780–788. https://doi.org/10.1177/1948550620939798.

12. Larsen, E. M., Donaldson, K. R., Liew, M., and Mohanty, A. (2021). 'Conspiratorial thinking during Covid-19: The roles of paranoia, delusion-proneness, and intolerance of uncertainty'. *Frontiers in Psychiatry, 12.*

13. Manson, J. H. (2020). 'Right-wing authoritarianism, left-wing authoritarianism, and pandemic-mitigation authoritarianism'. *Personality and Individual Differences, 167*, 110251.

14. Conway, L. G., III (2012). 'Knowing you are on to something real: Part IV'. *The Apologetic Professor.* http://www.apologeticprofessor.com/articles/2012/04/knowing-you-are-on-to-something-real-part-iv/.

15. From the WHO report in June 2020: 'At present, there is no direct evidence (from studies on Covid-19 and in healthy people in the community) on the effectiveness of universal masking of healthy people in the community to prevent infection with respiratory viruses, including Covid-19.' World Health Organization (2020, June 5). *Advice on the use of masks in the context of Covid-19.* https:// apps.who.int/iris/bitstream/handle/10665/332293/WHO-2019-nCov-IPC_ Masks-2020.4-eng.pdf. See also O'Brien, C. (2021). 'Former Biden Covid

adviser says cloth masks ineffective, suggests Americans start wearing N-95 masks'. FoxNews.com. https://www. foxnews.com/media/biden-covid-adviser-americans-need-to-wear-n95-masks.

16. From: https://en.wikipedia.org/wiki/Scott_Atlas#Covid-19_misinformation,_controversial_statements,_and_policy_influence. Accessed May 2022. Note that, by October 2022, the Wikipedia article had been updated to say 'Dr Atlas *at times* spread misinformation', which is, if we're being honest, hardly an improvement, as the 'at times' was presumably implied in the original.

17. Quoted in Geman, B. (2022, June). 'Top Biden aide prods big tech to crack down on climate change misinformation'. Axios. https://www.axios.com/2022/06/09/climate-gina-mccarthy-misinformation.

18. Simon, J. (2022, March 28). 'Misinformation is derailing renewable energy projects across the United States'. WITF. https://www.witf.org/2022/03/28/misinformation-is-derailing-renewable-energy-projects-across-the-united-states/.

19. https://www.facebook.com/permalink.php?story_fbid=1460411550817629andid=453311098194351.

20. Thoemmes, F. J., and Conway, L. G., III (2007). 'Integrative complexity of 41 US presidents'. *Political Psychology, 28*(2), 193–226.

21. Conway, L. G., III, Conway, K. R., and Houck, S. C. (2020). 'Validating automated integrative complexity: Natural language processing and the Donald Trump Test'. *Journal of Social and Political Psychology, 8*(2), 504–524.

22. Obtained from Box Office Mojo: https://www.boxofficemojo.com/chart/top_lifetime_gross_adjusted/?adjust_gross_to=2020.

23. For arguments against eating poison ivy, see University of Pennsylvania Medicine (https://www.pennmedicine.org/updates/blogs/health-and-wellness/2018/july/poison-ivysumac- oak) and backpaker.com (https://www.backpacker.com/gear-reviews/can-you-build-immunity-to-poison-ivy-by-eating-it/). For the argument that eating poison ivy is good for you, see Sanchez, A. (2015). 'Can you eat poison ivy?' https://anitasanchez. com/2015/04/04/can-you-eat-poison-ivy/.

Chapter 4

1. For the record, I'm not sure why it said that, and I make no strong claims about it. Subsequent discussions suggest it was most likely either sheep or lamb intestines, which *Huffington Post* assures me is apparently OK to eat (https://www.huffpost.com/entry/hot-dog-casings_n_5955008de4b05c37bb7c7208). While that sounds comforting, it turns out a deeper hot dog unknown might actually be worse. One report (https://www.medicaldaily.com/hot-diggity-

dog-14-hot-dogs-and-sausages-contain-unlisted-ingredients-including-human-358752) suggested that 2% of all hot dogs contain unreported human DNA. It's best not to ask too many questions about hot dogs.

2. West, S. G., Gunn, S. P., and Chernicky, P. (1975). 'Ubiquitous Watergate: An attributional analysis'. *Journal of Personality and Social Psychology*, *32*(1), 55.

3. Tajfel H. (1974). 'Social identity and intergroup behaviour'. *Social Science Information*, *13*, 65–93. https://doi.org/10.1177/053901847401300204.

4. Lemyre, L., and Smith, P. M. (1985). 'Intergroup discrimination and self-esteem in the minimal group paradigm'. *Journal of Personality and Social Psychology*, *49*(3), 660.

5. Conway, L. G., III, Houck, S. C., Chan, L., Repke, M. A., and McFarland, J. (2021). 'The agreement paradox: How pressures for agreement can ultimately divide us'. In J.-W. van Prooijen (ed.), *Current Issues in Social Psychology: Political Polarization* (pp. 112–126). New York: Routledge.

6. Altemeyer, B., and Hunsberger, B. (2005). 'Fundamentalism and authoritarianism'. In R. F. Paloutzian and C. L. Park (eds.). *Handbook of the Psychology of Religion and Spirituality* (378–393). New York: Guilford Press.

7. Interview on *The Ingraham Angle*, Fox News, November 9, 2021.

8. For the left-wing scale, see Conway, L. G., III, Houck, S. C., Gornick, L. J., Repke, M. R. (2018). 'Finding the Loch Ness Monster: Left-wing authoritarianism in the United States'. *Political Psychology*, *39*, 1049–1067. For the social dominance orientation scale, see Pratto, F., Sidanius, J., Stallworth, L. M., and Malle, B. F. (1994). 'Social dominance orientation: A personality variable predicting social and political attitudes'. *Journal of Personality and Social Psychology*, *67*(4), 741.

9. Rosenfield, K. (2021, November 4). 'Why the left can't let go of Brandon'. UnHerd. htpps://unherd.com/2021/11/why-the-left-wont-let-go-of-brandon/.

10. Ibid.

11. From an interview with Policy Exchange in November 2021, available here: https://www.youtube.com/watch?v=CZplF4qdwII.

12. Reuters Staff. (2020, June 25). 'Burnley fan behind "White Lives Matter" banner sacked from job – reports'. Reuters.com. https://www.reuters.com/article/uk-soccer-england-burnley-race-idUKKBN23V317.

13. Lee, M. (2021, August 8). 'Fauci berates mass outdoor gathering in South Dakota, but gives Obama's birthday bash a pass'. FoxNews.com. https://www.foxnews.com/politics/fauci-berates-mass-outdoor-gathering-in-south-dakota-but-gives-obamas-birthday-bash-a-pass.

14. ACLU on Twitter, September 2, 2021: https://twitter.com/aclu/status/1433433737304449024.

15. Quoted in Barnes, A. (2021, September 20). 'San Francisco mayor offers defense after video surfaces of her dancing indoors without a mask'. *The Hill*. https://thehill.com/policy/healthcare/573020-san-francisco-mayor-offers-defense-after-video-surfaces-of-her-dancing.

16. Crane, E. (2021, August 5). 'Cori Bush will pay $200K for private security – but still wants to defund the police'. *New York Post*. https://nypost.com/2021/08/05/cori-bush-will-pay-200k-for-private-security-but-still-wants-to-defund-police/.

17. Conway, L. G., III, Bongard, K., Plaut, V., Gornick, L. J., Dodds, D. P., Giresi, T., ... and Houck, S. C. (2017). 'Ecological origins of freedom: Pathogens, heat stress, and frontier topography predict more vertical but less horizontal governmental restriction'. *Personality and Social Psychology Bulletin, 43*(10), 1378–1398; Conway, L. G., III, Chan, L., Woodard, S. R., and Joshanloo, M. (2021). 'Proximal versus distal ecological stress: Socio-ecological influences on political freedom, well-being, and societal confidence in 159 nations'. *Journal of Social and Political Psychology, 9*, 306–320.

18. Conway, L. G., III, Zubrod, A., Chan, L., McFarland, J. D., and Van de Vliert, E. (2022). 'Is the myth of left-wing authoritarianism itself a myth?' *Frontiers in Psychology, 8*(13), 1041391.

19. Cooke, C. (2021, August). 'President Biden's extension of the eviction moratorium is unconstitutional and he knows it'. *USA Today*. https://www.usatoday.com/story/opinion/2021/08/05/eviction-moratorium-delta-variant-brett-kavanaugh-unconstitutional/5498649001/.

20. Interview on *Fox & Friends First*, Fox News, November 5, 2021.

21. 'Bracketology: Historical analysis of the RPI for at-large teams'. Steel City Blitz (2018, February 20). https://steelcityblitz.com/bracketology-historical-analysis-of-the-rpi-for-at-large-teams/.

22. From *Canceled in the USA* (Fox Nation show presented by Dan Bongino), July 25, 2022.

23. Interview ibid.

24. Interview ibid.

Chapter 5

1. Ostermeiqer, E. (2013). 'George H. W. Bush: Hater of broccoli'. Smart Politics. https://smartpolitics.lib.umn.edu/2013/07/09/george-hw-bush-hater-of-brocco/.

2. See: Conway, L. G., III, Conway, K. R., Gornick, L. J., and Houck, S. C. (2014). 'Automated integrative complexity'. *Political Psychology, 35*, 603–624.

3. Conway, L. G., III, Houck, S. C., Gornick, L. J., Repke, M. R. (2018). 'Finding the Loch Ness Monster: Left-wing authoritarianism in the United States'. *Political Psychology, 39*, 1049–1067.

4. For algorithmic predictions of a person's personality traits, see: Youyou, W., Kosinski, M., and Stillwell, D. (2015). 'Computer-based personality judgments are more accurate than those made by humans'. *Proceedings of the National Academy of Sciences, 112*, 1036–1040.

5. Suedfeld, P., and Tetlock, P. (1977). 'Integrative complexity of communications in international crises'. *Journal of Conflict Resolution, 21*(1), 169–184.

6. Jost, T., Glaser, J., Kruglanski, A. W., and Sulloway, F. J. (2003). 'Political conservatism as motivated social cognition'. *Psychological Bulletin, 129*(3), 339–375.

7. Conway, L. G., III, McFarland, J. D., Costello, T. H., and Lilienfeld, S. O. (2021). 'The curious case of left-wing authoritarianism: When authoritarian persons meet anti-authoritarian norms'. *Journal of Theoretical Social Psychology, 5*, 423–442. https://doi.org/10.1002/jts5.108; Costello, T. H., Bowes, S. M., Stevens, S. T., Waldman, I. D., Tasimi, A., and Lilienfeld, S. O. (2022). 'Clarifying the structure and nature of left-wing authoritarianism'. *Journal of Personality and Social Psychology, 122*(1), 135–170. https://doi.org/10.1037/pspp0000341.

8. This is complicated by the fact that left-wing authoritarians often have potential conflicts that create additional complexity for typical stems – as our own published model of authoritarianism predicts. There likely are issues on both sides where authoritarians may experience more or less complexity. Here, however, I focus on the simpler story – and yes, I do see the irony.

9. Conway, L. G., III., Thoemmes, F., Allison, A. M., Hands Towgood, K., Wagner, M. J., Davey, K., Salcido, A., Stovall, A. N., Dodds, D. P., Bongard, K, and Conway, K. R. (2008). 'Two ways to be complex and why they matter: Implications for attitude strength and lying'. *Journal of Personality and Social Psychology, 95*, 1029–1044.

10. Schaller, M., Boyd, C., Yohannes, J., and O'Brien, M. (1995). 'The prejudiced personality revisited: Personal need for structure and formation of erroneous group stereotypes'. *Journal of Personality and Social Psychology, 68*(3), 544.

11. Tetlock, P. E., Armor, D., and Peterson, R. S. (1994). 'The slavery debate in antebellum America: Cognitive style, value conflict, and the limits of compromise'. *Journal of Personality and Social Psychology, 66*(1), 115–126; Conway et al. (2008). 'Two ways to be complex and why they matter'.

12. For a review, see: Conway, L. G., III, Suedfeld, P., and Tetlock, P. E. (2001). 'Integrative complexity and political decisions that lead to war or peace'. In D. J. Christie, R. V. Wagner, and D. Winter (eds). *Peace, Conflict,*

and Violence: Peace Psychology for the 21st Century (66–75). Englewood Cliffs, NJ: Prentice-Hall.

13. Conway, L. G., III, Gornick, L. J., Houck, S. C., Hands Towgood, K., and Conway, K. R. (2011). 'The hidden implications of radical group rhetoric: Integrative complexity and terrorism'. *Dynamics of Asymmetric Conflict, 4,* 155–165.

14. Houck, S. C., Repke, M. A., and Conway, L. G., III (2017). 'Understanding what makes terrorist groups' propaganda effective: An integrative complexity analysis of ISIL and Al Qaeda'. *Journal of Policing, Intelligence and Counter Terrorism, 12,* 105–118.

15. See Twitter: https://twitter.com/sullydish/status/1413581043295297541?s=20.

16. To mitigate the risk of hurting this book's sales in other parts of England – or the wonderful people who frequent Old Trafford – I will relegate my affection for my beloved City to this footnote.

17. Kendi, I. X. (2020). 'The difference between being not racist and antiracist'. TED Talk, June 2020. Found at: https://www.ted.com/talks/ibram_x_kendi_the_difference_between_being_not_racist_and_antiracist?language=en.

18. Ibid.

19. Conway, L. G., III, Conway, K. R., and Houck, S. C. (2020). 'Validating automated integrative complexity: Natural language processing and the Donald Trump Test'. *Journal of Social and Political Psychology, 8*(2), 504–524

20. Kendi (2020). 'The difference between being not racist and antiracist'.

21. University of Montana resources (from May 11, 2022): https://libguides.lib.umt.edu/ResourcesAgainstRacism/GetStarted.

22. Lowery, W. (2016). *They Can't Kill Us All: Ferguson, Baltimore, and a New Era in America's Racial Justice Movement.* New York: Little, Brown; Anderson, C. (2016). *White Rage: The Unspoken Truth of Our Racial Divide.* New York: Bloomsbury USA; hooks, b. (1995). *Killing Rage: Ending Racism.* New York: Henry Holt.

23. Roberts, D. (2011). *Fatal Invention: How Science, Politics, and Big Business Re-create Race in the Twenty-First Century.* New York: New Press/ORIM; Kendi, I. X. (2016). *Stamped from the Beginning: The Definitive History of Racist Ideas in America.* New York: Nation Books; Ward, J. (2013). *Men We Reaped: A Memoir.* New York: Bloomsbury Publishing USA; Noble, S. U. (2018). *Algorithms of Oppression.* New York: New York University Press; Tourse, R. W., Hamilton-Mason, J., and Wewiorski, N. J. (2018). *Systemic Racism in the United States.* Cham, Switzerland: Springer International; Deer, S. (2015). *The Beginning and End of Rape: Confronting Sexual Violence in Native America.* Minneapolis: University of Minnesota Press; Saad, L. (2020). *Me and White Supremacy:*

Combat Racism, Change the World, and Become a Good Ancestor. Naperville, IL: Sourcebooks, Inc.

24. Saad, L. (2020, August 5). 'Black Americans want police to retain local presence'. Gallup. https://news.gallup.com/poll/316571/black-americans-police-retain-local-presence.aspx.

25. Rosalsky, G. (2021, April 20). 'When you add more police to a city, what happens?' NPR Planet Money. https://www.npr.org/sections/money/2021/04/20/988769793/when-you-add-more-police-to-a-city-what-happens.

26. Lilienfeld, S. O. (2017). 'Microaggressions: Strong claims, inadequate evidence'. *Perspectives on Psychological Science, 12*(1), 138–169.

27. University of Minnesota Public Health. 'Examples of racial microaggressions'. Retrieved May 11, 2022, from https://sph.umn.edu/site/docs/hewg/microaggressions.pdf.

28. Technically, the list did not say micro-aggressions only come from white people. Is it possible that the list is more balanced than my narrative gives it credit for? If you believe that it is, I suggest you try the following: Put out a parallel list where all people *engaging* in micro-aggressions are minority ethnicities and all *targets* of micro-aggressions are white. Then argue for the horrors of 'racial minorities micro-aggressing against white people'. I strongly suspect public reaction to your list will answer the question about whether the original list was intended as a one-sided narrative against white conservative micro-aggression.

29. https://genius.com/Rise-up-sing-out-cast-and-disney-junior-speak-up-lyrics.

30. Goodkind, N. (2022, June 20). 'Who decides if the US is in a recession? Eight White economists you've never heard of'. CNN Business. https://www.cnn.com/2022/06/30/economy/recession-economists-nber/index.html.

31. Associated Press (2021, June 30). 'Pete Buttigieg launches $1B pilot to build racial equity in America's roads'. NPR. https://www.npr.org/2022/06/30/1108852884/pete-buttigieg-launches-1b-pilot-to-build-racial-equity-in-americas-roads.

32. https://twitter.com/DailyCaller/status/1577353482415538177.

33. Abbott, C. (2021, March 2). 'Equity commission will root out systemic racism in USDA programs, says Vilsak'. *Successful Farming.* https://www.agriculture.com/news/business/equity-commission-will-root-out-systemic-racism-in-usda-programs-says-vilsack.

34. McCausland, P. (2021, July 1). 'Teaching critical race theory isn't happening in classrooms, teacher say in survey'. NBC News. https://www.nbcnews.com/news/us-news/teaching-critical-race-theory-isn-t-happening-classrooms-teachers-say-n1272945.

35. Stielglitz, B. (2021, July 4). 'America's largest teachers union supports teaching children critical race theory in schools'. *Daily Mail.* https://www.dailymail.co.uk/news/article-9754609/Americas-largest-teachers-union-says-supports-teaching-children-critical-race-theory-schools.html.

36. Carbado, D. W., and Roithmayr, D. (2014). 'Critical race theory meets social science'. *Annual Review of Law and Social Science, 10,* 149–167.

37. The Center on Race, Law and Justice (2021, March). 'Who's afraid of critical race theory?' Symposium presented at Fordham University. https://www.fordham.edu/download/downloads/id/15445/whos_afraid_of_critical_race_theory_cle_materials.pdf.

38. Jost, J. T., Banaji, M. R., and Nosek, B. A. (2004). 'A decade of system justification theory: Accumulated evidence of conscious and unconscious bolstering of the status quo'. *Political Psychology, 25*(6), 881–919. https://doi.org/10.1111/j.1467-9221.2004.00402.x.

39. Thusi, I. (2021, March). 'Blue lives and the permanence of racism'. In 'Who's afraid of critical race theory?'

40. Hoag, A. (2020). 'Derrick Bell's interest convergence and the permanence of racism: A reflection in resistance'. *Harvard Law Review Blog.* https://blog.harvardlawreview.org/derrick-bells-interest-convergence-and-the-permanence-of-racism-a-reflection-on-resistance/.

41. McPherson, J. M. (1997). *For Cause and Comrades: Why Men Fought in the Civil War.* New York: Oxford University Press.

42. American Psychological Association. (2018). 'Ethical principles of psychologists and code of conduct'. APA.org. Obtained October 6, 2022 from https://www.apa.org/ethics/code.

43. Chambers, J. R., Schlenker, B. R., and Collisson, B. (2013). 'Ideology and prejudice: The role of value conflicts'. *Psychological Science, 24*(2), 140–149.

44. Conway, L. G., III, Houck, S. C., Gornick, L. J., and Repke, M. R. (2018). 'Finding the Loch Ness Monster: Left-wing authoritarianism in the United States'. *Political Psychology, 39,* 1049–1067.

45. Saunders, B., Badaan, V., Hoffarth, M., and Jost, J. (2020, February 27–29). 'Spotting the Loch Ness Monster, or smiling for the surgeon's photograph? A critique of Conway and colleagues' (2018) research on left-wing authoritarianism' [part of the symposium 'Left-wing authoritarianism: Evidence on both sides of the debate', chaired by L. G. Conway III. Society for Personality and Social Psychology, New Orleans, LA, United States.]

46. Conway, L. G., III, Zubrod, A., Chan, L., McFarland, J. D., and Van de Vliert, E. (2022). 'Is the myth of left-wing authoritarianism itself a myth?' *Frontiers in Psychology, 8*(13), 1041391.

47. Diamant, J. (2018). 'Blacks more likely than others in US to read the Bible regularly, see it as God's word'. Pew Research Center. https://www.pewresearch.org/fact-tank/2018/05/07/blacks-more-likely-than-others-in-u-s-to-read-the-bible-regularly-see-it-as-gods-word/.

48. Newport, F. (2019). 'Americans' views of Israel remain tied to religious beliefs'. Gallup. https://news.gallup.com/opinion/polling-matters/247937/americans-views-israel-remain-tied-religious-beliefs.aspx.

49. Friedman, L. (2020). 'The American Jewish community and the 2020 US presidential election'. Arab Center Washington DC. https://arabcenterdc.org/resource/the-american-jewish-community-and-the-2020-us-presidential-election/.

50. Hutzler, A. (2021, April 29). 'Twitter blocks "Uncle Tim" trends after racist phrase goes viral'. *Newsweek*. https://www.newsweek.com/twitter-blocks-uncle-tim-trends-after-racist-phrase-goes-viral-response-tim-scotts-speech-1587456.

51. Flayton, B. (2022). 'My post-graduation plan? I'm immigrating to Israel'. Free Press. https://www.thefp.com/p/my-post-graduation-plan-im-immigrating.

Chapter 6

1. Saunders, B., Badaan, V., Hoffarth, M., and Jost, J. (2020, February 27–29). 'Spotting the Loch Ness Monster, or smiling for the surgeon's photograph? A critique of Conway and colleagues' (2018) research on left-wing authoritarianism' [part of the symposium 'Left-wing authoritarianism: Evidence on both sides of the debate', chaired by L. G. Conway III. Society for Personality and Social Psychology, New Orleans, LA, United States.]

2. Conway, L. G., III, Zubrod, A., Chan, L., McFarland, J. D., and Van de Vliert, E. (2022). 'Is the myth of left-wing authoritarianism itself a myth?' *Frontiers in Psychology*, 8(13), 1041391.

3. See: https://www.hollywoodreporter.com/tv/tv-news/the-mandalorian-star-gina-carano-fired-amid-social-media-controversy-4131168/.

4. Bill Watterson's cartoon *Calvin and Hobbes* amusingly illustrates this phenomenon, as illuminated in this blog piece: https://mindyourdecisions.com/blog/2012/02/01/3-things-calvin-and-hobbes-taught-me-about-money/.

5. Conway, L. G., III, Zubrod, A., Chan, L. (2020). 'The paradox of the tribal equalitarian'. *Psychological Inquiry*, 31, 48–52.

6. Volokh, E. (2015, December 28). 'Freedom and hypocrisy'. *Washington Post*. https://www.washingtonpost.com/news/volokh-conspiracy/wp/2015/12/28/freedom-and-hypocrisy/.

7. Conway, L. G., III, McFarland, J. D., Costello, T. H., and Lilienfeld, S. O. (2021). 'The curious case of left-wing authoritarianism: When authoritarian persons meet anti-authoritarian norms'. *Journal of Theoretical Social Psychology*, 5, 423–442. https://doi.org/10.1002/jts5.108.

8. Tetlock, P. E. (1994). 'Political psychology or politicized psychology: Is the road to scientific hell paved with good moral intentions?' *Political Psychology*, 15, 509–529.

9. Conway, L. G., III, Houck, S. C., Gornick, L. J., and Repke, M. A. (2016). 'Ideologically motivated perceptions of complexity: Believing those who agree with you are more complex than they are'. *Journal of Language and Social Psychology*, 35(6), 708–718.

10. Conway, L. G., III. (2021, July 7). 'The comedians are right: Authoritarian Democrats are also a problem'. *The Hill*. https://thehill.com/opinion/campaign/561825-comedians-are-right-authoritarian-democrats-are-also-a-problem.

11. Quoted in Dumas, B. (2021, March 12). 'Longtime Democrat Sarah Silverman not so sure she wants to be affiliated with a party anymore'. The Blaze. https://www.theblaze.com/news/longtime-democrat-sarah-silverman-not-so-sure-she-wants-to-be-affiliated-with-a-party-anymore.

12. From: 'Moving the goalposts'. TV Tropes (2022). https://tvtropes.org/pmwiki/pmwiki.php/Main/MovingTheGoalposts.

13. See, e.g., Wang, C. S., Whitson, J. A., Anicich, E. M., Kray, L. J., and Galinsky, A. D. (2017). 'Challenge your stigma: How to reframe and revalue negative stereotypes and slurs'. *Current Directions in Psychological Science*, 26(1), 75–80. Note that reframing isn't always bad and can sometimes involve looking at things differently and not inaccurately. Here, I highlight its negative potential.

14. Jost, T., Glaser, J., Kruglanski, A. W., and Sulloway, F. J. (2003). 'Political conservatism as motivated social cognition'. *Psychological Bulletin*, 129(3), 339–375.

15. Cain, C. (2021, August 14). 'Republicans claim to fear left-wing authoritarianism – but there is no such thing'. Salon. https://www.salon.com/2021/08/14/republicans-claim-to-fear-left-wing-authoritarianism--but-theres-no-such-thing/.

16. Conway, L. G., III, Chan, L., Woodard, S. R., and Joshanloo, M. (2021). 'Proximal versus distal ecological stress: Socio-ecological influences on political freedom, well-being, and societal confidence in 159 nations'. *Journal of Social and Political Psychology*, 9, 306–320; Conway, L. G., III, McFarland, J. D., Costello, T. H., and Lilienfeld, S. O. (2021). 'The curious case of left-wing authoritarianism: When authoritarian persons meet anti-authoritarian norms'. *Journal of Theoretical Social Psychology*, 5, 423–442. https://doi.org/10.1002/jts5.108.

17. For the 1990s, see McFarland, S. G., Ageyev, V. S., and Abalakina-Paap, M. A. (1993). 'The authoritarian personality in the United States and the former Soviet Union: Comparative studies'. In W. F. Stone, G. Lederer, and R. Christie (eds). *Strength and Weakness: The Authoritarian Personality Today*. New York: Springer Verlag. For more recent years, see Grigoryev, D., Batkhina, A., Conway, L. G., III, and Zubrod, A. (2022). 'Authoritarian attitudes in Russia: Right-wing authoritarianism and social dominance orientation in the modern Russian context'. *Asian Journal of Social Psychology*, *25*(4), 623–645. https://doi.org/10.1111/ajsp.12523.

18. McFarland, S. G., Ageyev, V. S., and Djintcharadze, N. (1996). 'Russian authoritarianism two years after communism'. *Personality and Social Psychology Bulletin, 22*, 210–217.

19. Mettler, S., Lieberman, R. C., Michener, J., Pepinsky, T. B., and Roberts, K. M. (2022). 'Democratic vulnerabilities and pathways for reform'. *The Annals of the American Academy of Political and Social Science*, *699*(1), 8–20. https://doi.org/10.1177/00027162221077516.

20. https://twitter.com/KeithOlbermann/status/1540346179548061698.

21. McFall, C. (2022, June 24). 'Roe v. Wade abortion decision: Democrats call Supreme Court illegitimate'. FoxNews.com. https://www.foxnews.com/politics/roe-v-wade-abortion-decision-democrats-call-supreme-court-illegitimate.

22. https://twitter.com/RashidaTlaib/status/1542567044339666946.

23. Devine, M. (2022, July 11). 'Majority of democrats, young people want to abolish the supreme court'. *New York Post.* https://nypost.com/2022/07/11/majority-of-democrats-young-people-want-to-abolish-supreme-court-poll/.

24. Interview on *The Faulkner Focus*, Fox News, January 13, 2022.

25. From: https://www.uncp.edu/sites/default/files/2019-01/Hilter%26%23039%3Bs%20Speeches%20Key.pdf.

26. For the full interview, see: https://www.youtube.com/watch?v=LJFsXycWBLE.

27. Garnier, N. (2021). 'End the gaslighting of Virginia'. *Washington Examiner.* https://www.washingtonexaminer.com/news/2881996/end-the-gaslighting-of-virginia/.

28. Wall Street Journal Editorial Board. (2021, October 26). 'About those domestic-terrorist parents'. *Wall Street Journal.* https://www.wsj.com/articles/about-those-domestic-terrorists-national-school-boards-association-merrick-garland-memo-fbi-11635285900.

29. Quoted in Brooks, E. (2021, September 29). 'McAuliffe says parents shouldn't tell schools what to teach, handing Youngkin a campaign ad'. Yahoo.com. https://www.yahoo.com/now/mcauliffe-says-parents-shouldn-t-173500644.html?guccounter=1.

30. Myers, S. L., and Sullivan, E. (2022, July 6). 'Disinformation has become another untouchable problem in Washington'. *New York Times.* https://www.nytimes.com/2022/07/06/business/disinformation-board-dc.html?smid=tw-share.
31. Gibson, J., and Singman, B. (2022, October 13). 'Dem operative admits he lied about the source Manfort, Lewandowski info included in dossier'. FoxNews.com. https://www.foxnews.com/politics/danchenko-trial-dem-operative-admits-lied-source-manafort-lewandowski-info-dossier.
32. Moore, M. (2022, May 10). 'DHS disinformation "czar" Jankowicz pushed Trump-Russia claims at center of Durham case'. *New York Post.* https://nypost.com/2022/05/10/dhs-disinformation-czar-jankowicz-pushed-trump-russia-claims/.
33. Dovere, E-I. (October 9, 2020). 'Hillary Clinton says she was right all along'. The Atlantic. https://www.theatlantic.com/politics/archive/2020/10/hillary-clinton-doing-now-2020/616668/.
34. To be fair to the authors of the article, they did note that the death blow to the 'Disinformation Board' came not from Republicans, but from three organizations – one of which is housed in Columbia – that are more liberal. They pointed out that those organizations said: 'In the wrong hands, such a board would be a potent tool for government censorship and retaliation.' But one gets the feeling that this was a tragic miscalculation rather than a good thing. Their conclusion wasn't that freedom won out. Their conclusion: 'The damage was done …' As with the rest of the article, this clearly comes from a place that has normalized censorship without awareness. Oh, how tragically damaging it is to stop censorship!
35. https://twitter.com/ChrisPolPsych/status/1544649874238590978?cxt=HBwWhMC-hY642e8qAAAAandcn=ZmxleGlibGVfcmVjjcw%3D%3Dandrefsrc=email (Twitter account now deleted).

Chapter 7

1. Stockmann, D., and Gallagher, M. E. (2011). 'Remote control: How the media sustain authoritarian rule in China'. *Comparative Political Studies, 44*(4), 436–467. https://doi.org/10.1177/0010414010394773.
2. Zhong, P., and Zhan, J. V. (2021). 'Authoritarian critical citizens and declining political trust in China'. *China Review, 21*(2), 117–152.
3. Hamerow, T. S. (1997). *On the Road to the Wolf's Lair – German Resistance to Hitler.* Cambridge, MA: Belknap Press of Harvard University Press.
4. Quoted in Manno, A. (2021, September 2). 'Jay Leno says cancel culture is now a fact of life and comedians "have to change with the times or you die" following criticism from Gabrielle Union for Asian jokes on AGT set'. *Daily*

Mail. https://www.dailymail.co.uk/news/article-9951337/Jay-Leno-says-cancel-culture-fact-life-change-times-die.html.

5. Carnahan, T., and McFarland, S. (2007). 'Revisiting the Stanford Prison Experiment: Could participant self-selection have led to the cruelty?' *Personality and Social Psychology Bulletin, 33*(5), 603–614.

6. Reicher, S., and Haslam, S. A. (2006). 'Rethinking the psychology of tyranny: The BBC Prison Study'. *British Journal of Social Psychology, 45*(1), 1–40.

7. Ibid.

8. Howard, P. K. (2019, January 26). 'It's time to blow up the bureaucracy that's killing America'. *New York Post.* https://nypost.com/2019/01/26/its-time-to-blow-up-the-bureaucracy-thats-killing-america/.

9. Wilson, J. Q., and Kelling, G. L. (1982, March). 'Broken windows'. *The Atlantic.* https://faculty.washington.edu/matsueda/courses/371/Readings/Wilson%20and%20Kelling%20(1982).pdf.

10. Goodwin, M. (2020, August 15). 'How NYC championed broken windows policing and thew it away'. *New York Post.* https://nypost.com/2020/08/15/how-nyc-used-then-tore-up-broken-windows-policing-goodwin/.

11. Ibid.

12. Freedman, J. L., and Fraser, S. C. (1966). 'Compliance without pressure: The foot-in-the-door technique'. *Journal of Personality and Social Psychology, 4*(2), 195.

13. Kanner, G. (2006). 'The Public Use Clause: Constitutional mandate or "hortatory fluff"?' *Pepperdine Law Review, 2,* 335–84.

14. Ledford, H. (2021). 'Deaths from Covid "incredibly rare" among children'. *Nature, 595,* 639. https://doi.org/10.1038/d41586-021-01897-w.

15. Malhotra, A. (2022). 'Curing the pandemic of misinformation of Covid-19 mRNA vaccines through real evidence-based medicine – Part I'. *Journal of Insulin Resistance, 5.* https://doi.org/10.4102/jir.v5i1.71.

16. Rothman, N. (2022, October 7). 'TGIF: War Games'. *Common Sense.*

17. Bat Removal Pro. (2020, January 16). 'What to do about bats in the attic during bat maternity season'. https://www.batremovalpro.com/bat-blackout-season/#:~:text=All%20Bat%20species%20in%20the%20US%20%26%20Canada,young%20bat%20pups%20which%20are%20unable%20to%20fly.

18. Altemeyer, B. (1998). 'The other "authoritarian" personality'. *Advances in Experimental Social Psychology, 30,* 47–91.

19. Feldman, S. (2003). 'Enforcing social conformity: A theory of authoritarianism'. *Political Psychology, 24*(1), 41–74.

20. Duckitt, J. (2013). 'Introduction to the special section on authoritarianism in societal context: The role of threat'. *International Journal of Psychology, 48*(1), 1–5.

21. Conway, L. G., III, McFarland, J. D., Costello, T. H., and Lilienfeld, S. O. (2021). 'The curious case of left-wing authoritarianism: When authoritarian persons meet anti-authoritarian norms'. *Journal of Theoretical Social Psychology*, *5*, 423–442. https://doi.org/10.1002/jts5.108.

22. Reicher and Haslam (2006). 'Rethinking the psychology of tyranny'.

23. Suedfeld, P., Steel, G. D., and Schmidt, P. W. (1994). 'Political ideology and attitudes toward censorship'. *Journal of Applied Social Psychology*, *24*(9), 765–781.

24. Conway, L. G., III, Repke, M. A., and Houck, S. C. (2017). 'Donald Trump as a cultural revolt against perceived communication restriction: Priming political correctness norms causes more Trump support'. *Journal of Social and Political Psychology*, *5*, 244–259.

25. Guo, J. (2015, December 12). 'The real reasons Donald Trump's so popular – for people totally confused by it'. *Washington Post*. https://www.washingtonpost.com/news/wonk/wp/2015/12/12/the-four-basic-reasons-that-explain-why-donald-trump-actually-is-so-popular/.

26. Thompson, D. (2016, March 1). 'Who are Donald Trump's supporters, really? Four theories to explain the front-runner's rise to the top of the polls'. *The Atlantic*. http://www.theatlantic.com/politics/archive/2016/03/who-are-donald-trumps-supporters-really/471714/.

27. Comment under Kilgore, E. (2021, May 20). 'The future could actually be bright for Republicans'. Intelligencer. https://nymag.com/intelligencer/2021/05/the-future-could-actuallybe-bright-for-republicans.html#comments.

28. Conway, L. G., III, and Zubrod, A. (2022). 'Are US presidents becoming less rhetorically complex? Evaluating the integrative complexity of Joe Biden and Donald Trump in historical context'. *Journal of Language and Social Psychology*, *41*(5), 613–625.

Chapter 8

1. See, e.g., Blass, T. (2009). 'From New Haven to Santa Clara: A historical perspective on the Milgram obedience experiments'. *American Psychologist*, *64*(1), 37.

2. Brehm, J. W., and Cole, A. H. (1966). 'Effect of a favor which reduces freedom'. *Journal of Personality and Social Psychology*, *3*(4), 420.

3. Levav, J., and Zhu, R. (2009). 'Seeking freedom through variety'. *Journal of Consumer Research*, *36*, 600–610.

4. Conway, L. G., III, and Schaller, M. (2005). 'When authority's commands backfire: Attributions about consensus and effects on deviant decision making'. *Journal of Personality and Social Psychology*, *89*, 311–326.

5. Contemplative Photography: Hope in a stone. For example, see https://commons.wikimedia.org/wiki/File:Nothing_is_Written_in_Stone_-_Flickr_-_brewbooks.jpg.

6. For example, see https://acidcow.com/pics/109046-ironic-signs-37-pics.html.

7. For a summary, see: Albarracín, D., Sunderrajan, A., Lohmann, S., Chan, M. P. S., and Jiang, D. (2018). 'The psychology of attitudes, motivation, and persuasion'. In D. Albarracín and B. T. Johnson (eds). *The Handbook of Attitudes* (pp. 3–44). New York: Routledge.

8. https://slidetodoc.com/an-escalator-leading-to-a-fitness-center-a-6/.

9. Conway III and Schaller (2005). 'When authority's commands backfire'.

10. Conway, L. G., III, Salcido, A., Gornick, L. J., Bongard, K. A., Moran, M., and Burfiend, C. (2009). 'When self-censorship norms backfire: The manufacturing of positive communication and its ironic consequences for the perceptions of groups'. *Basic and Applied Social Psychology, 31*, 335–347.

11. Conway, L. G., III, Repke, M. A., and Houck, S. C. (2017). 'Donald Trump as a cultural revolt against perceived communication restriction: Priming political correctness norms causes more Trump support'. *Journal of Social and Political Psychology, 5,* 244–259.

12. Quoted in Sterling, W., and Morse, B. (2021, October 6). 'Basketball star Andrew Wiggins on getting vaccinated: "Not something I wanted to do, but kind of forced to."' CNN. https://www.cnn.com/2021/10/05/sport/andrew-wiggins-Covid-19-vaccine-spt-intl/index.html.

13. Richard, L. (2022). 'Warriors' Andrew Wiggins regrets getting Covid-19 vaccine'. FoxNews.com. https://www.foxnews.com/sports/nba-champion-golden-state-warriors-andrew-wiggins-regrets-getting-Covid-19-vaccine.

14. Uslu, A., Lazer, D., Perlis, R., Baum, M., Quintana, A., Ognyanova, K., ... Qu, H. (2021, September 16). 'The Covid States Project #63: The decision to not get vaccinated, from the perspective of the unvaccinated'. https://doi.org/10.31219/osf.io/fazup.

15. Charlton-Dailey, R. (2021, November 30). 'Unvaccinated people are not oppressed – they're dangerous'. Verywell Health. https://www.verywellhealth.com/unvaccinated-people-are-not-oppressed-5210475.

16. Quoted in Bogart, N. (2021, March 25). 'Enforcing mandatory vaccinations for front-line workers would "undermine confidence and trust": UHN official'. CTVnews.com. https://www.ctvnews.ca/health/coronavirus/enforcing-mandatory-vaccinations-for-front-line-workers-would-undermine-confidence-and-trust-uhn-official-1.5361732.

17. Quoted in BBC Newsbeat. (2020, 7 June). 'Euros and taking the knee: Why

some England fans say they are booing players'. BBC News. https://www.bbc.com/news/newsbeat-57382945.

18. Quoted ibid.

19. Conway, L. G., III, Houck, S. C., Chan, L., Repke, M. A., and McFarland, J. (2021). 'The agreement paradox: How pressures for agreement can ultimately divide us'. In J.-W. van Prooijen (ed.), *Current Issues in Social Psychology: Political Polarization* (pp. 112–126). New York: Routledge.

20. See, for example: Schaller, M., Park, J. H., and Mueller, A. (2003). 'Fear of the dark: Interactive effects of beliefs about danger and ambient darkness on ethnic stereotypes'. *Personality and Social Psychology Bulletin, 29*(5), 637–649.

Chapter 9

1. Shapiro, B. (2010, April 21). 'Fighting Obama's fire with fire of our own'. Townhall. https://townhall.com/columnists/benshapiro/2010/04/21/fighting-obamas-fire-with-fire-of-our-own-n1318469.

2. Shapiro, B. (2021). *The Authoritarian Moment: How the Left Weaponized America's Institutions Against Dissent.* New York: Broadside Books.

3. Quoted in Stabile, A. (2021, January 5). 'George Mason law student blasts school's "incredibly unethical" Covid booster mandate'. FoxNews.com. https://www.foxnews.com/media/george-mason-law-student-unethical-covid-booster-mandate.

4. https://www.change.org/p/tell-gmu-president-gregory-washington-to-repeal-george-mason-university-s-vaccine-booster-mandate.

5. New Civil Liberties Alliance. (2022, January 31). 'George Mason Univ. ends student vaccine booster mandate following demand letter from NCLA'. Yahoo Finance. https://finance.yahoo.com/news/george-mason-univ-ends-student-233000072.html.

6. Bowles, N. (2022, June 24). 'TGIF: Buy your Juuls while you can'. Free Press. https://www.thefp.com/p/tgif-buy-your-juuls-while-you-can.

7. https://twitter.com/wesyang/status/1539907631166406656.

8. Colton, E. (2022, October 23). 'Canadian leader considers dropping Covid lockdown charges, apologizes to unvaccinated'. FoxNews. https://www.foxnews.com/us/canadian-leader-considers-dropping-covid-lockdown-charges-apologizes-unvaccinated.

9. Quoted ibid.

10. Quoted in Kellner, M. A. (2022, September 26). 'Mexican psychology graduate won't lose license over conservative remarks, school rules'. *Washington*

Times. https://m.washingtontimes.com/news/2022/sep/26/mexican-psychology-graduate-wont-lose-license-over/.

11. See: https://grammarist.com/idiom/fight-fire-with-fire/. Of course, no one knows for sure where phrases came from, and there are many different theories about this one. For our purposes, it is the metaphorical implication that matters.

12. Conway, L. G., III, Houck, S. C., Chan, L., Repke, M. A., and McFarland, J. (2021). 'The agreement paradox: How pressures for agreement can ultimately divide us'. In J.-W. van Prooijen (ed.), *Current Issues in Social Psychology: Political Polarization* (pp. 112–126). New York: Routledge.

13. Quoted in Van Brugen, I. (2021, November 19). 'JP Morgan backtracks on cutting ties with conservative group after outrage'. *Newsweek*. https://www.newsweek.com/jp-morgan-bank-backtracks-cut-ties-conservative-group-donald-trump-jr-event-backlash-1651090.

14. Quoted ibid.

15. Petty, R. E., Haugtvedt, C. P., and Smith, S. M. (1995). 'Elaboration as a determinant of attitude strength: Creating attitudes that are persistent, resistant, and predictive of behavior'. In R. E. Petty and J. A. Krosnick (eds.), *Attitude strength: Antecedents and Consequences* (pp. 93–130). Mahwah, NJ: Lawrence Erlbaum Associates.

16. Ibid.

17. For a summary, see: Conway et al. (2021). 'The agreement paradox'.

18. Howard, N. P. (1993). 'The social and political consequences of the Allied food blockade, 1918–19'. *German History*, *11*(2), 161–188.

19. Henig, Ruth (1995) [1984]. *Versailles and After: 1919–1933*. New York: Routledge.

20. DeLong, B. J., and Eichengreen, B. (1993). 'The Marshall Plan: History's Most Successful Structural Adjustment Program'. In Dornbusch, Rudiger; Nolling, Wilhelm; Layard, Richard (eds). *Postwar Economic Reconstruction and Lessons for the East Today*. MIT Press. pp. 189–230.

21. Price, H. B. (1955). *The Marshall Plan and Its Meaning*. Ithaca, NY: Cornell University Press.

22. DeLong and Eichengreen (1993). 'The Marshall Plan: History's most successful structural adjustment program'.

23. Joffe, A. R. (2021). 'Covid-19: Rethinking the lockdown groupthink'. *Frontiers in Public Health*, 98.

24. Suedfeld, P., Leighton, D. C., and Conway, L. G., III (2005). 'Integrative complexity and cognitive management in international confrontations: Research and potential applications'. In M. Fitzduff and C. E. Stout (eds). *The Psychology*

of Resolving Global Conflicts: From War to Peace. Volume 1, Nature vs. Nurture (pp. 211–237). New York: Praeger.

25. Conway, L. G., III, Bongard, K., Plaut, V., Gornick, L. J., Dodds, D. P., Giresi, T., ... and Houck, S. C. (2017). 'Ecological origins of freedom: Pathogens, heat stress, and frontier topography predict more vertical but less horizontal governmental restriction'. *Personality and Social Psychology Bulletin, 43*(10), 1378–1398.

26. Pappas, S. (2012). 'Liberals and conservatives more alike than you think'. *LiveScience.* https://www.livescience.com/25491-liberals-conservatives-not-that-different.html.

27. Graham, J., Nosek, B. A., and Haidt, J. (2012). 'The moral stereotypes of liberals and conservatives: Exaggeration of differences across the political spectrum'. *PloS one, 7*(12), e50092.

28. Druckman, J. N., Klar, S., Krupnikov, Y., Levendusky, M., and Ryan, J. B. (2022). '(Mis)estimating affective polarization'. *The Journal of Politics, 84*(2), 1106–1117.

29. Ahler, D., and Gaurav, S. (2018). 'The parties in our heads: Misperceptions about party composition and their consequences'. *The Journal of Politics, 80*(3), 964–981.

30. Lees, J., and Cikara, M. (2020). 'Inaccurate group meta-perceptions drive negative outgroup attributions in competitive contexts'. *Nature Human Behavior, 4*(3), 279–286.

31. Reyna, C., Tucker, A., Korfmacher, W., and Henry, P. J. (2005). 'Searching for common ground between supporters and opponents of affirmative action'. *Political Psychology, 26*(5), 667–682.

32. Conway, L. G., III, Woodard, S. R., Zubrod, A., and Chan, L. (2021). 'Why are conservatives less concerned about the coronavirus (Covid-19) than liberals? Comparing political, experiential, and partisan messaging explanations'. *Personality and Individual Differences, 183*, 111124.

33. Conway, L. G., III. (2020, April 30). 'Why conservatives and liberals are not experiencing the same pandemic'. Heterodox Academy. https://heterodoxacademy.org/blog/social-science-liberals-conservatives-covid-19/.

34. Durkee, A. (2022, June 26). 'How Americans really feel about abortion: The sometimes surprising poll results as Supreme Court overturns Roe v. Wade'. *Forbes.* https://www.forbes.com/sites/alisondurkee/2022/06/24/how-americans-really-feel-about-abortion-the-sometimes-surprising-poll-results-as-supreme-court-reportedly-set-to-overturn-roe-v-wade/?sh=7c7379af2f3a.

35. Lees and Cikara (2020). 'Inaccurate group meta-perceptions drive negative outgroup attributions in competitive contexts'.

36. Niella, T., Navajas, J., and Hodges, S. D. (2021). 'Polarizing moral discussions in the US and Argentina: People reach more agreement in face-to-face

conversations than we would expect'. Paper presented at the Annual Conference of the Society for Personality and Social Psychology.

37. Voelkel, J. G., Stagnaro, M. N., Chu, J. ... and Willer, R. (2022). 'Megastudy identifying successful interventions to strengthen Americans' democratic attitudes' (preprint). Strengthening Democracy Challenge. https://www. strengtheningdemocracychallenge.org/paper.

38. Stepman, J. (2021, March 8). 'Some liberals getting sick of cancel culture'. The Daily Signal. https://www.dailysignal.com/2021/03/08/some-liberals-are-getting-sick-of-cancel-culture/.

39. Lieblich, J. (1998). 'Conservative Christians protest anti-gay protestor'. *Lawrence Journal-World*.

40. Heine, S. J., Foster, J. A. B., and Spina, R. (2009). 'Do birds of a feather universally flock together? Cultural variation in the similarity-attraction effect'. *Asian Journal of Social Psychology*, *12*(4), 247–258.

41. Voelkel et al. (2022). 'Megastudy identifying successful interventions to strengthen Americans' democratic attitudes'.

INDEX

ABOUT THE AUTHOR

Luke Conway, PhD, is a Full Professor of Psychology at Grove City College. His lab is at the forefront of research related to authoritarianism more broadly – and left-wing authoritarianism (LWA) specifically. He is the author of over ninety academic articles and book chapters, and is a Fellow of the Society of Experimental Social Psychology and the Society for Personality and Social Psychology. His research has been featured in the *Washington Post*, the *New York Times*, the *Huffington Post*, *Psychology Today*, and others, as well as on the BBC and NPR. He lives in Western Pennsylvania.